Angels and Monsters

Angels &

Yale University Press   New Haven and London

Monsters

Male and Female Sopranos in the Story of Opera, 1600–1900

Richard Somerset-Ward

Published with assistance from the Mary Cady Tew
Memorial Fund.

Designed by Sonia L. Shannon.
Set in Sabon type by Tseng Information Systems, Inc.
Printed in the United States of America by Vail-Ballou Press.

Library of Congress Cataloging-in-Publication Data

Somerset-Ward, Richard.
Angels and monsters : Male and female sopranos in the story
of opera, 1600–1900 / Richard Somerset-Ward.
p. cm.
Includes bibliographical references (p.   ) and index.
ISBN 0-300-09968-1 (alk. paper)
1. Opera. 2. Sopranos (Singers)   I. Title.
ML1700.S69   2004
782.1′09—dc22
2003020227

A catalogue record for this book is available from the British
Library.
The paper in this book meets the guidelines for permanence
and durability of the Committee on Production Guidelines
for Book Longevity of the Council on Library Resources.

10 9 8 7 6 5 4 3 2 1

Gene Fairly and Paul Gottlieb urged me to write this book and helped me to plan it. Sadly, neither of them lived to see it completed. It is dedicated to their memory, with gratitude and great affection.

Contents

Introduction

I once made the mistake of describing a guest at my table as a prima donna. Her fellow guests were suitably impressed, but she was visibly annoyed. She was a singer, she said, an opera singer, and she didn't want people to think of her as "some sort of royal bitch with a chip on her shoulder."

Exactly when the term *prima donna* came to imply such a thing is hard to determine, but opera has existed for four centuries and I doubt if there has ever been a time when singers have been thought of as models of good behavior. Certainly not in the eighteenth century, when they were generally quite out of control—it took Gluck's legendary temper, or Mozart's charm and genius, to put them in their proper place—and the nineteenth century was not much better: Angelica Catalani at the beginning of the century, Giulia Grisi in the middle, and Nellie Melba at the end (to give just three examples) were legendary monsters.

But they could get away with it because they sang like angels. They held audiences—and therefore box offices, and therefore the managements of opera houses—in the palms of their hands.

This angel/monster dichotomy was a feature of opera until well into the twentieth century—which is not to say that it is entirely absent today, but it is certainly rare, and for very good reasons. To the extent that angels still exist they are more likely to be heard in concert halls than in opera houses, where stage directors often have as much power as conductors, and beautiful singing, per se, is no longer prized as the only, or even the greatest, virtue. By the same token, it is difficult, though not impossible, to behave like a monster. Those who have tried it recently, especially in American houses, have been slapped down hard, and sometimes publicly.

Whether this state of affairs represents progress or regression is not an argument with which I propose to get involved. This is a book about the first three centuries of opera, from 1600 to 1900, when by far the largest part of the opera repertory was created, and when the singers who created it were, almost always, angels—that is, they sang exquisitely, even if they were often (by our standards) undisciplined, willful, capricious, and self-serving. Acting skill was not essential, and very little attempt was made to direct the singers on stage. Their most important asset was an ability to capture the attention of a noisy and fidgety audience that generally treated the opera house more like a clubhouse than a theater. The resources they used to do this were, first, their voices, second, the music they were given to sing, and third, their own musicianship (most notably, their ability to improvise and ornament). So they really did need to sing like angels! For those who succeeded, it was a heady experience, and it is hardly surprising that it sometimes turned them into monsters.

What makes these singers important in the history of opera, and still of interest today, is that they were the *creators,* the ones for whose voices the great roles were written. They are long dead and we cannot hear them, but what we do have is the music that was written for them. Generally, composers were writing for singers they knew very well, so these scores provide us with the most detailed descriptions of these voices we will ever have. As to the personalities of the singers, we have to rely on contemporary reports and reviews, but there is no shortage of them: the writers of broadsheets, letters, diaries, and memoirs included a wide variety of avid operagoers.

So how did an angel sing? "In the Italian way" was the invariable answer. Only in France would you get a different response: the French created their own style of opera and opera singing and defiantly stuck to it for almost two hundred years. "The Italian way" was shorthand for the style of singing that began in Italy in the seventeenth century and dominated opera for three centuries—and even now, in its decline, is still a necessary part of an opera singer's training. Italians call it *bel canto* (beautiful singing), for that is what it is designed to produce—a stream of sound that is evenly produced over the full range of the voice, with beauty and contrast of tone, with smoothness and expressiveness, with accuracy, with agility—and above all, with purity.

The phrase itself—bel canto—is bland and uninformative: it can be applied to any form of vocal art there has ever been. It became part of the vocabulary of opera in the last quarter of the nineteenth century, in Adelina Patti's time, often with reference to Patti herself, to describe the style of singing in which she specialized. Today, we use it to define the operas she most often sang—"the bel canto operas," by which we generally mean the operas of Rossini, Bellini, and Donizetti. But that is far too narrow a definition, for it takes no account of the honor roll of eighteenth-century singers, teachers, and composers who established the tradition and were its greatest exponents. In any case, Rossini, Bellini, and Donizetti were quickly succeeded by a composer—Giuseppe Verdi—who believed passionately that opera should be concerned with a great deal more than just beautiful singing.

The trouble with bel canto was that it had only one objective, as its name implied, and that objective flew in the face of opera's original mission statement—*dramma per musica* (drama expressed through music). Beautiful singing was fine and admirable, but it didn't work well with the much more dramatic subject matter that was adopted in the nineteenth century in place of the myths and legends so beloved of the eighteenth century. As Verdi wrote to a theater director when advising him on the casting of one of his more dramatic characters: "Lady Macbeth's voice should have something devilish."[1]

What Verdi was battling was the deeply ingrained belief that Italian opera was defined not as a form of theater or drama, as it should have been, but as a style of singing—"beautiful singing," with its undramatic (some would say antidramatic) connotations. In the end, Verdi and his successors won the battle and the angels of bel canto began to disappear. Madame Marchesi trained the last big batch in the rue Jouffroy in Paris. After that, they appeared infrequently and erratically—a Callas, a Sutherland, a Sills, a Caballé—and the great Italian tradition withered, though it did not completely die.

Whether this was a good or bad thing is a matter of opinion, but what is indisputable is that bel canto provided opera with its sure foundation. By concentrating on its greatest exponents (and with a few detours into other traditions along the way), this book attempts to tell the story of its growth, and eventually its decline.

The angels and monsters were not all female. For the better part of two centuries the most famous (and notorious) of them were men. These were not tenors and basses: they were male sopranos, and they may have been the greatest virtuosi there have ever been. This was true in every European country other than France, which was different even then, and had no place in its operas for castrati.

Now that we can no longer hear them and have no authentic records of their singing (leaving aside the few discs made between 1902 and 1904 by a fairly ordinary castrato from the Sistine Choir, who was well past his prime at the time of the recordings),[2] it is easy to overlook the enormous part that male sopranos played in the creation of the opera repertory. To our modern ears, comfortably attuned to the female sound, the castrato voice would have been unearthly and disturbing—more virtuosic than today's countertenor, much more powerful than any female voice. It was generally very musical as well, because the castrati had the best of all musical educations, beginning when they were very young and uninterrupted by puberty. The most constant part of this training was breath control: they developed lungs of astonishing power to fuel a technique that concentrated on evenness and purity of tone throughout the entire compass of the voice, which was sometimes as much as three octaves. It was for these amazing voices that many, if not most, of the great roles of the eighteenth century were composed—the backbone of the bel canto tradition.

During the castrato ascendancy (which is to say, until quite late in the eighteenth century), women were singing under a grave disadvantage. By and large, society did not consider their profession—singing, on the stage, in public—as respectable. They were very often regarded as no more than "kept women," and many of them were just that. They lived dangerous and difficult lives, traveling from theater to theater, sometimes from country to country, in uncomfortable stage coaches, and then appearing in front of rowdy and unpredictable audiences, some of whose members regarded women who appeared onstage as fair game offstage. They were in need of protection. Yet some major talents did emerge—female singers whose vocal abilities were comparable with those of the best castrati and who sometimes contested top billing with them—singers like Cuzzoni, Bordoni, Gabrielli, Mignotti, and later Madame Mara and the incomparable Catalani. They prepared the way for the great *prime donne* of the nineteenth century, from Colbran at the beginning of the century to Melba at its end. These nineteenth-century ladies, of course, were competing on entirely different terms: they now controlled the whole soprano repertory, since the castrati had finally reached their due date and been retired from opera for good, leaving their vocal category and most of their roles to the distaff side.

The beginning of the twentieth century is not an arbitrary cutoff point. It was quite clear by then that the bel canto tradition was no longer preeminent—Italian opera was dominated by the dramatic singing demanded by Verdi, Puccini, and the verismo composers; French opera, both grand and lyric, had finally gone international, and become immensely popular in the process; Wagner was not just respectable but a craze in cities as far apart as New York and St. Petersburg; and there were important new traditions of opera demanding attention, particularly Bohemian and Russian. The bel canto operas were still in demand (those of the nineteenth century, at any rate) but few sopranos could afford to base a career on them alone: there was too much else going on. So the angels began to disappear. Madame Marchesi closed her school on the rue Jouffroy in 1908, and although many of her pupils in turn became teachers and torchbearers for her method (Estelle Liebling was Beverly Sills's teacher), the bel canto era was over and there was not much the twentieth century could do (or wished to do) to bring it back.

By coincidence, the new century also happened to be the time when recording became a factor in the lives of leading singers. Inevitably, posterity will judge twentieth-century singers by their recordings rather than their stage performances, and that is a very different standard of judgment. Nevertheless, it enables us to get a glimpse (but only a glimpse, because the technology was still very primitive in the first decade of the century) of what real bel canto was like. Patti, alas, was already sixty-two when she first experienced "singing in a Gramophone," as she charmingly put it,[3] and her discs can only represent what Herman Klein, the critic and historian, lovingly described as the "beaux restes" of her voice.[4]

Melba, on the other hand, was still in her prime. There are several examples of this, but one will do. In 1907, she recorded Violetta's "Ah! fors' è lui," from *La traviata*. She was in her mid-forties at the time, and the result is stunning for the accuracy of its coloratura, the precision with which she realizes all the markings in the score, and the astonishing purity of tone throughout. It is a thing of beauty—a precious example of the style that is rightly called "beautiful singing," and a worthy tribute to the generations of singers who had preceded her.

This is their story.

Angels and Monsters

CHAPTER ONE

Caccini's Pupils

The soprano voice arrived on the scene surprisingly late. In Italy, where the princely courts and the Church were generally responsible for establishing standards of acceptable behavior, singing was not thought of as a proper activity for women until the early sixteenth century. What caused it to become acceptable then was the extraordinary popularity of the madrigal, which became the focus of all kinds of secular music-making—in courts, in formal and informal groups, and within families. For the first time, singing was recognized as a social grace for women—but still not as something to be displayed in public. It took another fifty or sixty years, until the last quarter of the sixteenth century, before women were seen regularly in concerts and court entertainments, and composers began writing female soprano roles as a matter of course.

Coincidentally, the male soprano arrived at almost exactly the same time.

And hard on the heels of both of them came the first experiments in dramma per musica, which quickly developed into "opera."

As a singer, teacher, and composer, Giulio Caccini played an important role in all these events. He was a member of the Florentine group that developed the idea of dramma per musica; he was largely responsible for two of the original operas (*Il rapimento di Cefalo* and *Euridice*, both dated 1600); he was an accomplished instrumentalist and singer, frequently heard in court entertainments; and he was, above all, the teacher of some of the finest singers of the time, including several of the first "opera singers." Among them were two of his own daughters, Francesca and Settimia, and two of the male

singers who took leading roles in Monteverdi's *Orfeo*, the first really successful opera and the one that established the genre in Mantua in 1607—Francesco Rasi, a tenor, created the title role, and Giovanni Gualberto Magli, a
castrato, sang three smaller roles.

Born in 1551, Caccini grew up in Rome—a poor boy who was saved
from obscurity by the quality of his voice. He sang in the choir of the Cappella Giulia in St. Peter's, and it was there that he was heard by the Florentine ambassador and quickly recruited to the Medici court. He was fourteen
when he arrived in Florence, and what he found there was something very
different from the church-dominated musical world of Rome.

For a start, it was not inconceivable that female singers might perform
in public in Florence. Rome, the epicenter of the Catholic Church, was a
strict observer of St. Paul's admonition that women should "keep silence in
the churches."[1] Nor were they allowed to appear on the stage or in other
public entertainments, and that ban would continue in force until 1798. If
you wanted to hear a woman sing in Rome, or in any other part of the Papal
States, you would have to be one of the privileged few who got invitations
to private functions at the houses of great princes and noblemen.

Florence was different. It was the capital city of the independent dukedom of Tuscany, ruled by the Medici family. It was rich, powerful, closely
allied to the crown of France, and not (in temporal matters, at least) subject to the diktat of Rome. Its court, even in the fading years of the Renais-
sance, when most of Italy was sinking into economic depression, was still a
glittering affair, with music playing a central role. Many of the people Caccini came to know there were more than just good musicians: they included
the leading theorists of music—men like Vincenzo Galilei (father of the as-
tronomer), Count Giovanni de'Bardi, Jacopo Corsi, and Emilio de'Cavalieri.
These men were all members of the Accademia degli Alterati, a society that,
true to its name, existed for the "alteration" or improvement of society. One
of the things they wanted to alter was the prevailing style of music.

Not far to the north of Florence, the court of Ferrara was also celebrated for its music. In the 1580s it featured an innovative group known as
the *concerto di donne* (the concert of ladies). The three women who made up

this group performed only "secret music"—that is, they performed for the prince and his court, but not for the general public. They were not aristocrats themselves, though they appear to have come from respectable families, which was necessary since their duties involved not just singing but making "agreeable conversation."[2] They were the ancestors, no doubt, of Fiordiligi and Dorabella, Mozart's *dame ferraresi* in *Così fan tutte*, but they were light-years removed from those flirtatious creatures (though it appears that one of them was later murdered by her jealous husband).[3] They were, in fact, the first cautious experiment we know of in which the female soprano voice was featured as an instrument in its own right. Their fame spread across northern Italy, and Florence could not be far behind.

The first great female star of the Medici court was Vittoria Archilei. A Roman lady (she was popularly known as "La Romanina"), she arrived in Florence in 1588. With her husband, who was an accomplished composer and lutenist, she quickly became a member of the group of musicians and singers who devised and performed the entertainments the Medici commissioned to celebrate great events. Most often, these were *intermedi*—musical performances that took place "in the middle" of other entertainments (a feast, a tournament, a stage play). They were tableaux rather than dramas, often very lavish, and this was certainly the case with the intermedi of 1589, commissioned by Grand Duke Ferdinand to celebrate his marriage to Christine of Lorraine. There were, in this instance, six intermedi, designed to fit before, after, and during the intermissions of a five-act play (a long evening!). La Romanina sang two principal roles, Harmony and Amphitrite. Harmony's opening aria, "Dalle più alte sfere" (From the Highest Spheres), with its very ornate embellishments, leaves no doubt that she was a considerable virtuosa.

Caccini had several roles in these intermedi of 1589—as a singer and harpist, as the composer of an extremely florid aria, and as the architect of Florence's riposte to Ferrara's concerto di donne. For Vittoria Archilei was not the only female singer on hand: there were two others. One was Caccini's wife, Lucia, the *seconda donna* who sang the Sorceress's aria composed by her husband. The other was a young pupil of the Archileis, identified only as Margherita (almost certainly the same Margherita who later became Caccini's second wife). Together, at the very end of the final *intermedio*, Vittoria, Lucia, and Margherita performed a trio for *tre donne,* and Florence became the proud possessor of its own concerto di donne.

Caccini's principal mentor in Florence was Count Bardi. Caccini must therefore have been closely involved with the group of amateur and professional musicians who met regularly at Bardi's house and who were collectively known as a *camerata* (a club or gathering). It was these men who developed the blueprint for the new form of dramma per musica. It was based on what they believed to have been the practice of the ancient Greeks—the use of music to accompany and emphasize the words of a play. But the musical style of the sixteenth century was basically polyphonic—that is, music of "many sounds," in which various different melodies and harmonies were blended to produce an overall effect. The camerata reasoned that this would only serve to drown out the words, so they developed instead a monodic style—a reciting line, or recitative *(stile rappresentativo),* accompanied by occasional chords on a harpsichord or lute. Caccini later claimed to have been the inventor of this style.[4] If that was so, it is notable that no one else gave him credit for it. The real inventor is likely to have been Galileo Galilei.[5]

Galilei died in 1591, and it was another seven years before the new style was demonstrated in Jacopo Peri's *Dafne,* which is generally credited as the first "opera." In the meantime, Caccini had lost his position in the Florentine court. He was always a difficult man, and litigious, too, but it is probably significant that his misfortune coincided with the departure in 1592 of his mentor, Count Bardi, to be chamberlain to Pope Clement VIII in Rome.

Caccini left Florence for a time and worked in Genoa, but he eventually reestablished himself with the Medici and became a major contributor to two of the musical events commissioned to celebrate the grandest wedding the Medici ever staged—the marriage of Maria de'Medici to the King of France, Henri IV, in 1600. *Il rapimento di Cefalo,* the centerpiece of the celebrations, was part intermedi, part newfangled dramma per musica, with Caccini as its principal composer (though three others made contributions). *Euridice,* by contrast, an altogether smaller work, was a genuine dramma per musica by Jacopo Peri. The version performed at the wedding, however,

A woodcut on the title page of Giulio Caccini's score of *Euridice*,
published in Florence in 1600. In his introduction, Caccini wrote: "The
style of singing I have called for contains a certain casualness *[sprezzatura]*
which I think suggests nobility and with which I have endeavored to
approach natural speech." (Lebrecht Collection.)

was not entirely Peri's, for Caccini had also written (or was in the process of writing) an alternative setting of Ottavio Rinuccini's libretto. Since several of the singers at the first performance were Caccini's pupils, he apparently insisted that they perform his settings of their solo numbers, not Peri's. Caccini also contributed three of the choruses. At all events, *Euridice,* in its mongrel edition, was not a great success at the wedding, but it was much admired at later performances in Florence, when Peri reverted to his own original score. Caccini's version, with its somewhat more lyrical, less declamatory, less dramatic style, had to wait more than two years for its single performance. If Caccini was disappointed, he compensated himself by rushing his version into print six weeks ahead of Peri's.[6]

The truth of the matter, however, was that neither Caccini nor Peri, nor any of their Florentine colleagues, was talented enough to launch this new form of musical drama on his own—hours and hours of "dry recitative" interrupted by occasional choruses and slightly more embellished songs was not a prescription for a lively evening. *Dafne* and *Euridice* were innovative and interesting, no doubt, but the Medici, whose decisions were final in Florence, decided to revert to intermedi for subsequent events. Luckily for the future of opera, Claudio Monteverdi was waiting in the wings in Mantua, ready to add his musical and dramatic genius to the basic idea that had been pioneered in Florence.

We do not know if Vittoria Archilei performed in either the Caccini or Peri versions of *Euridice*—probably not, for she turned fifty in 1600 and the evidence suggests that she was increasingly specializing in sacred music. But she was still the first lady of Florentine music, and both Peri and Caccini went out of their way to acknowledge their debt to her in prefaces to their published editions of *Euridice.* Peri wrote about the way she had ornamented his earlier scores—"those charms and graces that cannot be notated, and, if notated, cannot be deciphered"[7]—while Caccini praised her for having "long ago" mastered the new forms of passage-work and recitative he claimed to have invented.[8]

Caccini may not have invented them, but he probably did as much as anyone else to develop them. In 1602, just a year after the publication of

Euridice, he issued a collection of his solo madrigals and airs, *Le nuove musiche*. There would be a further collection in 1614 *(Nuove musiche e nuova maniera di scriverle)*. In these publications—and more important, in the didactic introductions he wrote for each of them—he articulated the ideas that had been developed by Count Bardi and the camerata. He proclaimed the importance of words. The music, he said, was written to accompany and emphasize the words, not to overcome them. He therefore sought to "introduce a kind of music in which one could almost speak in tones." There was, nevertheless, a role for ornamentation, for it was through carefully regulated embellishments and ornaments, he argued, that singers were able to "move the affections" of their audiences.[9]

This ability to affect the audience was the key to opera, and when, in 1607, Caccini traveled to Mantua to hear Monteverdi's *Orfeo*, he may have been amazed by what he heard (eleven principal singers, chorus, ballet, an orchestra of thirty-eight, and a wind band as well), but he would also have appreciated the artful way in which Monteverdi used his music to pluck the heartstrings of his audience. And if Caccini returned to Mantua a year later to hear Monteverdi's next opera, *Arianna*, he would have been even more amazed by the effect of Arianna's Lament—"No one hearing it was left unmoved," wrote the court archivist.[10]

Caccini had a personal reason for wishing to develop the role of the female voice—his family. Over the years, the concerto di donne created for the 1589 intermedi had changed in character and personnel: it had become more of a family ensemble, directed by Caccini himself and featuring his second wife, Margherita, who had been part of the original concerto, and his two daughters, Francesca and Settimia. Their fame had spread well beyond Florence. In 1603, and again the following year, they had been invited to Paris to perform at the court of Maria de'Medici, and there is no doubt that much of Caccini's fame in his final years (he died in 1618) came from his association with his daughters.

Francesca, the older daughter, was more than just a fine singer: she followed in her father's footsteps and became a very distinguished composer. *La liberazione di Ruggiero dall'isola d'Alcina* (1625) is the first opera we know of that was written by a female composer. It made use of lyrical recitatives in her father's style, though it contained more tuneful arias than he would have used. Written to an essentially feminist libretto, it featured an ensemble of women's voices, and introduced an idea that was to become very important in opera—the idea that the different genders and social standings of the characters in an opera could be represented musically by contrasting the tones in which they were set. Thus, Alcina and her women all sing in flat keys, while Ruggiero and the men sing in sharp keys.[11] *La liberazione* was so admired by the Medici's guest in whose honor it was written, Prince Wladislaw of Poland, that he had it copied and performed at his court in Warsaw in 1628. He also commissioned two more operas from her, though neither has survived, if in fact they were ever written.

Francesca appeared on the payroll of the Medici court for the first time in 1607, when she was twenty. In that year she composed the music to accompany a tournament in Pisa, but by then she had already been performing at court for at least seven years: in 1600, she had sung with the concerto di donne during the wedding festivities for which Jacopo Peri and her father wrote *Euridice*. She must quickly have developed into a virtuosa, because there is evidence that both Cardinal Montalto in Rome and Prince Ferdinand Gonzaga in Mantua tried to steal her away from the Medici court. She elected to stay in Florence, and she was well rewarded for doing so: by 1622 she was the highest paid musician of either sex on the Medici payroll.

The pity is that we know so little about Francesca.[12] As singer, teacher, and composer, she was clearly a major force in the development of the soprano voice, on the one hand, and dramma per musica, on the other. Very little of her work survives—a few dramatized pieces in addition to *La liberazione;* a collection of her own songs published in 1618; and a handful of letters that show her as a very cultivated and practical woman. But there is no doubt that her influence in northern Italy was profound. By the time she died (sometime after 1637), the musical world observed by her father when he first arrived in Florence seventy years before had been turned upside down. Opera was being performed in most of the courts and cities of northern Italy, and was about to begin its commercial career in Venice, while female singers like Francesca had won for themselves a major role, if not yet a very highly regarded one, in its performance.

Francesca Caccini (1587–after 1637). Known as "La Cecchina," Francesca
was a famous singer and teacher in Florence and Rome, and the first
female composer of opera. (John Minnion/Lebrecht Collection.)

In Mantua, Monteverdi had his own corps of singers. They included the Baroni family, of which Adriana (the mother) and Leonora (her daughter) were the most gifted. The poet John Milton, hearing Leonora sing in 1638, quickly penned three Latin sonnets in her praise. But neither Adriana nor Leonora ever sang in opera, and there was a reason for this. Despite the concerti di donne, despite the examples of Vittoria Archilei and the Caccini sisters, it was still not respectable for women to appear on the stage, and it would be many years before those barriers were finally removed. Adriana's husband was a minor nobleman, and it is clear from her well-documented negotiations with the Duke of Mantua and his agents that she was determined to be treated as a lady. During one such negotiation she was reported to have wept bitterly while declaring, "If the Lord Duke wants to have me killed or raped he can do so, I know, I believe it, but rather than go and serve anyone I will bear all these ills."[13] Leonora was as firm as her mother. When Cardinal Mazarin, an old friend, invited her to perform at the French court in 1644 she refused to go unless she received a personal invitation from the Queen Regent, and then only to give concerts at court.[14] Appearances were important: singing on the public stage (as opposed to taking part in a private concert before royalty) was not the sort of risk a well-bred woman could afford to take with her reputation. Any woman who appeared on stage, it was widely believed, was probably a courtesan.

Adriana Baroni may have been a better singer than Francesca Caccini (Monteverdi thought so), but Francesca's sister, Settimia, was better than both of them. Four years younger, and the daughter of Caccini's second wife, Margherita, Settimia was taught by her father and appears to have become a member of the concerto di donne when she was only eleven. But Settimia was a singer first and last (even those few songs attributed to her were more likely written by her husband, Alessandro Ghivizzani), and her career was made not in Florence, but in Mantua where Adriana Baroni was her contemporary. By the time she arrived there, in 1613, Monteverdi had already left for Venice, but she was clearly well known to him—in 1628 she sang the role of Aurora in his *Mercurio e Marte,* composed for the wedding celebrations of the Farnese Duke in Parma. Writing in 1649, Severo Bonini, who was an acute observer of the changing styles in music, declared that Settimia had "an immortal reputation" and had "mastered to perfection the art of singing."[15]

Among all these women pioneers, there was one whose brief life had given promise that she would be the greatest of them all. Caterina Martinelli died in a smallpox outbreak when she was only eighteen, but her legend lived on, perpetuated in requiem masses that were said for her every month and that were endowed by the Duke of Mantua himself. As a thirteen-year-old, Caterina had gone from her home in Rome to the Gonzaga court in Mantua where she lived in the Monteverdis' household. It was for her that Monteverdi composed the role of Arianna in 1608, but she died just weeks before the première. The poignancy of Arianna's Lament (perhaps the first "hit tune" in opera) was made all the greater by the circumstances in which it was first performed.

The woman who stepped in at short notice for Caterina was Virginia Ramponi (she had only six days to learn the role). She, too, must have been a formidable singer, but her career was closely tied to that of her husband, Giovanni Battista Andreini. Under the patronage of the Gonzaga dukes, he had founded a group known as Comici Fedeli. It specialized in entertainments that were a cross between traditional commedia dell'arte and the emerging form of opera. In many ways, its influence was as profound as that of Caccini and the Florentine school, or even of Monteverdi himself, because, as a touring company, the Fedeli gave popular performances throughout northern Italy and made several visits to France, as well as to Vienna and Prague. They did as much as anyone to spread the idea of dramma per musica, and the part women had to play in it.

Male singers also benefited from these developments, none more so than Francesco Rasi. He was a minor Tuscan nobleman who very early became a pupil of Caccini in Florence. It was from Caccini that he learned the art of embellishing and ornamenting the singing line. Rasi was a tenor—"a sweet and robust voice," according to Severo Bonini, which "made his singing seem angelic and divine."[16] He took part in the Florentine entertainments of

1600—both *Euridice* and *Il rapimento di Cefalo*—and he went on to create the title role in Monteverdi's *Orfeo,* and an almost equally important role in *Arianna* the next year, singing opposite Virginia Ramponi. His subsequent career was somewhat tarnished by his exile from Florence in 1610 for having been involved in a murder: he had to move to Turin.

There were tenors and there were basses (baritones did not become a separate category until the middle of the nineteenth century), but the most popular type of male voice at the turn of the seventeenth century was one that included within its range both tenor and bass registers. To judge from the evidence of most of the music that was written for Rasi (though *Orfeo,* with its lyric tenor range, is an exception), and some that he wrote for himself, his voice was somewhat below that of the modern tenor.[17] Such a singer would always be in demand, but henceforth it would more often be for the lower roles, more bass than tenor, because the tenor as *primo uomo* was now threatened by the emergence of the male soprano, or castrato.

The practice of castrating young boys before they reached the age of puberty in order to preserve the purity of their voices coincided with the development of opera in Italy, but it was a genuine coincidence of timing. There was nothing new about eunuchs, of course: they existed in many early civilizations, sometimes as "safe" servants or slaves in royal and princely households, sometimes as a result of punishment. But the idea of a young boy being emasculated for musical purposes originated with the Church, probably in Spain in the fifteenth century, though its later practice was confined almost entirely to Italy, where it began somewhere around 1560. For the next three and a half centuries, boys were castrated because there was a demand for soprano voices in church choirs, from which women were banned. Opera was an incidental beneficiary, though a very considerable one because there is no doubt that the castrati were among the greatest attractions of opera right up to the time of Rossini.

To the modern ear, the sound would undoubtedly be off-putting, to put it mildly—but then we have never heard the real thing.[18] At its best, it was a virtuoso instrument with a range, a reach, and a flexibility that no ordinary voice could duplicate—it was the result, after all, of basically female equipment powered by massively developed male lungs. We think of it as artificial, but seventeenth- and eighteenth-century Italians described it as *sincero* (natural, or true).

The Church, of course, was in a bit of a bind. It *had* to condemn castration—it always had—but, at the same time, it wanted the castrati in its choirs. So it did both things: it issued edicts damning the practice of castration, and it recruited the best of the castrati into its service. The justification for this paradoxical policy was issued by Pope Clement VIII (1592–1605): castration could be authorized, he wrote, solely "ad honorem Dei"—for the glory of God.

The official who probably drafted this policy for the pope was Count Giovanni de'Bardi, the same man who had played such an important role in the origins of opera in Florence. Clement had summoned him to Rome in 1592 to be the chamberlain of the papal court, so Bardi was almost certainly on hand when the first castrati were auditioned for the Sistine Choir and admitted in 1599. The appointments were furiously opposed by the *falsetti* who had dominated the choir for years. Some of these were men with genuinely high voices (what we would now call countertenors), but most were natural tenors who used the artificial "head voice" to approximate the treble range. At all events, the pope, who had been greatly impressed by the castrati, intervened to ensure that he got his way.[19] The falsetti, of course, were right to be alarmed: by 1624 all these so-called "sopranists" had been replaced by castrati. Falsetti continued to sing in the choir as contraltos for another half century, but by 1675 they too were being replaced by castrati. Siface, who had a famous career in opera, was one of the first. By that time, the falsetto voice had come to be thought of as unnatural—*contro natura*.

The princely courts were not slow to capitalize on this new resource. The Medici in Florence had a castrato on their payroll by 1604, Giovanni Gualberto Magli. He was a pupil of Caccini's, and one Caccini was evidently proud of, because he recommended Magli to Monteverdi in Mantua and helped to negotiate his loan for the performance of *Orfeo* in 1607. Magli had learned the role of La Musica in advance, but it appears that when he arrived in Mantua he was asked to learn two other roles, Proserpina and Speranza, while rehearsals were taking place. It is also probable—though we cannot know for certain since no firsthand record of the 1607 performance has sur-

vived—that the principal female role of Euridice was sung by another castrato, Girolamo Becchini.[20] Such *travesti* casting would have come as no surprise to an early-seventeenth-century audience accustomed to seeing female
leads in the straight theater played by boys. This was the time of Shakespeare.

At all events, the male soprano had arrived. He quickly became dominant in church choirs, and just as quickly he took his place beside the newly
promoted female soprano on the opera stage. From now on, composers like
Monteverdi would write female roles for men *or* women to sing, depend-
ing on which happened to be available—Monteverdi's *Il ritorno d'Ulisse in
patria,* for example, had no significant castrato parts, whereas both the leading men in *L'incoronazione di Poppea,* only two years later, were castrati.

By the time Giulio Caccini died in 1618, all these different strands—the
female soprano, the male soprano, and the new art form now referred to
as *opera in musica,* or just "opera"—were coming together to launch a new
epoch in musical development. Through his teaching and performing, and
to some extent through his compositions, Caccini had played a major role
in all of them. Like many great teachers, however, he had an abrasive, com-
petitive personality, and it often got in his way. As early as 1588 he had been
in danger of losing his position in Florence—he was actually recommended
to the court of Modena in that year for the post of superintendent of gar-
dens (apparently he was very good at citrus horticulture, and had "excellent
handwriting as well").[21]

Even though he spent much of the 1590s without a court position,
his survival was probably guaranteed—partly by the growing reputation of
his concerto di donne, partly by the continuing patronage of Count Bardi
(absent in Rome but always a hovering presence in Florence). When, at last,
the position of *maestro di cappella* became open at the Medici court in 1609,
Caccini was passed over in favor of the much younger Marco da Gagliano,
who had already established himself as the central figure in Florence's first
formal music academy, the Accademia degli Elevati. We know that Peri,
Bardi, the poet Ottavio Rinuccini, and several of the other founding fathers
of opera belonged to the Academy, but there is no record of Caccini having
been a member. Instead, he had to be content with playing a vicarious role

in the careers of his pupils as they began to achieve the successes for which he had trained them. If he liked to claim that he had invented the style of composition and singing that made it all possible . . . well, he had done more than most to make it happen.

CHAPTER TWO

Getting Away with Murder

The Prima Donna Comes of Age

Anna Renzi was a model prima donna. She was also one of the first of the species in the story of opera, and certainly the first to be promoted by a press campaign.

She began her career in Rome, taking part in private performances of operas at the house of the French ambassador. In 1640, as a twenty-year-old, she arrived in Venice and made her reputation immediately in Francesco Sacrati's opera *La finta pazza* (The One Who Feigned Madness). If any single work can be said to have enabled opera to "take off" with the public, it was this one. It was eventually performed all over northern Italy, and in Paris as well.

For a start, it was (in part, at least) a comedy—something totally new to opera and clearly a welcome development for the Venetian audience. It also contained the first mad scene in opera—an opportunity for Anna Renzi, as Deidamia, to demonstrate impressive vocal powers, negotiating whole series of arpeggios, as well as octave leaps both downwards and upwards, and to show off her remarkable prowess as an actor. Just as amazing for the audience, it seems, was the work of Giacomo Torelli, the master builder of sets and stage machines.

Venice was where opera came of age. In 1637, less than four decades after Jacopo Peri and Giulio Caccini had presented the new "invention" in Florence, the first public opera house opened in Venice—not a subsidized theater propped up by princely patronage, but a genuine commercial venture, dependent on its box office.

It worked. Within thirty years, there were sixteen or seventeen parish theaters operating in this way in Venice, and nine of them regularly or occasionally presented opera. Historians reserve most space for the three operas Monteverdi wrote for these public theaters at the end of his long life, and for the works of Francesco Cavalli, which pretty well dominated the scene thereafter, but it was Sacrati's *La finta pazza,* and Anna Renzi's performance in it, that made the deepest impact at the time.

La finta pazza was commissioned for the opening of a new theater, the Novissimo. This theater was distinguished from its neighbors by the fact that it was founded and managed by members of a powerful and semisecret Venetian organization, the Accademia degli Incogniti. The organization was powerful because it included among its members almost all the leading intellectuals of Venice, and it was semisecret because its underlying philosophy was, to the Church at least, subversive—its motto, *Ignoto Deo,* proclaimed "an unknown god" that valued the physical pleasures of the here and now above the more mystical values of Christian morality. Only in Venice, an independent republic notoriously at odds with the Church, could such a society have existed freely. Venice, to its considerable satisfaction, had been excommunicated by the Vatican in 1600 for banning Jesuits from operating within its territories.

Several members of the Incogniti were actively involved in opera, most of them as librettists, and one of them was Giulio Strozzi, who was commissioned to write the text of *La finta pazza.* It was evidently Sacrati's idea to bring Anna Renzi from Rome to sing the role of Deidamia, but it was Strozzi who promptly became Renzi's chief promoter in Incogniti publications. One of these, *Le glorie della signora Anna Renzi romana,* published in 1644, is the first in a long line of "diva books" that have sought to deify their subjects.

Strozzi was not a newcomer to opera. A few years earlier, he had collaborated with Monteverdi on a very similar project, *La finta pazza Licori.* It never saw the light of day, but Monteverdi's extensive correspondence has survived as a remarkable testament to the need for close collaboration between librettist and composer (and the need of the composer to prevail).[1] Strozzi was also a good judge of singing. His adopted daughter, Barbara Strozzi, was one of Venice's most celebrated composers and chamber singers, though she never sang in opera. And in Anna Renzi, Strozzi found a protégée worthy of his pen.

She had a low soprano voice, what we would now call a mezzo-soprano —Monteverdi later wrote the role of Ottavio for her in *L'incoronazione di Poppea*. She was clearly not one of those blazing singers whose sole purpose is to amaze her audience. Certainly, according to Strozzi, she had "a full sonorous voice, not harsh, not hoarse" and capable of "felicitous passages, a lively trill, both double and *rinforzato*," but her real genius was as a singing actress—"Our Signora Anna is endowed with such lifelike expression that her responses and speeches seem not memorized but born at the very moment. In sum, she transforms herself completely into the person she represents."[2] This was particularly necessary at this early stage of opera's development because there was still a great reliance on recitative. Ellen Rosand, the most learned historian of early Venetian opera, has estimated that the average number of arias written for an opera in 1640 was not more than a dozen; ten years later, this had doubled, and by the 1670s it was not unusual to find as many as sixty.[3] Anna Renzi continued singing at least until 1657, so she would have become familiar with the demand for more "set pieces" and more ornamentation, but at the beginning of her career, in the early 1640s, she was clearly the ideal prima donna for composers like Sacrati and Monteverdi, and librettists like Strozzi, all of whom were interested in opera as drama empowered by music. The singers had not yet taken control.

But that day was coming, and quickly. Rosand notes that, by 1658, even Cavalli, an unusually well paid composer, was receiving only about half the amount paid to Signora Girolama, the leading singer in his opera *Antioco*.[4] It is true that a singer's fee generally included traveling and living expenses, but impresarios were in no doubt that it was the singers who sold the box office, not the composers. By 1669, Giulia Masotti was getting six times the composer's fee,[5] and if the impresarios wanted evidence that it was money well spent they could see it in the number of *applausi* that were showered on the leading ladies at curtain calls. Applausi were little gift packages containing sonnets in praise of the singers. The French diplomat Saint-Disdier, writing in 1680, described how "partisans of these admirable singers have quantities of sonnets printed in their honor, and during the applause that these singers inspire, they shower thousands of them from the heights of Paradise, filling the loges and parterres."[6]

Competing with the scenery has always been a problem for singers, and never more so than in seventeenth-century Venice, where Giacomo Torelli was king. Torelli was an engineer as well as a designer: he was responsible for the building of the Novissimo Theater in 1640–41, and for its remarkable stage machinery, which enabled the entire set to be changed in one operation by a system of rails, rollers, and pulleys. He also designed most of the productions during the brief existence of the theater (it was demolished in 1647), including *La finta pazza,* with which the Novissimo and Anna Renzi made their debuts, and Giovanni Rovetta's *Ercole in Lidia* five years later, which was reported on by the English diarist John Evelyn. He noted thirteen scene changes and the performances of the leading singers, who included "the best treble of women," Anna Renzi. "This held us by the Eyes and Eares til two in the Morning." Evelyn also reported a fish dinner with Renzi: "she entertained us with rare musiq."[7]

Venice's preeminence in opera did not last very long. By 1660 it had reached its high-water mark; by the end of the century it was over. Writing in 1681, Cristoforo Ivanovich, the first historian of opera, did not hesitate to blame the singers: "Instead of the former profits, debts are incurred because of the excessive payment to singers. At the beginning, two exquisite voices, a small number of delightful arias, and a few scene changes sufficed to satisfy. Now, one objects if one hears a voice that is not up to European standards; one expects every scene to be accompanied by a change of setting, and that the machines be brought in from another world."[8]

"European standards" had arrived. The singers (and who can blame them?) were exploiting the economics of the new medium. Driven by box office, the system required impresarios to compete for the most popular singers, to pressure composers and librettists to write showy arias for them, and very often to allow the singers to dictate what they would and would not sing, and with whom they would appear. One of the most popular castrati of the time, Antonio Cavagna, laid down conditions for his performances in the 1666 season: "I intend to sing with the instruments tuned to Roman pitch" (which was a whole tone lower than Venetian pitch); one of the ariettas written for him was "mannered and beggarly, and unless you get [the composer] to write new music for it I won't sing it at all"; and he was concerned about having "to sing between two angels, Signora Antonia and Signora Giulia."[9]

He might have been even more concerned had he read Signora Giulia's contract (she was the same Giulia Masotti who would be paid six times the composer's fee only three years later): it stipulated that she should always have "la parte prima" and that she should be able to examine her parts before agreeing to sing them. Increasingly, singers were having arias changed to suit them, sometimes even abandoning arias written by the composer and replacing them with arias from other operas and other composers. Indeed, Giulia Masotti did not hesitate to demand the replacement of a whole opera already announced for the season on the grounds that her rival, Antonia Coresi, was billed to sing, if not "la parte prima," then certainly a role of almost equal importance. Signora Masotti got her way.[10]

The spiral was a familiar one. In order to fill the theaters, impresarios had to lower seat prices to attract a wider audience. At the same time, they had to pay ever higher fees to the singers, and stage ever more spectacular productions in order to keep the new audience happy. The initial burst of enthusiasm for opera was followed by a period of much less activity. Carnival, with all its foreign guests, was still important, especially to a city so obviously in decline as Venice was throughout the seventeenth century, but between 1650 and 1670 there were generally only two or three theaters performing opera at any one time, and that meant there were rarely more than three or four new operas being produced each season.[11] Box offices performed well below capacity. The natural order of things was restored to some extent in 1678 with the opening of the grand new Teatro S. Giovanni Grisostomo, which was bigger and better equipped than its rivals, and featured the best Italian singers, with seat prices to match. By that time, Venice's position as the opera capital of Italy was already being challenged: Naples was preparing to assume the mantle.

Nevertheless, it was in Venice, at the S. Giovanni Grisostomo, early in the new century, that the greatest stars of a new style of singing were introduced. Faustina Bordoni made her debut there in 1716, and Francesca Cuzzoni joined Bordoni in Pollarolo's *Ariodante* in 1718. The achievements and the rivalry of these two ladies would place the image of the prima donna indelibly in the European consciousness, and not always in the most flattering light.

By the last quarter of the seventeenth century, Italian opera had established itself in London, Vienna, Madrid, and several of the German territories. In Paris, however, it had been repulsed. Cardinal Mazarin, himself an Italian even though he was first minister of France, had made several attempts to import it, staging works by Sacrati, Rossi, and Cavalli, with all the spectacular effects Giacomo Torelli could dream up. But Italian opera was not a great hit in Paris, and Mazarin was eventually outflanked by his young king, Louis XIV, and yet another Italian resident in France, Giovanni Battista Lulli. In the same year that Mazarin died, 1661, Lully (to give him his French name) was appointed *surintendant et compositeur de la musique de la chambre du roi,* and from that time right up to his death in 1687 he worked single-mindedly to create a new and very distinctive art form—French opera.

It was different from Italian opera in many respects. First, and always, it was in the French language. Second, it was designed for a particular audience—the king and his court—so it unashamedly glorified Louis and his concept of kingship *(la gloire).* Third, it always included dance, because that was Louis's favorite art form and the one in which Lully had made his reputation.

In all these respects, Lully doubtless designed his operas specifically to win the king's approval. But he was better than that. The form of opera he created, *tragédie en musique,* long outlasted him, and anyone who compared it with the Italian model (which a lot of French writers and philosophes did a lot of the time) found that French opera had a good deal in its favor. It was more dramatic; it put greater emphasis on staging and spectacle; it gave more prominence to the chorus and orchestra (grand overtures and occasional *symphonies*); it tended to meld recitatives directly into *airs* (or arias), thus giving singers less opportunity to improvise and audiences less opportunity to stage noisy demonstrations of support or disapproval; and it never made use of castrati, who were not welcome in France after Cavalli's *Ercole amante,* the last of Mazarin's commissions to Italians (though a few castrati were retained to sing in the choir of the royal chapel).

French sopranos were therefore female—*dessus* (or "top") was the term used to describe them: *haut-dessus* and *bas-dessus*. They sang at the Académie Royale de Musique, later known as the Paris Opéra, and that meant they sang under court patronage for Lully, to whom King Louis had granted a patent (in effect, a monopoly) for the commissioning and performing of opera in the French language. A career at the Académie depended, first, on being in Lully's favor, and second, on having a private life that would stand up to the scrutiny of court officials whose job was to protect the king and his family from scandal of any sort. It is for this reason, perhaps, that the résumés of female French opera singers of the period quite often included time spent in convents—sometimes permanent retirement to the cloisters for outrageous behavior, more often temporary absences occasioned by dalliances thought to be inappropriate.

The amorous adventures of "les filles de l'Opéra" were not exactly private: they were celebrated in popular *chansons* of the time, written by musicians as famous as François Couperin, the king's organist and the royal family's harpsichord teacher. He had a particular fascination for Fanchon Moreau—"la tendre Fanchon," as he called her in the title of one of his harpsichord pieces. She was one of Lully's last discoveries, and she created roles in several of his final operas, as well as in post-Lullian works like Charpentier's *Médée*. Her credentials as an opera singer were not in doubt, but her greatest fame, alas, was as the "lady between the sheets" immortalized in Couperin's ballad *La femme entre deux draps*. Fanchon escaped the convent because she had friends in high places—she was the mistress of the dauphin, the king's son and heir, though she had very nearly forfeited his protection in an identity mix-up. She was the victim of the Paris Opéra's custom of listing singers by their second names only—cast lists invariably referred to "Mlle Moreau," "Mlle Desmatins," and so forth. Unfortunately, there were two Mlles Moreau. Fanchon had an older sister, Louison, who also sang at the Opéra, and it is often hard to tell from the records which sister sang which part. It also meant, as the dauphin discovered, that letters addressed to Mlle Moreau could end up in the wrong hands. One of the codirectors of the Opéra was asked to invite Fanchon to a liaison with the dauphin. By mistake, the letter went to Louison, and she, probably quite innocently, accepted the invitation. Indeed, she became the dauphin's mistress for a time—until the mistake was rectified and her more glamorous sister took her place.

Not all the Opéra's female singers behaved like the Moreau sisters. Mlle de Saint-Christophle was one who definitely did not. It is true that she retired to a convent, but she did so for reasons of vocation rather than disgrace. She was described as "grande, bien faite, belle et vertueuse,"[12] and she was clearly one of Lully's favored singers during his early years as a composer of *tragédies en musique*. She sang the title role in *Alceste,* the first of Lully's tragedies to be performed at the Palais Royal, which he had persuaded the king to give him rent-free as a home for the Académie (it had previously housed the troupe run by Molière, a longtime collaborator of Lully's, who had died the previous year). Mlle de Saint-Christophle went on to create many more roles for Lully—in *Atys, Psyché, Persée,* and several others—until her departure to the convent in 1682.

Saint-Christophle's successor was Marie Le Rochois (more often known as Marthe), and we know much more about her because she was Lully's own protégée and created more of his leading roles than any other. The most famous of them was Armide in 1686, in the opera that revealed Lully and his librettist, Phillipe Quinault, at the height of their powers. It was one of those stories much loved by Louis XIV (who chose it personally for Lully) about crusader knights, medieval chivalry, and a magician, Armide, who seeks to destroy Renaud, the Christian knight, but falls in love with him instead. One observer, Le Cerf de la Viéville, said Rochois's performance made him shiver with delight.[13] Another, Titon du Tillet, wrote of the moment in the first act when "Mademoiselle Rochois spread her arms and raised her head with a majestic air" to sing her first aria: "One no longer saw anyone but her on the stage, and she seemed to fill it alone."[14] Clearly she was a fine singer, but she was also a great actress—one who could compete effectively with the astonishing sets constructed by Jean Berain, including the stage-machine palace that imploded in the final scene of the opera, as Armide departed in her flying chariot.

Marthe Le Rochois belongs to a very select group of prime donne in the story of opera—Anna Renzi, María Malibran, and Jenny Lind also belong to it—whose magnetism onstage and personal qualities offstage inspired the love and respect of colleagues and audiences alike. Rochois's virtue was un-impeachable (other than a nasty accusation that she was having a flirtation with a bassoonist, but she quickly produced a promise of marriage written by the gallant bassoonist on the back of an ace of spades, and all was well).[15] She spent her retirement passing on her art and her experience to a new gen-eration of Lullian and post-Lullian singers.

The life of a dessus at the Paris Opéra was not an easy one. The Parfaict brothers, François and Claude, compiled a *Histoire de l'académie royale de musique* for the years 1645 to 1741. Their breezy descriptions of the singers, many of whom they knew, portray an atmosphere of gossip and conspiracy not unlike that of most opera houses today, but it is clear that French singers had nothing like the economic power and influence enjoyed by their counter-parts in Italy. They worked for a state monopoly (the Opéra) that was much more like the musical establishment of the court of Mantua in Monteverdi's early days than the freewheeling public theaters of Venice, where box office depended on the drawing power of singers. Like Monteverdi himself in those early days, they were appallingly badly paid. Marie Aubry and Marie Ver-dier, two of Lully's stalwarts at the beginning of the Académie, are recorded as having had to share not just a room, but a bed as well.[16] That they escaped to liaisons with the rich and powerful is hardly surprising. Aubry became the mistress of Henry Guichard, the man who went to court to contest Lully's right to be the sole person entitled to present opera in Paris. Lully's victory in the trial was ensured by Aubry's sensational evidence that Guichard had hired her brother to murder Lully by mixing arsenic with his tobacco. Much later, Aubry was forced into retirement, according to the Parfaicts, "not be-cause of her age but because she had assumed such a prodigious size that she could not walk and that she appeared to be *toute ronde*."[17]

But all these ladies had one contemporary whose fame and infamy far outran their own. Mlle de Maupin was a *bas-dessus* (a contralto)—"the most beautiful voice in the world," as one stagestruck marquis wrote in his jour-nal. She first sang at the Opéra in 1690, three years after Lully's death, but it was only when Marthe Le Rochois retired in 1698 that her career took off. Unfortunately, other parts of her life had also taken off—so much so that 130 years later, Théophile Gautier would write a best-selling novella about her exploits.[18] The eighteenth-century English music historian Dr. Burney succinctly summed up her adventures: "She was equally fond of both sexes, fought and loved like a man, resisted and fell like a woman."[19]

She married young but promptly ran away with a fencing master. With a voice that was untrained but possessed of great natural beauty, she began a singing career, but fell in love with a young girl whose parents hurriedly confined her to a convent in Avignon. Maupin got into the convent by posing as a novice, set fire to the building, and escaped with the girl. Captured and put on trial, she was condemned to be burned alive. How she got out of that one no one quite knows, but she appeared soon after at the Paris Opéra and began her career as one of the company's outstanding singers, most stunning actors, and most dangerous enemies. When she thought herself insulted by the Opéra's leading tenor, Dumesnil, she waylaid him in the street disguised as a man, thrashed him, and stole his watch and snuff box—items which she returned the next day in front of his colleagues at the Opéra. Another male singer hid in the cellars of the Palais Royal for three weeks before summoning up the courage to make a public apology for having incurred her wrath. She delivered her pièce de résistance at a ball given by Monsieur, the king's brother. Dressed in men's clothing again, she insulted a countess and was challenged to duels by no less than three men. Outside, according to legend, she killed all three of them and immediately returned to the ballroom, where Monsieur obtained an instant pardon for her from Louis XIV.

Paris was getting a bit hot for her. She moved to Brussels and became mistress to the elector of Bavaria—an ill-starred romance that ended with another very public scene. But now Le Rochois had retired from the Paris Opéra, and Maupin returned to become the company's leading lady for several years. Her distinctive low voice and her stunning appearance, allied to formidable acting skills, made a deep impression on the Paris audience—never more so than in 1702 when she appeared as Clorinde in André Campra's *Tancrède,* an opera famous for the low-lying nature of all its male roles, as well Clorinde's. Three years later, still only thirty-two, she retired from the stage, reunited with her original husband (the one she had left for the fencing master), and became, we are told, very devout. Alas, she died only two years later.

Mlle de Maupin was the first (but not the last) lady to give prime donne a reputation for "getting away with murder."

The generation that succeeded her—the generation that bridged the gap between Lully, who died in 1687, and Jean-Philippe Rameau, whose first successful work for the Opéra was in 1733—may not have been so colorful, but that was partly because short trips to the convent were more often used as "cover-ups." Marie Antier, who had a great and long career, was one example. She was a pupil of Le Rochois, making her debut in 1711 at the age of twenty-four. She was still singing in 1741, by which time she had performed a succession of major roles for Rameau, including the very difficult part of Phaedra in *Hyppolyte et Aricie*. She was a favorite of the royal family, too: she appeared with Louis XV himself in court performances of *opéras-ballets* (Louis was one of the dancers), and she was showered with gifts from Louis's family when she married in 1726. Her fall from grace came only one year later: an unwise liaison with a high-profile lover became public knowledge and she was confined to the Convent of Chaillot for a time, though she continued to perform at the Opéra.

There was a time in the 1720s and 1730s when Parisian operagoers were divided into *mauriens* and *pélissiens*. Respectively, these were supporters of Catherine-Nicole Lemaure and Marie Pélissier. Lemaure had been the first to establish herself at the Opéra in 1720, and had quickly acquired a reputation for using her voice and her body to transform herself into the character she was singing—"miraculeuse," was how one critic described it.[20] But she was highly emotional and temperamental, and liable to announce sudden cancellations, even retirements, without notice. Returning from one such retirement in 1726, she found she had been overtaken in the audience's esteem by Marie Pélissier. The two ladies came head to head in *Pirame et Thisbé*. This was the first opera to be cowritten by two young men, François Rebel and François Francoeur, who had joined the Opéra orchestra while in their early teens, and eventually, in the 1740s and 1750s, became its artistic and administrative directors. *Pirame et Thisbé* was helped not a little by the warfare that ensued between mauriens and pélissiens.

The warfare continued through much of the 1730s, and when the two singers weren't fighting each other, they were generally fighting the Opéra administration. Lemaure refused to appear in the 1735 revival of Monté-clair's *Jephté*, then spent a night imprisoned at Fort l'Evêque (in full costume) when she deliberately sang poorly and was booed by the audience. Pélissier, for her part, was dismissed by the Opéra following a scandal with her lover, and fled to London. But she returned the following year to resume her career as one of Rameau's leading ladies. Lemaure and Pélissier may not have been the equals of Marthe Le Rochois, nor even of Mlle de Maupin, but they certainly had their supporters. Voltaire was one of their most devoted fans: he wrote glowingly of Lemaure's emotional vocal performances and Pélissier's supreme technical artistry.[21]

With Rameau in the ascendant and Lully's posthumous hold over the Opéra beginning to loosen, a new generation of singers was coming to the fore. Marie Fel was one of them, and her pupil Sophie Arnould would eventually be the most important of them all, for it was Arnould who became the voice of Gluck when he arrived in Paris in 1774. By then, the French opera tradition that Gluck sought to reform—the one that had been founded by Lully and continued in his image for almost a hundred years after his death—was greatly in need of regeneration.

There were many people, particularly in England, who thought that Francesca Cuzzoni, like Mlle Maupin, had gotten away with murder. In September 1741, the *London Daily Post* reported: "We hear from Italy that the famous singer, Mrs. C-z-ni, is under sentence of death to be beheaded for poisoning her husband." But Cuzzoni continued to sing all over Europe, and even returned to London in 1749. In fact, her husband, Pietro Sandoni, a minor composer and singing teacher, died in 1748, seven years after she was supposed to have poisoned him. Francesca Cuzzoni got away with many things during her lifetime, but murder was apparently not one of them.

Together with her great rival, Faustina Bordoni, Cuzzoni represented a new kind of Italian opera that required new kinds of singers. It was described, perhaps unfortunately, as *opera seria* (serious opera) and it had developed out of the Arcadian reform movement that began in Rome in the 1690s and infected many forms of art—poetry, drama, and opera, in particular. Its aim was to purify these arts, to make them more serious by eliminating comedy and concentrating on themes derived from nature and the more heroic moments in history. In opera, it was immensely successful: for the best part of a hundred years, operatic characters poured forth paeans of praise to humble trees, the setting sun, bumblebees, and other phenomena of the natural world. Poets like Apostolo Zeno and Pietro Metastasio provided the words in spare and elegant verse, but it was the music that made this a singer's paradise.

The showpiece aria might have been frowned on by the French, but it was the sine qua non of Italian opera. Every principal character in an opera seria took time out to ponder his or her predicament, to liken it to happenings in Bountiful Nature, and to do so in a blaze of what we would now call coloratura (a word that was rarely, if ever, used in the eighteenth century)—florid ornamentation, trills, embellishments, "shakes," and improvisations; in a word, virtuosity. The first important composers of this new kind of opera were Alessandro Scarlatti, Francesco Gasparini, and Giovanni Bononcini, all of whose styles became increasingly elaborate as opera seria took hold. Handel was one of several foreign musicians who spent time in Italy at the beginning of the century, studying the new form of opera and becoming as adept at it as the natives. His first Italian opera, *Rodrigo,* was written for Florence in 1707, but it was his second, *Agrippina,* that established him as a master of the form, only three and a half years after arriving in Italy.

Agrippina was written for Carnival in Venice in 1710, with a strikingly amoral libretto attributed to "Anonymous." In fact, it was written by Cardinal Grimani, a member of one of Venice's most powerful families and a controversial diplomat who operated in the interests of the Habsburg family (which very often meant opposing the interests of the Vatican: the portrayal of Emperor Claudius in *Agrippina* was widely believed to be a satirical representation of Grimani's boss, Pope Clement XI). The cast included two castrati as Nero and Narcissus, but its stars were probably the finest female singers in Italy at that time—Diamante Maria Scarabelli, whose role of Poppea required real virtuosity and a range of more than two octaves, and the much younger Margherita Durastini. Handel had first met Durastini in Rome in 1707 when they were both in the service of Marquis Ruspoli, and he must now have been delighted to find her ensconced in Venice as prima donna at the S. Giovanni Grisostomo. The title role in *Agrippina* was the first operatic role he wrote for her, but there were many more to come—she would have a longer association with Handel than any other singer, right up to 1734. In the meantime, it was the writing of Handel and Grimani, and the singing of Scarabelli and Durastini, that assured *Agrippina* of significant success. Handel left Venice with an international reputation.

He made good on that reputation in London—a German composer writing Italian opera for an English audience. English opera had surfaced briefly at the end of the seventeenth century, most notably in the "semi-opera" works of Henry Purcell, and it would maintain a small presence through composers like Thomas Arne and impresarios like John Rich. It was Rich who built the first theater at Covent Garden in 1732. Even though he gave Handel a home there for three seasons, Rich didn't much like Italian opera: he preferred the popular ballad operas, like *The Beggar's Opera*, which he staged in 1727. But London's fashionable society—the people who could afford the most expensive entertainments—favored Italian opera, on condition that it featured high-priced Italian stars.

This was not a subsidized court theater, as in France. It depended on subscriptions and box office, although it was an annual donation of a thousand pounds from the new Hanoverian monarch of England, George I, that provided the economic foundation for the Royal Academy of Music, which was established in 1719 to perform Italian opera at John Vanbrugh's new theater in the Haymarket. The Academy was never without financial problems; it went through several manifestations and had to fight off competitors like the short-lived Opera of the Nobility. But it had some great years, all of them between 1720 and 1741, when that other Hanoverian in London, Handel, was composer-in-residence, and when the greatest Italian singers of the time were performing there.

What they performed, for the most part, were new operas written by Handel (thirty-five of them for the London theaters), as well as the works of Giovanni Bononcini, Attilio Ariosti, Nicola Porpora, and other leading Italian composers of the day. Handel's aristocratic backers sent him to the continent to find singers, and he soon accumulated a distinguished roster. They included several castrati, whose style of singing had already been made popular in England by one of the greatest of the breed, Nicolini. He had first performed in London in 1708 and was held in something close to veneration by critics and audiences alike (and paid accordingly: an astonishing eight hundred guineas a season). Besides overseeing, and often arranging, most of the Italian operas heard in London in those early years, he showed the British public that the castrato voice, however artificial, was a vital and exciting part of Italian opera—and they fell in love with it. By the time the Academy of Music was established in 1720, Nicolini's London career was over, but he had already created two of the most fiendishly difficult title roles ever written by Handel, Rinaldo in 1711 and Amadigi in 1715. Burney called him "this great singer, and still greater actor," and Joseph Addison, writing in *The Spectator,* called him "the greatest performer in dramatic Music that is now living or that perhaps ever appeared on a stage."[22] It was quite natural, therefore, that Handel would sign up for London the best of Nicolini's successors—Carestini, Berenstadt, Bernacchi, Caffarelli, and most of all, Senesino.

However important these castrati were in London, it was the ladies who eventually made most of the headlines. When Italian opera arrived in England at the very beginning of the eighteenth century, it did so in the person of Margherita de l'Epine. Whether she was Italian or of French Huguenot extraction is not clear, but before she first came to London in 1692 she had certainly been singing, without much acclaim, in Venice and other Italian cities. Her last known performance was as late as 1733, so she had a long career, but most of it was contained within the period between 1702, when she settled permanently in London, and 1722 (not coincidentally the year in which Handel brought Francesca Cuzzoni to England). To begin with, at least, L'Epine spoke very little English and declined to sing in that language. When Thomas Clayton's *Arsinoe, Queen of Cyprus* was given in 1705—an English translation of an Italian libretto set by a journeyman English composer who had studied in Italy—she sang Italian songs between the acts but had no part in the opera. The following year, in *Camilla,* a genuine Italian opera with music by Antonio Maria Bononcini (brother of the composer who would later become Handel's rival), she sang her role in Italian while the rest of the cast sang in English.

On both these occasions, the principal English singer was Mrs. Tofts (female singers in London were customarily billed as Mrs., whether or not they were married). Katherine Tofts was beautiful, where L'Epine was plain (some said ugly), and the two ladies' supporters were quickly at odds. In

1704, when they appeared together on the concert platform, L'Epine was hissed, booed, and hit by an orange thrown from the audience. When a certain Ann Barwick was taken into custody for having thrown the offending orange, Mrs. Tofts was forced to write to the *Daily Courant,* admitting that Barwick "was lately my servant" and hoping that "you will cause her to be prosecuted, that she may be punished as she deserves."[23] Mrs. Tofts enjoyed huge popularity, but it was short-lived. By 1709 she was apparently quite mad, convinced that she was really one of the royal and aristocratic figures she portrayed on the stage. "This lady," wrote Richard Steele in *The Tatler,* "entered so thoroughly into the great characters she acted that when she had finished her part she could not think of retrenching her equipage, but would appear at her own lodging with the same magnificence that she did upon the stage."[24] Partially recovered, she later married Joseph Smith, the British consul in Venice, and lived out her fantasies in Smith's very grand palazzo.

Mrs. Tofts's mental state did not allow her to take part in the Handelian revolution that now engulfed London. Had she still been around, she would certainly have been required to sing in Italian, for that was the language and style that dominated opera in London from the time of Handel's *Rinaldo* in 1711 (his first work for London) until the resurrection of English opera in the twentieth century. But Anastasia Robinson was very much a part of the revolution. Though she was English (and therefore "Mrs.") she had probably been born in Italy and she certainly spoke Italian. She became a singer in her late teens, when her father, a portrait painter, went blind and she needed to support the family. To begin with, she sang as a soprano—one of the parts Handel wrote for her was Oriana in *Amadigi*—but somewhere around 1717 her voice seems to have dropped, and all the parts thereafter were contralto. They included Matilda in *Ottone* and Cornelia in *Giulio Cesare.* In these operas, and several others, she was part of Handel's "dream team," singing alongside Senesino, Cuzzoni, and Durastini.

Mrs. Robinson endured none of the ailments that afflicted poor Mrs. Tofts, and she was no wilting violet. She had a champion, the Earl of Peterborough, a politician much given to conspiracies and a military leader who had made his reputation in the War of the Spanish Succession, but who was better known in his later years as an amateur cook. He and Mrs. Robinson were secretly married in 1722, though he refused to acknowledge the marriage until the very end of his life thirteen years later. He had not hesitated, however, to leap to her defense during rehearsals for *Ottone* when she had complained of "ridiculous protestations of love, followed by unseemly familiarities" from the castrato Senesino. Arriving backstage, the mighty hero thrashed the quailing castrato into submission and forced him "to confess upon his knees that Anastasia was a non-pareil of virtue and beauty."[25] Soon after the first (hugely successful) performances of *Giulio Cesare,* Mrs. Robinson, still not thirty, retired from the stage and left the way clear for the legendary confrontation between Cuzzoni and Bordoni.

These were two of the greatest singers there have ever been. If the story of their epic competition in London sometimes takes pride of place, then it should not be forgotten that they, alongside the greatest of the castrati, were more responsible than any others for promoting and popularizing the new form of opera seria, both within Italy and outside.

Nor should it be forgotten that Margherita Durastini arrived in England two years before either of them. Handel doubtless had fond memories of her performance in *Agrippina* ten years earlier, but he would also have known that she was more than just a very good singer: she was a fine actor as well, and one capable of characterizing her roles in vocal as well as physical acting. Her voice started out in the soprano range *(Agrippina),* but it got noticeably lower until, by the 1730s, she was singing mezzo-soprano. In London, Handel wrote a wide variety of parts for her, including a number of "trouser roles" (male roles acted by women)—Radamisto was one, Sextus in *Giulio Cesare* was another. Castrati were all very well, but in an age when tenors and basses were generally limited to minor parts, it did not make dramatic or musical sense for castrati to perform all the principal men's roles.

Handel was one of several composers who frequently wrote these roles for female singers—singers like Diana Vico. She was a contralto with not much range but a magnificent, sonorous sound, and Handel used it to good effect when she sang for him in London between 1714 and 1716. He cast her mainly in men's roles—in fact, he had her take over the title role in *Rinaldo,* which he had originally written for the castrato Nicolini. One critic cruelly dismissed Vico as "some He-she thing or other,"[26] but she continued singing successfully in Italy up until 1726. Francesca Vanini was another specialist in trouser roles. She had a very low contralto voice, and Handel wrote both

Otho in *Agrippina* and Goffredo in *Rinaldo* for her. Both roles had a very narrow range, with exceptionally low *tessitura* (texture).

As for Durastini, Dr. Burney wrote that "her person was coarse and masculine"—in which case she appears to have projected it very accurately on the stage—but Burney's description does not tally well with an announcement in the *Evening Post* in March 1721: "Last Thursday, His Majesty [King George I] was pleased to stand godfather, and the Princess and the Lady Bruce godmothers, to a daughter of Mrs. Durastini, chief singer in the opera house."[27] Just before Durastini went home to Italy at the end of the 1724 season (she would return to London for the 1733–34 season), the Earl of Peterborough, Anastasia Robinson's secret husband, commissioned an address for Durastini to read to the audience after the curtain fell on her final performance. It was written by Alexander Pope, and it ended: "But let old charmers yield to new; / Happy soil, adieu, adieu."[28]

Two years earlier, in 1722, Francesca Cuzzoni had arrived in London to join the newly formed Royal Academy of Music. She found a company in which the castrato Senesino was clearly the star, with Durastini and Anastasia Robinson the principal female attractions. Her arrival changed everything. She already had a great reputation, and it had preceded her, hence her improbably large salary of two thousand guineas a season. But she came from Italy, and in Italy things were done rather differently from the way Handel was busily establishing them in London. For a start, Italian singers did not expect to sing anything they did not personally approve. So rehearsals for *Ottone,* the first opera in which Cuzzoni took part, were difficult. The role of Teofane had not been composed with her specifically in mind, and she informed the composer that she would not sing the first aria, "Falsa immagine." It did not suit her voice, she complained. "Madam," Handel informed her, "I know that you are a veritable devil, but I want you to know that I am Beelzebub, the chief of the devils—and I intend to throw you through that open window."[29] Cuzzoni sang the aria as written (in fact, she had great success with it), and apparently avoided defenestration as well, but it was, at best, a simmering truce. Handel continued to write great music for her—Emilia in *Flavio,* Cleopatra in *Giulio Cesare,* Asteria in *Tamerlano,* Berenice in *Scipione,* the title role in *Rodelinda,* and much more—and she had equal success in operas by Ariosti and Giovanni Bononcini. But it was a vicious circle—the greater her success, the more outrageous her behavior. Rival bands of supporters, hers and Senesino's, disrupted performances and made life miserable for the other performers. By the end of the 1725 season it was clear that something had to be done.

What Handel did was to recruit Faustina Bordoni. She was a year younger than Cuzzoni, and their careers had taken parallel courses. Bordoni's mezzo-soprano voice was a whole tone lower than Cuzzoni's, so they had frequently appeared together on the stage in Italy. But Handel must have known that they would clash in the rarified air of London's elitist opera world. In fact, he probably relied on it, and if so he was not disappointed. He joyfully composed a series of operas to show off their voices, and that of their chief protagonist, Senesino—*Alessandro, Admeto, Riccardo Primo, Siroe,* and *Tolomeo*—and there were works by Ariosti and Bononcini as well. In the meantime, both ladies acquired, through no fault of their own, groups of supporters that were as aggressive as any other claques in the story of opera. Cuzzoni's supporters were led by the formidable Countess of Pembroke, Faustina's (for that was how she was always known) by the Countess of Burlington and Lady Delawar. There was also a strong gender division. Faustina was beautiful and had charming manners, and men flocked to her banner. Cuzzoni was plain, with manners that left much to be desired, and there were more women than men among her supporters. The diarist Horace Walpole, chauvinist to the last, wrote of Cuzzoni that she was "short and squat with a doughy, cross face, dressed badly, and was silly and fantastical."[30] Ambrose Philips, an even more virulent detractor, described her as "a little stage siren" and "corrupter of all manly arts"; he pleaded with her to "leave us, the British, rough and free."[31] Eventually, he got his way.

The punch-up, when it came in the summer of 1727, just over a year after Faustina's arrival in London, was as spectacular as it was predictable. For several weeks the rival groups of partisans had been getting increasingly raucous. In April, the Princess of Wales was reported to have been upset by their behavior at Handel's *Admeto*. She was nevertheless back in the house on June 6 when it boiled over during a performance of Bononcini's *Astianatte*. The premiere of that opera had been postponed several times owing to the "indisposition" of one or other of the singers, which suggests that they may have had premonitions of what might happen. There is no actual evidence that the two ladies themselves came to blows on the stage, but that was how it was famously parodied a few months later in *The Beggar's Opera,* when Lucy Lockit and Polly Peachum went at each other hammer and tongs in the prison scene. Everyone knew what that scene referred to, and it became the stuff of legend. What is undeniable about the events of June 6 is that the audience got totally out of control and the performance had to be suspended at the end of act two; the subsequent uproar caused everything else to be omitted except for a desultory rendering of the final chorus. Mercifully, perhaps, King George I died a few days later and the opera house was closed for the compulsory period of mourning.

The directors of the Academy decided to dismiss Cuzzoni, but they were thwarted by the new king, George II, who threatened to withdraw his subscription if she was not reengaged. So Cuzzoni and Faustina had one final season together in London—an altogether quieter season that began with the new king's coronation and proceeded with the premiere of Handel's *Riccardo primo, re d'Inghilterra,* a happy choice for the beginning of a new reign. When the season ended, however, the directors, uncomfortably aware that expenses were going up and attendance was not, disbanded the Academy and set Handel free to form a new company, known as the Second Academy, with the impresario John Jacob Heidegger. Handel immediately set out for the continent to recruit a whole new set of singers.

Henceforth, Cuzzoni and Faustina pursued different paths—Cuzzoni's slowly downward, Faustina's steadily upward. Cuzzoni, ever her own worst enemy, went first to Vienna, where she sang with success but could not get a permanent job because her financial demands were astronomic. Italian opera houses were more willing to pay her fees and she had significant successes, notably performing the works of a young German composer, Johann Adolf Hasse, who, like Handel before him, had gone to Italy to learn his art. But the association with Hasse was short-lived, because in 1730 Hasse married Faustina. The following year the newlyweds departed for the Saxon court at Dresden, where they enjoyed a magnificent thirty-year ascendancy, he as *primo maestro di cappella,* she as resident prima donna.

Cuzzoni's path was much more erratic. She returned to London in 1734 and sang for two seasons with the Opera of the Nobility, the company set up by a group of aristocrats in opposition to Handel's. It was a star-studded company that included Farinelli, the greatest of all the castrati, and was led by the Neapolitan maestro Nicola Porpora. But the weight of two Italian opera companies, each of them performing twice a week (idiotically, on the same days), was too much for London to bear. Handel's company barely survived; the Opera of the Nobility went under after four short seasons. For Cuzzoni, it had been a mixed success: she was well paid, but enthusiasm for her was notably reduced, and she *hated* being billed beneath Farinelli. Her subsequent peregrinations around Europe included a spell in a debtor's prison in the Netherlands. Though she kept at it gamely, by 1750 her aging voice was no longer an instrument capable of earning a living. The ending was sad: almost twenty-five years spent in Bologna, much of it making and selling buttons to keep a roof over her head. She died there in extreme poverty in 1778.

Few eighteenth-century prime donne approached the fame of Cuzzoni and Faustina, but one that did was their contemporary Vittoria Tesi. Aside from appearances in Dresden, Vienna, and Madrid, she made her career entirely in Italy, and it was a career against which she sometimes rebelled. In contrast to Cuzzoni and Faustina, she was a contralto with a low and very distinctive voice, and as a result she was frequently cast in travesti roles—indeed, she created a long line of them. If appearing on the stage was still not a respectable activity for a woman, then appearing dressed as a man was even more questionable. The Church had much to say about transvestism, none of it encouraging, and Tesi clearly felt the heat of disapproval. In 1738, at the height of her fame, just after she had starred at the opening of the Teatro San Carlo in Naples, she refused to sing any more travesti roles on the grounds that "acting a male part was bad for her health."[32] The refusal turned out to be temporary: within a short time she was back in trousers.

Whether she was playing a man or a woman, Tesi was an impressive actor, and it was her stage presence that critics and diarists remarked on, rather than her singing, about which opinions were divided. But composers liked her. In her forties she was creating roles for Gluck (Ipermestra and Semiramide) and Jomelli (Achilles and Dido); and in her fifties, when she was still creating roles for Gluck, including Lisinga in *Le Cinesi* (The Chinese Ladies), she was comfortably settled in Vienna with the official title of costume director to the court theaters and living, as a respected friend, in the palace of the Prince of Saxe-Hildburghausen, who just happened to be Gluck's employer as well. Tesi's longtime husband, a Signor Tramontini (it was a marriage of convenience, but it provided good cover for her many liaisons), was a former barber who made himself useful by keeping the faro bank in the prince's gaming rooms. One of Tesi's lovers—a young nobleman who was also a priest—became much more famous than he would have wished (though long after his death) when her letters to him were published, providing fascinating insight into the life and thinking of a highly literate and articulate woman who defied the low opinion of female singers held by most of her contemporaries.[33]

If Vittoria Tesi is remembered, somewhat unfairly, as a liberated woman rather than as a great singer, then the reverse is true of Cuzzoni and Faustina. They were, quite simply, the finest exemplars of a new kind of singing, one that required superb technique and great daring, and that truly deserved the description *bel canto*. The *da capo* aria, with its repetitions and invitations to embellish, sometimes to improvise, was the outstanding innovation of opera seria. It was the vehicle that enabled singers to amaze their audiences and to show off their very real virtuosity, but it required training and techniques unknown to previous generations. Handel allowed his singers less room for improvisation than most Italian composers, but that was because he knew exactly what embellishments he wanted, and he wrote them into the score—quite a fright for an Italian singer accustomed to extemporizing more or less whatever she felt would show off her voice to best effect. It clearly annoyed Cuzzoni on her first visit (hence the Beelzebub confrontation), but she could cope—she was in a class of her own. Dr. Burney certainly thought so: "A native warble enabled her to execute divisions with such facility as to conceal every appearance of difficulty . . . The art of conducting, sustaining, increasing and diminishing her tones by minute degrees acquired her, among professors, the title of complete mistress of her art . . . Her shake was perfect . . . Her high notes were unrivalled in clearness and sweetness."[34]

The most difficult of coloratura arias seem to have come naturally to her ("Da tempeste" in *Giulio Cesare*), but she could also move an audience to tears by her rendition of arias such as "Ombre, piante" in *Rodelinda* and

"Falsa immagine" in *Ottone* (the very aria she had originally refused to sing). She had a range of more than two octaves, an unusual gift for *rubato* (in which a singer temporarily disregards strict time), and a famous trill that was slow and sensuous.

Faustina, with a lower voice, had contrasting gifts but no less technique. She was essentially a dramatic artist ("born for singing and for acting," Burney wrote), but she was also capable of taking greater liberties than Cuzzoni. Hearing her in 1721, one critic wrote: "She always sang the first part of an aria exactly as the composer had written it but at the *da capo* repeat introduced all kinds of *doublements* and *maniere* without taking the smallest liberties with the rhythm of the accompaniment."[35] That was before she began singing for Handel, of course, but it is probable that her musicianship, and her great sense of the dramatic, enabled her to improvise more than most singers without ever upsetting the integrity of the music.

As for Handel, he was not sorry to see the backs of the two ladies who had caused him so much trouble. One of his librettists, Paolo Antonio Rolli, reported that "one of them [Faustina] never pleased him at all and he would like to forget the other [Cuzzoni]."[36] The lady he acquired to replace them combined some of the virtues of each—Cuzzoni's warble and Faustina's flair for drama. Her name was Anna Maria Strada del Pò. Burney attributed her success almost entirely to Handel's training, calling her "a singer formed by himself and modeled on his own melodies." Between 1729 and 1737 he wrote fourteen major roles for her, and she took over eight of Cuzzoni's old roles and one of Faustina's. The London public came to like her but never to love her. "Strada's personal charms did not assist her much in conciliating parties," wrote Burney, "for she had so little of Venus in her appearance that she was usually called the Pig. However, by degrees she subdued all their prejudices, and sang herself into favour."[37]

Because of its wealth, and because of the fortuitous presence of Handel, London had assumed an unlikely role in the development of opera, and particularly of opera singing. But Handel wrote no new operas after 1741 (he turned to composing English oratorios instead), and though London would remain an important center for performance, it was on the European mainland, in Italy, France, and the German states, that most of the principal developments took place. Nowhere was more important than Naples.

CHAPTER THREE

Porpora's Pupils

Nicola Porpora of Naples was probably the most famous singing teacher of the eighteenth century—and a very successful composer, too, though his forty-five operas are rarely, if ever, performed today. For the most part, they were predictable pieces that exploited a well-worn formula of simple recitatives and high-flying arias, but they fulfilled the most basic requirement of eighteenth-century Italian opera, which was to give the singers ample opportunity to amaze.

More than any other period in the story of opera, this was a time when singers were supreme. The prevailing style of opera was statuesque, short on drama, and serious—it was, after all, known as *opera seria*. More than anything else, it was a platform for those singers who possessed the vocal equipment to silence a noisy, often inattentive audience by the power and range of their singing—more than two octaves for most singers, almost three for some. Not unnaturally, popular taste favored the higher registers, the ones in which singers could best show off their vocal acrobatics. Porpora and his fellow Italian composers provided the music for these operas, though they did not generally write the most acrobatic sections, which were improvised by the singers themselves, joyfully adding their own trills and ornaments, often whole cadenzas. At its worst, it was self-indulgent and repetitive. At its best, it was exciting and virtuosic.

To our modern way of thinking, such a scheme of things would naturally favor sopranos and tenors, but in Porpora's time (which was also Handel's time) the tenor voice was not much admired—it tended to be used for small parts, and often for unattractive characters. Yet eighteenth-century opera was far from being a female preserve, and that was especially true in

Nicola Porpora (1686–1768) defined and taught the vocal style that became known as *bel canto*. It was the classical Italian style of singing, and it dominated opera for two hundred years. (Lebrecht Collection.)

Italy. The prima donna was a star, certainly, and she had considerable draw-ing power at the box office, but she almost always had to share top billing with the primo uomo, the male star: indeed, she quite often had to accept second place to him. The male star was also a soprano, of course—a cas-trato—and it was that artificial, musical, and intensely powerful voice that gave baroque opera its peculiar quality and its enormous popularity.

What made Porpora such a pivotal character in all this was not just that he wrote operas singers liked to perform, but that he taught so many of the most important singers and musicians of the century, male and female. His influence spread far beyond Italy, to Vienna, London, Madrid, and Dresden. He visited all these places himself, and wrote operas for them, but his influence was spread most of all by the fame of his pupils—an honor roll of eighteenth-century opera. They included two of the greatest castrati of the age, Farinelli and Caffarelli; two of the outstanding female sopranos, Regina Mingotti and Caterina Gabrielli; the master librettist of the century, Metastasio; and two of the most important opera composers, Johann Adolf Hasse and Joseph Haydn.

Timing and geography helped. Porpora was born in Naples in 1686, a time when the city was fast becoming the opera capital of the world. Alessandro Scarlatti was the leading composer, and he, more than anyone, established opera seria as the dominant format, with the da capo aria as its showpiece. Literally, *da capo* means "from the top" or "from the beginning," and it referred to the three-part structure of the aria (ABA) in which the last part was a reprise of the first ("from the top"). Each part allowed singers to interpolate their own decorations and vocalises, but it was in the final section, the reprise, that the most ornate variations and cadenzas were added. Since most of these were "exit arias," the general idea was that the singer would save the best for last and leave the stage to a noisy demonstration of support. A principal character might have five or six such arias in a single opera, so it was hardly surprising that the singers loved the format, and often played fast and loose with it. Most of them owned at least one *aria di baule,* or "suitcase aria," which traveled around in the singer's baggage and was blithely inserted into a performance if the existing arias were felt to be inadequate—regardless of its suitability, and generally without the composer's permission.

Porpora was more than a journeyman composer. He was a skilled exponent of the format Scarlatti had pioneered, yet he could hardly be compared to some of his younger contemporaries in Naples. Sadly, Leonardo Vinci (1690–1730) and Pier Luigi Palestrina (1710–36) both died very young, whereas Porpora, by virtue of longevity (he died in 1768 at the age of eighty-one), and because of the continuing influence of his pupils, was pervasive in a way that they were not. The one man whose talents were greater than all of theirs, George Frideric Handel, was based in faraway London. He and

Porpora went head to head in that city for three years in the 1730s (Porpora came off second best and retreated to Naples), but Handel's work was little known in Italy, even though it was Italian in both language and style.

Porpora was the son of a Neapolitan bookseller. He landed on his feet at the age of ten when he won a place in the Conservatorio dei Poveri di Gesù Christo. This was one of the city's four charitable institutions founded in the sixteenth century for the education of orphans and poor children. Their emphasis was on music and they were responsible, more than any other places in Italy, for the training of castrati. But Porpora was neither a castrato nor particularly poor. For his first three years at Gesù Christo he was a paying pupil: it appears that only thereafter was he given a scholarship to cover his expenses, probably because he was deemed an outstanding pupil. By the time he left, at age twenty, he was widely recognized as an up and coming composer. He was commissioned to write operas for the Neapolitan Royal Palace, the Portuguese ambassador, the Prince of Hesse-Darmstadt, and, in 1714, for the imperial court in Vienna.

Composing operas and having them performed in prestigious venues was important and good for the résumé, but it did not pay well. By 1715 Porpora had taken up a full-time teaching position as maestro di capella at another of the Neapolitan conservatories, Sant'Onofrio, and it was at this time that he gave lessons to two of the young men who would help to make him famous throughout the world of opera—Farinelli and Metastasio.

The three of them collaborated for the first time on a serenata, *Angelica e Medoro,* commissioned for a party at the palazzo of the Prince de la Torella in 1720. The twenty-two-year-old Metastasio provided the text, Porpora the music, and fifteen-year-old Farinelli made his debut before the public. For Porpora, it was just another commission, gratefully received and well executed. For Metastasio and Farinelli, it was the beginning of a friendship that would span their lives. Though they rarely saw each other in the years ahead, they corresponded regularly for six decades—sending letters that invariably began "Caro gemello" (Dear twin).[1] The evening of their meeting in 1720 was remembered in a dedication to Farinelli with which Metastasio began one of his later dramas:

Appresero gemelli a sciorre, il volo
La tua voce in Parnaso e il mio pensieri.

Your voice over Parnassus, twinned with my thoughts,
Learned at the same time to unleash their flight.[2]

No one knows quite why Carlo Broschi, known as Farinelli, was a castrato. His father was a minor aristocrat who became a provincial governor in the kingdom of Naples shortly after Carlo's birth. He lost his job three years later, so it is possible he had his son castrated for the normal reason—money. "Farinello" means "rogue" or "rascal" in Italian, and "farinelli" was apparently a nickname applied collectively to the family—perhaps because that was Governor Broschi's reputation in politics. At all events, Farinelli became a pupil at Sant'Onofrio when he was very young, probably only four or five, and it was there that Porpora became his teacher, when he was ten years old. In later life, Porpora always maintained that the somewhat younger Cafarelli was a better singer, though a vastly inferior human being, but Farinelli was clearly promising enough as a teenager to be entrusted with first performances of the master's own compositions. Within a year of his debut and his meeting with Metastasio at the Palazzo Torella, Porpora took him to Rome and cast him in a succession of operas he had been commissioned to write for the Aliberti Theater. It was in one of these, *Flavio Anicio Olibrio,* that Farinelli, now seventeen, had his legendary confrontation with the German trumpet player, so famously described by Dr. Burney—a night-after-night contest to see which of them could outlast and outperform the other. It climaxed on one amazing night when the trumpet player stopped, exhausted, thinking he had fought Farinelli to an honorable draw, "when Farinelli, with a smile on his countenance, showing he had only been sporting with him all that time, broke out all at once in the same breath, with fresh vigor, and not only swelled and shook the note, but ran the most rapid and difficult divisions, and was at last silenced only by the acclamations of the audience."

"From this period," wrote Burney, "may be dated that superiority which he ever maintained over all his contemporaries."[3]

Metastasio, on the other hand, took private lessons from Porpora, not in singing but in composition. He was a poet, of course, but to write poetry that would be set to music he had to know the basics of composition. He had grown up in Rome, where his father was a grocer and his education had been looked after first by his godfather, who was a cardinal, and then by a wealthy man of letters named Gravina, who eventually left him a small fortune, which he blew in a remarkably short time. He had written his first play under Gravina's supervision when he was only fourteen, and, also at Gravina's suggestion, he had Hellenized his name (it had originally been Trapassi, which literally means "transition"). More important for the long term, he had come under the influence of the Arcadian Academy, which had been founded in Rome in 1690 by the literary circle surrounding Queen Christina, the former Queen of Sweden. The Arcadian "reform" movement encouraged a return to the simplicity of antiquity, on the one hand, and to Cartesian values—"all the passions of the human heart"—on the other. Descartes had been Christina's tutor in Sweden when she was in her early twenties. She had succeeded to the throne when she was only six, and she abdicated and moved to Rome when she was twenty-eight.

So in 1719, once again impoverished but knowing that he was born to write, Metastasio moved to Naples and got a job in a law office. It was there that he met Porpora and began his music lessons, and it must very soon have become clear to both of them that Metastasio's spare and elegant writing, with its emphasis on moral dilemmas and the triumph of those who succeed in controlling their passions, was tailor-made for the style of opera seria championed by Porpora and his colleagues. Metastasio's characters all had to express their feelings, and the da capo aria was the ideal vehicle, especially when the words were written in elegant Italian, full of vivid imagery and recognizable passions.

The little serenata on which he collaborated with Porpora and Farinelli in 1720 was just the beginning. Within three years, Metastasio was writing full-length operas for Naples, and very soon for Rome and Venice as well. By the 1729–30 season in Rome, when no fewer than three of his operas were given premieres, all in settings by Leonardo Vinci, he could accurately be described as the leading librettist of Italian opera. That fact was recognized in the same year, 1729, when he was invited to succeed Apostolo Zeno as

Pietro Metastasio (1698–1782). A follower of Descartes's treatise
Les passions de l'âme, Metastasio believed the passions were "the necessary
winds by which one navigates through the sea of life," and he ensured that
his dramas projected the triumph of characters who learned to control
their passions and to use them for positive (that is, moral) ends.
(Beinecke Rare Book and Manuscript Library, Yale University.)

Caesarian court poet in Vienna, and that was where he remained for the last fifty-two years of his life. It was where he wrote most of his twenty-seven opera librettos—but, more important, it was where he watched as those same librettos were set and reset by more than three hundred different composers, some of them more than fifty times (*Grove* lists no fewer than eighty-six settings of *Ataserse*).

Aside from the "twins," Porpora's most important pupil was Gaetano Majorano, known as Caffarelli. Five years younger than Farinelli, he had a voice described as a high mezzo-soprano, whereas Farinelli's was generally described as soprano. Most composers concentrated on the medium register when writing for castrati—Patrick Barbier, one of the most authoritative historians of singing in this period, notes that "the public enjoyed being amazed by virtuosity, but . . . by choice, they definitely preferred low notes sung by a high voice, for they were warmer, more sensual, endowed with a far superior emotional quality."[4] Porpora's own compositions, mostly written within the compass of an octave and a fifth, are evidence that this was true. Most people who heard Caffarelli in person remarked on the sweetness of his voice, on his ability to seduce audiences by the sheer beauty of his singing, on his talent for "pathetic song," and on his brilliance as a musician (he was a fine harpsichordist and could read almost anything on sight)—whereas Farinelli, especially in his early years, had a propensity to amaze, especially in the trills, ornaments, and cadenzas he interpolated for himself. It was eventually the Emperor Charles VI who advised him, "Adopt a more simple style, and gradually you will win hearts."[5]

Farinelli's stage career effectively ended in 1737 when he began his twenty-two-year odyssey at the Spanish court of Philip V, but Caffarelli's went on much longer. His last professional engagement appears to have been in 1756 in Madrid, where, fittingly, he spent time with Farinelli. We do not know what the two great castrati thought of each other (Farinelli's side of the correspondence with Metastasio has been lost) but we can make an educated guess from the scathing tone of Metastasio's occasional, and gleeful, reports of the troubles Caffarelli got himself into, almost always because of his bad behavior.[6]

If ever there was a monster of the opera stage, it was Caffarelli. He was vain, arrogant, and frequently contemptuous of his colleagues. He fought at least one duel, and was rescued from another only by the intervention of the contralto Vittoria Tesi, who fearlessly placed herself between the combatants, much to the relief of Caffarelli, who quickly gave up his sword to her. He was imprisoned in Naples for (according to the official report) "lasciviousness on stage with one of the female singers, conversing with the spectators in the boxes from the stage, ironically echoing whichever member of the company was singing an aria, and finally refusing to sing in the *ripieno* with the others."[7] On another occasion, he got into a fight with a rival castrato in the middle of a church while they were meant to be performing in a motet during "the solemn celebration of Profession" of a lady taking the veil. A visit to Paris ended when Louis XV gave him three days to leave the country, for impertinence: he had implied that a gift from the king, a snuffbox, was inadequate.

The only person who appears to have found an effective way of overcoming Caffarelli's temperament was the Prince of Savoy, who was marrying the Infanta of Spain. As a wedding present, the King of Naples had sent Caffarelli (all expenses paid) to sing at the ceremony. But Caffarelli did not want to sing, perhaps because the Infanta was a pupil of Farinelli's. The prince approached the reluctant singer and told him his young wife could not believe that any singer other than Farinelli could really please her. Caffarelli immediately vowed that he would prove himself "two Farinellis in one." He sang, and he did please her.[8]

Matters of character aside, as Burney reported, "Porpora, who hated [Caffarelli] for his insolence, used to say that he was the greatest singer Italy had ever produced."[9]

Porpora's fame as a teacher was such that any powerful patron with a promising young singer as his protégé might seek to engage him. This was certainly the case with two of the finest female singers of the period, Regina Mingotti and Caterina Gabrielli. They were, in a way, the successors to Francesca Cuzzoni and Faustina Bordoni, the prime donne who had proved such a handful for Handel in London. Mingotti, in fact, became a rival of Bordoni in Dresden in the late 1740s. Bordoni, married to the Saxon Court's musical director, Johann Adolf Hasse, was the reigning prima donna; the much younger Mingotti, introduced by Porpora, threatened her position. Hasse attempted to solve the problem by writing an opera that blatantly featured what he deemed to be the weak points in Mingotti's voice, but the scheme backfired: Mingotti scored a triumph.

"A perfect mistress of her art," was the way Dr. Burney described Mingotti. He had heard her in London, and later visited her in retirement in Munich. Much of what we know about her is dependent on Burney's description—that she spoke about music with as much authority as any maestro di capella he had ever met (and that was praise indeed, coming from Burney), and that she was trilingual in German, French, and Italian, as well as speaking very acceptable English and Spanish, and reading Latin.[10] A well-educated lady, by any standard. She had been born Caterina Valentini, probably in Naples, and had apparently spent much of her early life as a "servant-pupil" in a Silesian convent—why, we do not know. She hated the drudgery of the convent, and she knew she had a good voice. So, at the age of twenty-five, she used her voice and her good looks to get herself a place in the touring company of Pietro Mingotti, whom she hastily married, and almost equally hastily parted from. It was Mingotti who introduced her to Porpora, and Porpora who introduced her to the Saxon court at Dresden in one of his own operas, much to the displeasure of Bordoni. Obviously, Dresden, at the height of the ascendancy of Hasse and Bordoni, was not a place where Mingotti could make a career, but she was there long enough to make a startling impression—which, in turn, launched her on a glittering career in Naples, Prague, Madrid, Paris, and London.

It was in London that she fell from grace. Engaged to sing at the King's Theatre during the winter season of 1764, she quarreled with Vaneschi, the reigning impresario, and took over the management of the theater herself. She quickly lost her entire investment.[11]

Caterina Gabrielli was another matter altogether. Her reputation for tantrums, cancellations, and general bad behavior was rivaled only by Caffarelli's. But then, like Caffarelli, she had talent enough to get away with it. Her father was a cook—in fact, rather a well-placed cook, because he worked for Cardinal Gabrielli in Rome. Knowing his daughter to be musical, but lacking the money to pay for singing lessons, the cook took her occasionally to the Teatro Argentina. Back home, Caterina would sing some of the arias she heard from memory. One day, the cardinal, walking in his garden, heard her.[12] The rest, as they say (including Caterina's customary gesture of taking her patron's name), is history.

She was probably only fourteen when the cardinal sent her to Venice to study. Porpora, now almost sixty and very famous, was teaching at the Ospedaletto, one of Venice's four orphanages for girls. These orphanages had a reputation for teaching music that was greater even than that of the Neapolitan conservatories (where the emphasis was on boy castrati rather than girls, and where Porpora had taught right up to his departure for Venice in 1741). The Venetian orphanages were at the peak of their fame—Vivaldi, who taught at the Pietà for most of his life, had died in 1741; the much younger Galuppi was the reigning maestro at the Mendicante; and now Porpora was lending his name to the Ospedaletto. It is hardly surprising that the cardinal chose to send Caterina to Venice.

She studied with Porpora and others for most of three years, before making her stage debut in Lucca at the age of seventeen. Gaetano Guadagni, less than a year older than Caterina, sang in the same performance. He would later take acting lessons from David Garrick and go on to become Gluck's favorite castrato—the original Orpheus in *Orfeo ed Euridice* and one of the most important reasons for that opera's stunning and revolutionary success. Young Caterina, it is said, was smitten, and her infatuation with the castrato transformed her "from a thin, fretful girl into a beauty."[13]

It wasn't long before she was capitalizing on her looks, and getting into trouble. Not the least of her conquests were the Austrian Chancellor and the reigning Duke of Parma (a hunchback who was so jealous of the attention paid her by other men that he placed her under house arrest in his own palace). In Sicily, where she insulted the viceroy by failing to attend a dinner and then "singing her airs in a whisper" at the evening performance at the opera house, she was thrown into prison for twelve days. She passed the time singing for the prisoners (full voice) and passing out money to pay their debts—until she was released amidst universal rejoicing. In Vienna, the French and Portuguese ambassadors competed for her affections. In a fury at finding the Portuguese in her house, the Frenchman attacked Gabrielli, and wounded her. Saved from serious injury by the whalebone of her corset, Gabrielli confiscated the sword "as a trophy." Metastasio later negotiated its return to its remorseful owner.

Metastasio was one of Gabrielli's most important champions. It was on his recommendation that she was appointed court-singer to the Emperor Francis in Vienna, and it was he who gave her lessons in declamation and was probably responsible for transforming her from a very good singer into an outstanding singing actress. She was highly esteemed by the two most important composers of the period—Gluck (not a man who tolerated tantrums from his singers), for whom she created the title role in *Tetide*, and Traetta, for whom she sang in many premieres, including *Armida*. It was Traetta who persuaded the Empress of Russia to invite her to St. Petersburg, where she sang for four seasons—Catherine was horrified by the size of her fee, but she paid it all the same.

Gabrielli continued singing into her fiftieth year, although her powers were clearly declining. Mozart, hearing her in 1778, wrote that, for all her fluency in runs and roulades, she "was unfortunate in being unable to *sing*."[14] Two years later, in one of her final performances, she was booed off the stage at La Scala because she declined to sing an encore. But the ubiquitous Burney, meeting her in her prime, described her as "the most intelligent and best bred virtuosa" he had ever met. Burney's daughter, Fanny, however, contented herself by counting Gabrielli's entourage as she left the theater—one servant carrying her train, another her little dog, another her parrot, and another her monkey.[15]

One way or another, the cook's daughter from Rome had done very well for herself. Whatever mayhem she left in her wake, her three years with Porpora in Venice and the time she spent with Metastasio in Vienna a few years later had not been wasted. As an actor and a singer she ranked with the greatest of the century, along with her first love, Guadagni, and with her slightly younger contemporary in Paris, Sophie Arnould.

So what was it that Porpora taught his pupils that made them so outstanding?[16] First and foremost, it was breathing—more precisely, breath control.

It is, of course, the most basic requirement for all singing, but for castrati its importance was magnified by the nature of the operation that had been performed on them (customarily between the ages of eight and ten). Two of its principal effects were to enlarge the rib cage and to maintain the position of the larynx. Normally, when a boy's voice breaks at puberty, the larynx moves downward, causing the timbre and pitch of the voice similarly to move downward. In the case of the castrato, the larynx maintained its position and the vocal cords therefore remained close to the cavities of resonance. In this way, the range and quality of the treble voice was maintained, and they were augmented by the much more powerful lungs and diaphragm of a grown man.

But the operation on its own could not guarantee that the castrato voice would have either the power or the control that was necessary to develop its potential. That was done by expanding the muscular system of the vocal cords, and that, in turn, required several hours—every day, for years on end—of breathing exercises. What Porpora and his colleagues at the conservatories taught the boys was to *filar il suono* (spin the tone)—to convert breath into a whisper, then into a tone; to swell the tone on the breath and then develop it naturally, without any constriction or stutter, into a stream of sound. Eventually, it was hoped, the boy would abandon the natural abdominal breathing of childhood and develop the ability to control his breathing through the ribs as well as the abdomen (what is called "deep costal-abdominal breathing"). Spinning tone through this highly developed equipment was what enabled the castrati to perform vocal feats that were impossible for normal human beings.

Breath control was essential, but the castrato needed much more than that. He had to be able to "color" his voice, to give it breadth and variety of expression. That was achieved by his command of several different registers, from the high register (the head voice), which remained his natural domain, to the lower registers of the chest. The operation would have arrested the normal downward shift to a lower pitch, so it was necessary to develop these chest registers in the same way that a female singer might. The castrati could do it better than most women because their male larynxes were bigger and stronger than a woman's. So singers like Senesino and Carestini (in the second part of his career at least) were described as contraltos and were most famous for the power and beauty of their chest registers. Even Farinelli, a high soprano, was renowned for his ability to swoop down into these lower registers. What they all had in common, whether they were described as sopranos or contraltos, was this wide compass that was the hallmark of the castrato voice. After breathing, it was probably the most important thing they had learned from their teachers in long hours of study and training during their teenage years.

There were many other refinements of technique and interpretation the castrati had to learn. Many of these were doubtless taught by Porpora and his colleagues, but some of the most important did not truly take effect until the singers were out on the road, experimenting for themselves in ways in which they could move and affect their audiences. One of these was the use of *legato* (the ability to "bind together" or connect the notes and phrases of their music): it is the quintessential quality of bel canto, but it was one that many castrati developed only when they had gotten over the first rush of self-wonder at their ability to astonish audiences by technique alone (and some of them never got over it).

The art of singing was not the only thing Porpora taught his pupils. He also instilled in them the rudiments of composition. At its most basic, singing is, and always has been, a collaboration between singer and composer (whether the composer is dead or alive), and that has never been more true than it was in the eighteenth and early nineteenth centuries, when operas were being written at a pace, and in quantities, that have never been equaled. Almost always, they were written for specific singers and specific occasions, so there was quite frequently an element of genuine collaboration between the composer and the singer. Singers often requested changes; sometimes they even suggested what those changes should be. Composers were accommodating (they had to be), but they worked best with singers who themselves had a grounding in composition. Within eighteenth-century operas there are hundreds of examples of arias singers claimed to have composed themselves—a more proper credit would generally be "suggested by"—but whether they actually wrote music or not, they were certainly expected to improvise on what they were given. The da capo aria was an invitation to the singers (virtually a command) to add their own ornaments, embellishments, and whole cadenzas. This was a disaster area for the unmusical, and it was also the reason why Porpora's pupils needed to know the basics of composition.

Porpora taught in the Neapolitan conservatories, on and off, for most of his life. It is said, somewhat improbably, that he confined Caffarelli to performing the same set of exercises, all written on one sheet of paper, for six years, at the end of which time he dismissed him with the admonition, "Go now, my son: I have nothing more to teach you. You are the greatest singer in Europe." That may not be literally true, but it illustrates the intensity of the training to which the young boys were subjected.[17] They spent hours and hours perfecting the *messa di voce* (placement of the voice) before they were allowed to sing a single melody; they learned and practiced every kind of vocalization technique on their way to mastering the ornate and intricate requirements of the baroque style; they took daily lessons in counterpoint; later, they were required to sing in front of a mirror in order to avoid ugly grimaces and unsuitable gestures. They studied literature as well as music, instruments as well as singing. It was repetitive, highly concentrated, and very disciplined.

Their living conditions were at best basic, at worst shocking. They earned money for the conservatories by performing at concerts, funerals, and masses—most famously as the "cherub children" who stood vigils beside the bodies of dead children. Occasionally, if they were very lucky, they got to sing at one of the Neapolitan theaters as members of a children's chorus. No one seems to have pondered the psychological complexities of their lives: they were generally referred to as eunuchs—or worse, as *non integri* (not whole).

Out of this hell came a few young men who enchanted the courts and cities of Europe, and who were generally the best educated and the best trained singers of their time. They made a lot of money, and a few hung on to it. Caffarelli bought himself a dukedom in Calabria and built himself a splendid house in Naples just off the Via Roma (it still exists).[18] Farinelli, vastly enriched by his long service to the crown of Spain, purchased an estate outside Bologna and had a fine villa constructed on it.

But for every Farinelli or Caffarelli who succeeded, there were literally hundreds who either failed completely or settled for minor positions in obscure church choirs.

As for the ladies—La Regina and La Gabrielli, as they were known —we know very little about the way Porpora taught them, but it is fair to conjecture that for them, too, breathing was the most fundamental and repetitive part of their training. After all, they were being trained to compete onstage, night after night, with the most virtuosic of the castrati—that is, with men who were singing in the same registers as they were, but who had what amounted to supercharged female equipment. Such an unequal contest could only be essayed by women whose breath control was as good as (or, as was probably often the case, better than) that of most castrati.

Whether they were angels or monsters, or, more likely, a mixture of the two, these women were tough. They had to be. The eighteenth century had little regard for women who appeared on the stage. In the Papal States, which extended across a large part of central Italy, the practice was banned altogether (so was castration, but the Church managed to have it both ways and all ways: the Sistine Chapel was one of the first employers of castrati, and almost certainly the last, using them up until shortly before the First World War). Female singers were therefore members of a greatly abused profession. They were often referred to as "courtesans." They generally had "protectors," and they were much in need of them, as any reading of police court proceedings in cities such as Naples, Venice, Rome, and Bologna at this time will illustrate.[19] The great ones, Mingotti and Gabrielli among them, had entourages and lived extravagant lives. Their later years were not necessarily impoverished, but they tended to be quiet and rather lonely. Gabrielli retired to Rome and lived with her sister, while Mingotti settled in Germany, first in Dresden, then in Munich, then in Neuburg, where her illegitimate son, grandly known as Samuel von Buckingham, was inspector of forests.

The best singers at least had the opportunity to make their fortunes. Composers and singing teachers did not. If they were lucky, they would marry well, like Gluck, or find a generous patron, like Haydn. For Porpora, it was always a matter of finding employment. His facility as a composer and his reputation as a teacher were such that he was normally welcome wherever he went—for a time—but his life was itinerant and often difficult. Again and again he fell back on teaching appointments at the Neapolitan conservatories and Venetian orphanages. Along the way, he owed much to the influence of his pupils. Farinelli, Caffarelli, Gabrielli, and Mingotti all performed in his operas and gave them a currency they might not otherwise have had. But it was Metastasio who helped him most, not just by providing texts he could set, as he did for every composer of the time, but also by intervening on numerous occasions to get him work at the imperial court in Vienna and to act as intermediary when he got into scrapes. It was Metastasio who arbitrated in the dispute between Bordoni, Hasse's wife, and Mingotti, Porpora's protégée, in Dresden; it was Metastasio who found him work in Vienna when he had to leave Dresden; and it was Metastasio who introduced him to his last important pupil, Joseph Haydn.

In the mid-1750s, Haydn, a superannuated chorister at St. Stephen's, was in his early twenties and busy surviving in Vienna. He lived in an attic, but the attic happened to be in the house where Metastasio lived, so it was the eminent court poet who instructed him in Italian and also found him jobs. One of these jobs was as valet to Porpora, which Haydn combined with acting as keyboard accompanist when his master gave singing lessons to the wives, daughters, and mistresses of the Viennese elite. Not unnaturally, Haydn also became a pupil of Porpora's, and was grateful for the experience: "I wrote fluently, but not wholly correctly, until I had the good fortune to learn the true foundations of composition from the celebrated Porpora who was in Vienna at that time."[20]

Much the same sentiments might have been expressed by Hasse. He, too, had taken lessons from Porpora, but thirty years earlier in Naples. He had quickly moved on to become a pupil of the much better known Alessandro Scarlatti, but not before he had made the acquaintance of two of Porpora's other students—Farinelli, who sang one of the title roles in *Antonio e Cleopatra*, the serenata that brought Hasse to the attention of the Italian music world; and Metastasio, who became a lifelong friend. Indeed, Hasse set all but one of Metastasio's twenty-seven original librettos (*Temistocle* appears to have been the only exception).

It was at the Saxon court of Dresden that Hasse prospered most greatly, working in tandem with his wife and prima donna, Faustina Bordoni. Like all Europeans of that generation, their lives were cruelly disrupted by the ravages of the Seven Years' War (1756–63). The Hasses saw out the war in Venice and Vienna (the Saxon court had moved to Warsaw); when they finally returned to Dresden in 1763 it was to find that the library of sacred music manuscripts, including many of Hasse's, had been burned down, while the opera house and their home had been virtually destroyed. They returned to Vienna, which was always a happy hunting ground for Hasse—partly because of Metastasio's friendship, partly because he became one of the favorite composers of the Empress Maria Teresa, who gave him several commissions. The last of these was a setting of Metastasio's *Ruggiero*, commissioned by the empress for the wedding of her son, the Archduke Ferdinand, in Milan in 1771. She also commissioned a companion piece, an opera called *Ascanio in Alba*. It was when he heard this work that the seventy-three-year-old Hasse is reported to have said of its sixteen-year-old composer: "This boy will cause us all to be forgotten." The boy's name was Mozart.[21]

In a way, Hasse was right: he *was* more or less forgotten after his death. For 150 years, his operas were rarely, if ever, performed; only his sacred music was heard, and even that was generally confined to Dresden. The rediscovery of his operas was one of the more interesting musical developments of the late twentieth century.

Porpora, Hasse's onetime teacher, rival, and sometime friend, had no such reinstatement in the pantheon. Even in his own lifetime, his operas had seemed old-fashioned and lacking in invention—useful frameworks for singers to improvise on, perhaps, but not much more than that. With the possible exception of the works he wrote in London in the 1730s, when a more dramatic style was dictated by his composing in direct competition with Handel, there is no reason to believe that his operas will ever be resuscitated. His influence, however, was remarkable. He helped to create a generation of singers and musicians that took the baroque style to its zenith, that seduced and amazed eighteenth-century Europe and raised the art of singing to one of the greatest peaks in its history. That that style was artificial and ephemeral, no one now doubts. There is no true record of it, and it cannot be accurately reproduced—but we know it existed, and we know that Nicola Porpora played a most important part in it.

Almost inevitably, he died in poverty. Like Hasse, he had been a victim of the Seven Years' War—his pension from the Saxon court had been cancelled. He went home to Naples, taught for a year or two in the conservatories where he had begun his career more than seventy years before, then retired to die in obscurity.

CHAPTER FOUR

The Castrato Ascendancy

The province of Apulia is on the Adriatic side of Italy, in the southeast corner. In the seventeenth and eighteenth centuries it accounted for a large part of the kingdom of Naples and it faithfully reflected the economic and social conditions of the time—widespread poverty, the dominance of the Church, and an economy in which owning land was the only real source of security. These were also the conditions that gave rise to the phenomenon of the castrati, and it is not surprising that Apulia was one of the places from which many of them came, including Farinelli from Andria and Caffarelli from Bitonto.

Why would a family allow one of its sons to be emasculated in order to retain his childhood voice into adulthood? For many families it must simply have been a matter of money. Castrati could become very rich (perhaps one out of a hundred did so), but even those who didn't might be expected to support themselves and send money home to their families. In truth, very few of them—perhaps ten or fifteen out of a hundred—were able to do even this, but in largely impoverished communities those were attractive odds nonetheless. And unfavorable odds could be further discounted by the knowledge that the boys would be serving a "higher cause," the Church—they would be working *ad honorem Dei,* as Pope Clement VIII's edict had put it. Naturally, the Church condemned the practice of castration, but everyone knew it was prepared to turn a blind eye so as to ensure that church and monastic choirs had a good supply of male soprano voices to take the place of the female voices it had banned. For some families, especially those that owned land, there was a further piece of contorted reasoning: celibacy was the most effective means of birth control, and enforcing celibacy on a younger son, who just happened to have a God-given voice, must sometimes have seemed an attractive way of safeguarding the family's property rights and avoiding the subdivision of land that would be necessary to support another family. Greed, desperation, and cruel calculation were frequently dressed up in practical or high-minded rationales.

It was never a widespread practice. Even at its height, between 1650 and 1730, there would not have been more than a few hundred castrati in the whole of Italy at any one time.[1] But it was difficult to be a churchgoer (which most Italians were) and remain ignorant of this practice. It was part of the culture, and most Italians approved of it. Only in the middle years of the eighteenth century, when writers like Burney were investigating it and writing disparagingly, did it come to be questioned to any significant degree. By that time, in any case, it was in retreat. Economic revival had set in around 1730, prospects for younger sons were brighter, and Christian asceticism began to decline in most parts of Italy—church and monastic choirs were fewer and smaller, and there was less demand for castrati. By the end of the eighteenth century they were becoming a rarity, a shift aided by Napoleonic reforms and the Church's surrender of temporal power. It is true that Rossini and Meyerbeer both composed roles for them in the first quarter of the nineteenth century, and it is true that a castrato could still be heard in the Sistine Choir as late as 1913, but these were exceptions.[2] In the nineteenth century the idea was generally found repugnant.

If the Church was the chief sponsor of castrati, then it was opera that provided their most glittering showcase. It was pure coincidence that castrati had become a feature of the religious world at the very time that opera was coming into existence, but opera was very glad to have them. In the Papal States, which made up a large part of central Italy, they were a necessity because women were not allowed on stage at all. Elsewhere in Italy women were allowed to perform, but they were often thought of as courtesans, and treated as such: castrati were welcome substitutes.

Singing female roles was certainly not their principal raison d'être. Most of the time they were used to sing male roles. Tenors and basses were useful additions to a cast (playing small roles, villains and so forth), but they were not thought of as virtuosi—whereas castrati were. Only the very best of them got to perform in opera, of course, but those who did had considerable advantages over other singers. They had been trained from a very early age, with no interruption for puberty. Their larynxes had not moved downwards, as normally happens at puberty, and their training, as we have seen, had concentrated on the development of the muscular system around the vocal cords so that the high, flexible, and brilliant sound of the voice could be augmented by prodigious power and almost superhuman breath control. Such a voice could produce crowd-pleasing pyrotechnics, but it was also capable of great subtlety and shades of emotion that could move listeners to tears. We may think of the castrato voice as artificial, but it was undeniably a virtuoso instrument.

It is hardly surprising, therefore, that the form of opera in which the castrati shone was the most artificial and virtuosic form there has ever been —opera seria. Castrati had been a perceptible presence at the very beginning of opera, in the time of Peri and Caccini, but it was the arrival of opera seria in the last two decades of the seventeenth century that made them indispensable. The Italian castrato became an international phenomenon, and would remain one for the best part of 130 years. Siface and Pistocchi were among the first to become famous outside Italy.

High noon for the castrati, as well as for opera seria, was the first half of the eighteenth century. This was when singers like Nicolini, Bernacchi, Senesino, Farinelli, Caffarelli, and Carestini vied for supremacy with female stars like Cuzzoni and Bordoni, and generally had top billing. It was also the time when the most prolific composers of opera seria—Scarlatti, Giovanni Bononcini, Vinci, Leo, Handel, Hasse, and Porpora—were writing major roles for them in almost every opera they composed.

The second half of the century was hardly less glorious. Guadagni, Pacchierotti, and Marchesi were as famous as most of their predecessors, and a generation of new composers led by Jommelli, Galuppi, Traetta, and Gluck continued to write for them, but there were signs that the tradition was ending. From about 1730 onward, opera seria had had to compete with *opera buffa*. Audiences liked comic opera: it was more realistic, less artificial, less demanding. But opera buffa did not generally involve castrati, who specialized in portraying noble and heroic characters—essential to high-minded opera seria but virtually unknown to opera buffa unless they were being sent up rotten. Opera seria was still where one went for virtuosity, to hear the greatest singers performing the most dazzling and most moving arias, but the Metastasian format of opera seria, which had always been stylized and rather predictable, quickly became ossified. It was a vehicle for singers, not for drama, and Gluck, who had been one of its most distinguished exponents, had the necessary eminence and foresight to put on the brakes and eventually to institute reforms that spelled the end.

But not quite the end, because it was still a format that princes and wealthy sponsors liked to patronize. Why venture into risky and irreverent opera buffa when a reliable Metastasian libretto was always available to be set yet again? Haydn, Mozart, and Rossini added a last luster to the genre—and some of its greatest examples—and major composers like Piccinni, Sarti, Sacchini, Salieri, Paisiello, and Cimarosa made very successful careers in both opera seria and opera buffa. So the last of the great castrati, among them Crescentini and Velluti, were able to perform into the nineteenth century—but they were becoming an oddity, and audiences tended to view them as such. "The manly British public should have been spared the disgust of such an appearance as that of Velluti," thundered the London *Times* in 1825.[3]

So the castrati disappeared from opera, leaving us with no reliable record of what they actually sounded like. (The recordings made in 1902–03 by Alessandro Moreschi, one of the last castrati in the Sistine Chapel choir, are no yardstick by which to measure the likes of Farinelli and Caffarelli.)[4] But there is no doubting the importance of the castrati. For the first two centuries of opera's four-hundred-year existence they were a major presence, and for over a hundred of those years they were generally its principal attraction. From Dublin to St. Petersburg, from Naples to Stockholm, they were the film stars of their time. And even if we cannot hear them, then at least we can judge something of their virtuosity and technical ability from the music the great composers wrote for them. Today, when this music is generally performed by female sopranos and contraltos, we get almost no idea of what it sounded like three hundred years ago. Only when it is performed by the most talented of male countertenors can we get an echo (and that a distant echo) of the other-worldly quality, the ethereal beauty, with which the great castrati invested it.

Even while they pursued fame and fortune in the opera houses of Europe, most of these castrati kept up their church connections. Nicolini constantly returned to Naples to sing in the churches where he had made his reputation as a teenager; Caffarelli remained a lifetime member of the Naples royal chapel; Gaetano Guadagni was sacked from the choir of San Antonio in Padua at the age of sixteen because of his repeated and unauthorized absences, yet he kept up a barrage of pleas to be readmitted, and finally succeeded, eighteen years later, when he was already famous as Gluck's Orfeo. Singing in church was a basic activity for almost all the castrati: it was where they began, and where most of them ended their careers. It was probably an insurance policy as well, because the life of a touring castrato was no easier, and no more secure, than that of a prima donna.

Few of them suffered the misfortune that eventually overtook Giovanni Francesco Grossi in 1697: he was assassinated by the relatives of a Modenese widow with whom he had had an indiscreet affair. Castrati may have sounded effeminate in their singing, and many of them looked somewhat incongruous because of the aftereffects of the operation (the Frenchman Charles de Brosses, traveling through Italy in 1739–40, wrote that "most sopranists become big and fat like capons, their mouths, their rumps, arms, breasts and necks rounded and chubby as in women"),[5] but this was not universally true—Carestini, Crescentini, and Marchesi were handsome men, the matinee idols of their day. And it was certainly not true that castrati were incapable of having sex (the fact that it was "safe" sex must often have made it more tempting for their lovers).

That said, Giovanni Francesco Grossi was not an attractive man, either physically or in any other way. He was known as Siface—a nickname he had acquired at the age of eighteen when he sang Syphax in Cavalli's opera *Scipione africano*. That was in 1671, when opera was still in its infancy and the public theaters of Venice were less than thirty-five years old. Castrati like Antonio Cavagna were already making names for themselves and were demanding large fees, but Siface and his contemporary Domenico Cecchi (known as Cortona) were the first to become superstars. It was not easy— there was no career ladder to climb—and Siface had to fall back on singing in the papal choir for three years in his early twenties, but his career eventually took off when he became an employee of the Duke of Modena in 1677. The next year he sang the title role in Carlo Pallavicino's *Vespasiano* at the grand opening of the new S. Giovanni Grisostomo theater in Venice.

Siface's career over the next twenty years was a commentary on the growth of opera at the end of the seventeenth century. For the first time, there was a network of opera houses that a singer could take advantage of—in Venice, Rome, Florence, Modena, Reggio d'Emilia, Naples, and several other cities—and international fame was suddenly a consideration, too. Siface's employer, the Duke of Modena, was the brother of the Queen of England (James II's wife): Siface was sent to London in 1687 as a "present" to the queen. But success had gone to his head. Already in 1683 there had been an infamous contretemps with the French ambassador in Rome, as a result of which the Duke of Modena had felt obliged to place Siface under house arrest for several weeks (he had sung for the ambassador but afterwards he had demanded "doubloons for his singing, and not merely ices, which was all one ever got from the French").[6] In England, he behaved no better. The diarist John Evelyn, who heard him at Samuel Pepys's house and much admired his singing, wrote that he was "a mere wanton, effeminate child, very coy and proudly conceited . . . much disdaining to show his talent to any but princes."[7]

Siface's career bridged the gap between what one might call "early opera" (Cavalli) and the arrival of opera seria near the end of the century. Because of his premature death, and because of an unexplained gap in his career in the early 1690s, probably caused by ill health, it is hard to judge his true importance. But it is clear that he was the first castrato to win genuine star status for himself. Alessandro Scarlatti recognized that as early as 1684, when he adapted the tenor role of Mithridates in his opera *Pompeo* so that Siface could sing it in Naples—it was a huge success. Queen Christina of Sweden was another of his admirers. From her adoptive home in Rome, where she orchestrated the movement that became, just after her death, the Arcadian reforms of the 1690s, and that led almost directly to the full flowering of opera seria, she held a special brief for the castrati, and particularly for Siface and Cortona. She kept a number of lesser castrati on her personal staff and waged constant warfare against the papacy to keep the Roman theaters open and the castrati performing in them—Innocent XI, popularly known as Papa Minga (*minga* being the word for "no" in Innocent's native Milanese dialect), was one of several popes who were determined to close the theaters but eventually admitted defeat when faced with Christina's vitriolic campaigns.

Siface had some accomplished contemporaries, particularly Cortona and Matteuccio (who spent several years in the middle of his career at the Spanish court singing for the half-mad Carlos II—a portend of the way Farinelli would end his career half a century later), but the one who made the greatest impact, as a teacher if not a singer, was Francesco Antonio Massimiliano, known as Pistocchi. Until Mozart appeared on the scene a century later, Pistocchi was widely thought to be the greatest musical prodigy there had ever been. He was a published composer by the time he was eight, a contralto castrato in the cathedral choir of Bologna in his early teens, and an opera singer of repute for more than twenty years. He wrote at least five full-length operas, though very little of them survives. His greatest contribution, however, was to found his own school for singers in Bologna. Among those he taught were the castrato Gaetano Berenstadt, who would sing for Handel in London, and one of the very few tenors to make an impact on the eighteenth century, Annibale Pio Fabri. But his greatest pupil was Antonio Maria Bernacchi, a castrato blessed with amazing technique and the ability to perform vocal acrobatics like no other. Pistocchi was not particularly amused by this—"My sadness is that I taught you to sing and you want to play"[8]—but had he still been alive in 1727 (he died the previous year) he would doubtless have felt a certain pride in Bernacchi's performance during the vocal duel that ensued when he and Farinelli appeared on the same stage. Bernacchi was forty-two, Farinelli twenty years younger, yet there is no doubt from contemporary accounts that the older man won the day, first imitating Farinelli's ornamentations, then adding much more astonishing ones of his own—and this was five years after Farinelli had won his equally famous contest with the German trumpet player in Rome. An unexpected outcome of the duel was that the two castrati became firm friends, and remained so to the end of Bernacchi's life.

Partly because Pistocchi was much loved and universally respected, and therefore not much criticized in Italy, it is hard to know quite what he taught his pupils. Pier Francesco Tosi, whose treatise on singing was published in 1723, during Pistocchi's lifetime, wrote of him as the defender of a "pure" style of singing, not necessarily devoid of ornamentation (which he said should be worked out by the singer, not written down by the composer), but certainly not obsessed with technique at the expense of all else. Others, taking their cue from Bernacchi's fireworks, assumed that Pistocchi was responsible for the corruption of the pure style and the encouragement of the singers to add more ornamentations and more of their own improvisations. Whatever the truth of the matter, the divide between "pure" and "corrupt" is a faithful reflection of the argument that continued in opera until the time of Gluck, and even beyond. For most of the castrati, it was more tempting to rely on technique and try to thrill their audiences with their leaps and trills. It was also the easiest way to silence a generally noisy auditorium. The alternative—attempting to engage the emotions of the audience—was much more difficult and could only be achieved by the greatest singers. Farinelli's career was a good example of how such a singer matured. As a young man, rejoicing in his powers, he liked nothing better than to perform breathtaking feats of vocalism that would get the audience screaming in the aisles, but not long after the confrontation with Bernacchi (and acting on the advice of the Emperor Charles VI), he changed his style radically: he began to play on the emotions of his audiences, often using pathos where once he had relied on vocal agility. It required just as much technique, and a lot more dramatic commitment.

Bernacchi remains something of a mystery. To judge from the parts Handel wrote for him in London (Arsace in *Partenope*, for instance), he had a low alto voice with a range of about two octaves. No one seems to have regarded the voice itself as in any way remarkable—certainly not when they compared it with Senesino's, which was slightly lower and of much greater natural beauty. But almost everyone commented on his technique, and not always admiringly. There were those who said he used it in an instrumental way, "imitating flutes and oboes and other agile but inhuman agencies."[9] To these critics Bernacchi was an acrobat, not an artistic singer, one who could excite his audiences but rarely move them. Eventually, however, after a thirty-year career as one of Europe's leading castrati (and this was during the "high noon" period when Senesino, Farinelli, and Caffarelli were at the zenith of their careers) he chose to follow in the footsteps of his teacher Pistocchi: he too established a singing school in Bologna.

The school appears to have owed more to Pistocchi's teaching than it did to Bernacchi's athletic style of singing—certainly, his best known pupils were renowned for refinement rather than explosiveness. One of them, the castrato Tommaso Guarducci, was admiringly described by Burney as "the plainest and most simple singer of the first class I ever heard."[10] Another, the great German tenor Anton Raaff, for whom, in his sixty-seventh year, Mozart would compose the title role in *Idomeneo,* was renowned for the smoothness of his legato technique—and legato, it seems, was the central theme of Bernacchi's teaching. It means "bound together" or "connected." A singer achieves it through *portamento*—the ability to carry the sound smoothly from note to note, without any break.

This legato technique was one of the defining characteristics of the style of singing that sopranos, male and female, brought to opera during the first century of its existence. We call the style, in retrospect, bel canto, and we can date it more or less from the introduction of opera seria in the late seventeenth century. Even today, there is a tendency to think bel canto can only be achieved by a display of astonishing agility and technical virtuosity. Like the young Farinelli, Bernacchi may once have thought that, but in his teaching, at least, he placed legato high on the list of priorities, and it would remain there right through the nineteenth century, through the era when Rossini, Bellini, and Donizetti added new luster to the genre by composing what are often known as "the bel canto operas." The fact that such works could be composed, and that there were singers trained and ready to perform them, was testament to the tradition of bel canto that had been established more than a century earlier by the men and women who taught the sopranos their intricate art—and taught that legato was an essential part of it.

Bernacchi was about the same age as Senesino, twenty years older than Farinelli and Carestini, twenty-five years older than Caffarelli. His career overlapped with all of them and there is evidence that he gave lessons to both Farinelli and Carestini. These five were the greatest stars of the greatest age of the castrati.

They were often identified simply as "sopranists," but most of them had voices that were slightly lower in texture and range than the true female soprano. Like Caffarelli, they would be described nowadays as mezzo-sopranos. Others, like Senesino and Bernacchi, were lower still—altos or contraltos. Farinelli's high soprano was truly exceptional, though Carestini started out as "a powerful and clear soprano" (in Burney's words), only later becoming "the fullest, finest and deepest counter-tenor [contralto] that has perhaps ever been heard." Nor were they famed for their acting skills. Of the five, only Carestini, a very handsome man, was renowned for his dramatic interpretations, though Senesino was generally thought to be "graceful" in his movements,[11] and Farinelli (another quite handsome man) was a striking presence onstage, if somewhat statuesque and immobile. What they all had in common was their musicianship, a product of their long and intense training from a very early age—and it was, of course, their voices that made them extraordinary. Although we have no recordings of those voices, and the first-hand descriptions that have come down to us are often highly subjective and don't tell us a great deal about the improvisations and ornamentations the singers interpolated, what we do have are the scores that were written for them by the great composers of the time. From these, we can get a very good idea of the singers' range and the composers' expectations of their voices.

Porpora's pupils, Farinelli and Caffarelli, were widely believed to be the most accomplished. Farinelli's astonishing range (three whole octaves) was unmatched by any singer of the time. Few composers actually wrote for that range, of course (why write a part that would be impossible for any other interpreter?), but the flexible format of the da capo aria gave the singers ample opportunity to show off their wares in improvised cadenzas. In Farinelli's case, however, there was one composer who was always prepared to write for him, and him alone. Riccardo Broschi was Farinelli's brother, not a composer of the first rank but an able technician. His opera *Idaspe,* written for Carnival in Venice in 1730 and starring his brother, contains an extraordinary aria ("Qual guerriero in campo armato") that required Farinelli to explore all his three octaves in a series of leaps, trills, and slides that would have been unthinkable for any other singer. Later, in London, Broschi wrote another aria, "Son qual nave che agitata," that was designed to show off his brother's messa di voce. This was the technique, beloved of castrati, that began with a pianissimo note, swelled it to a climax, then slowly allowed it to die away. Even if we allow for a little exaggeration in reports that Farinelli could hold

Farinelli (née Carlo Broschi; 1705–1782). In 1734, when this portrait was painted by Bartolomeo Nazari, Farinelli was at the height of his fame and on his way to London, where he would sing for three seasons in the Opera of the Nobility. Sir John Hawkins wrote, "It became a proverbial expression, that those who had not heard Farinelli sing, and Foster preach, were not qualified to appear in genteel company." (Royal College of Music, London.)

such a note for a whole minute, it must have been an amazing effect. But the messa di voce that introduced "Son qual nave" was only the beginning: it went straight into fourteen consecutive bars of vocalises, ending with "an interminable trill"—and all of it performed "without any obvious signs of breathing."[12]

Farinelli's career was short—only seventeen years on the stage—but that was of his own choosing. He retired at the end of his London contract in 1737, still at the height of his powers, in order to accept an invitation to go into the service of Philip V, the King of Spain. He remained at the court of Madrid for twenty-two years, becoming a very rich and powerful man in the process. His initial task was to sing for the melancholic king—reputedly the same four arias every night—but he gradually assumed other duties, both for Philip and his successor, Ferdinand VI. He was in charge of a scheme to divert the River Tagus; he redesigned the royal opera house; and he produced a long series of opulent stagings of operas for which he recruited the best Italian singers and composers. His influence on the court was enormous, but never, it seems, sinister. When he finally retired to the villa he had built outside Bologna he became a popular guru and éminence grise. His visitors book contained the names of Gluck, Mozart, Casanova, the Emperor Joseph II, and many others.

Tastes in singing varied. Porpora, who taught them both for several years, thought Caffarelli was better than Farinelli. Another good judge, Handel, thought Carestini was better than Farinelli: in 1833 he heard both of them sing in Bologna, then chose Carestini to be part of his London company (this may have been because Handel generally preferred lower voices, like Senesino's). Londoners had the opportunity to compare all four of them during the next few years, with Carestini, and later Caffarelli, singing for Handel, while Farinelli and Senesino were employed by the rival company, the Opera of the Nobility. Senesino's relationship with Handel had been lengthy but never very friendly, so it was hardly surprising that he was now one of the chief proponents of setting up the new company in opposition to Handel's. His expectations of being the main attraction were given a nasty jolt when Farinelli was engaged as well. The first time they sang together, however, Senesino was so overwhelmed by the beauty of Farinelli's singing that at one point, early in the first act, he actually stopped the performance to rush over and embrace his fellow castrato—an action that did not go down well with the audience, which thought it was watching an implacable tyrant (Senesino) refusing to grant mercy to an enslaved prince (Farinelli).[13]

Senesino was always best as hero or tyrant: he was much less effective as supplicant or lover. He was a large, imposing man who naturally dominated the stage—Julius Caesar, Alexander the Great, and King Richard I of England were the sort of roles he thrived on; Admeto and Orlando, both of them deceived in love, were less to his liking. Johann Quantz, who would later be Frederick the Great's court composer, was in London in 1727 when

Senesino (née Francesco Bernardi; c.1680–c.1759). Considering how famous he was between 1715 and 1740, it is remarkable that we know almost nothing about Senesino's origins and later life, other than the assumption that he was born, and probably died, in Siena (hence the nickname Senesino). (Royal College of Music, London.)

Senesino was at his best: "He had a powerful, clear, equal and sweet contralto voice, with a perfect intonation and an excellent shake [trill]. His manner of singing was masterly and his elocution unrivalled. Though he never loaded adagios with too many ornaments, yet he delivered the original and essential notes with the utmost refinement. He sang allegros with great fire, and marked rapid divisions, from the chest, in an articulate and pleasing manner. His countenance was well adapted to the stage, and his action was natural and noble. To these qualities he joined a majestic figure."[14]

It was a peculiarity of Senesino's career, of course, that he sang so little in Italy. We hear of him first in 1707 in Venice, and he was certainly a star in Naples by 1715, when he was creating roles for Scarlatti. But in 1717 he went to Dresden, and from there to London, where he remained for seventeen years until the breakup of the Opera of the Nobility, with only occasional visits to Italy. When he did finally return there in 1737, the Naples audience found that he sang "in an antique style," and he had little success.[15] In the interim, however, it had been his good fortune to be the castrato of choice during the period of Handel's greatest productivity. In all, he sang twenty roles for Handel, of which seventeen were written specially for him. The compass of these roles was quite narrow—mainly within an octave and a half—but they always contained opportunities for him to show off the brilliant coloratura for which he was famed in the great heroic arias, and the equally brilliant *mezza voce* in what were known as "pathetic" (or slower) arias.

By contrast, Caffarelli was not a success in London. He arrived in 1738, aged twenty-eight, with a twelve-year career in Italy already under his belt, and a huge reputation. Aside from the fact that he took an instant dislike to the climate, his timing was unfortunate. Although the Opera of the Nobility had recently collapsed, the English public had just spent three years listening to, and deifying, Farinelli—"One God, one Farinelli!" as an enthusiastic female supporter had shouted from her box one night. There was no way the newfound god was going to be deposed in favor of another. What made it worse was that Farinelli had already left for Madrid, so Caffarelli found himself competing with a legend rather than a singer. He stayed only one season, just long enough to create two title roles for Handel, Faramondo and Xerxes. The music the composer wrote for him tells us something about Caffarelli's voice. It may have been categorized as mezzo-soprano rather than soprano, but it was certainly a high mezzo. Handel gave him a range of almost two octaves and some very beautiful music, including what is generally known as "Handel's Largo"—Xerxes' aria to the plane tree, "Ombra mai fù."

Angel or monster? The stories about Caffarelli's ugly behavior were legion and they preceded him wherever he went, but so did reports of his angelic singing. Baron Grimm, writing in 1782, recalled hearing him at the Louvre on King Louis's name day: "It would be difficult to give any true idea of the degree of perfection to which this singer has brought his art. The charm and love which can convey the idea of an angel's voice . . . , combined with the finest execution and surprising facility and precision, exert over the senses and the heart an enchantment which those least responsive to music would find it hard to resist."[16]

Very occasionally, Caffarelli came up against someone whose need to be respected was as great as his own, and it is not surprising that Gluck was one of them. The two men clashed in Naples in 1753 when Gluck conducted his opera *La clemenza di Tito*. Caffarelli demanded that Gluck pay him his humble respects before rehearsals began. Gluck declined and said that, on the contrary, Caffarelli should pay respects to him. Amazingly, that is what happened: the castrato, sensing perhaps that Gluck's determination was even greater than his own, offered to pay his respects to "the divine Bohemian," and the two of them became fast friends![17] We do not know what happened when Caffarelli met Farinelli in Madrid three years later, but there is no reason to believe there was not a considerable amount of respect between them, too.

The bookends of Caffarelli's career provide interesting insights into his determination to control his own destiny. It seems likely that he was originally castrated at his own insistence. A contractual agreement of 1720, when he was ten years old, stated that his grandmother had given him the income from two vineyards so that he could study grammar, and especially music, "to which he is said to have a great inclination, desiring to have himself castrated and become a eunuch."[18] The end of his opera career was no less remarkable. He was in Lisbon in 1755 and would probably have been a victim of the great earthquake that devastated the city had he not chosen that day to visit Santarém. It was in thanksgiving for his escape that he made the decision to retire from the opera stage immediately, though he was only forty-five and continued singing in churches for another fifteen years.

Of all these great castrati, Giovanni Carestini may be the least known to posterity, but that does not mean he was any less famous than the others in his day. He clearly created excitement wherever he went — partly because he was exceedingly handsome and had a remarkable stage presence, partly because his idea of his own importance was at least as great as Caffarelli's (greater, in fact, if his demand to be paid eight hundred doubloons for appearing in Naples was anything to go by: he was passed over in favor of Caffarelli, who wanted only five hundred).[19] Carestini was the same age as

Farinelli and appears to have started out with the same type of high soprano voice. In 1721, when he was seventeen, he was singing opposite the contralto Bernacchi in Scarlatti's *La Griselda* in Naples. Two years later he was in Prague as the star attraction in one of the greatest operatic productions there has ever been—Fux's *Costanza e Fortezza,* staged for the coronation of Charles VI with a cast of two hundred singers and a hundred musicians, in a magnificent outdoor auditorium that seated four thousand people. During the next few years he was clearly thought of as a phenomenon. Johann Adolf Hasse, for whom he sang in Naples in 1728, said of him: "He who has not heard Carestini is not acquainted with the most perfect style of singing."[20]

For reasons that are unknown, the high soprano of his early years turned into a low contralto in mid-career—still a very beautiful voice and still accompanied by astonishing technique that enabled him to perform prodigious feats. The German composer Johann Quantz heard him in the 1730s and later recalled: "He had extraordinary virtuosity in brilliant passages, which he sang in chest voice, conforming to the principles of the school of Bernacchi and the manner of Farinelli."[21] In London, Handel composed exceedingly brilliant parts for him, including the title role in *Ariodante* and Ruggiero in *Alcina*. The extended arias and great duets of these operas gave Carestini the sort of opportunities to shine that all singers crave. Not the least of them was Ruggiero's aria "Verdi prati," which Carestini at first rejected as being insufficiently brilliant: like Francesca Cuzzoni before him, he wilted before Handel's famous temper and performed it as written, with huge success.

Carestini, Caffarelli, Farinelli, Senesino, and Bernacchi were just the most outstanding castrati of the first half of the eighteenth century. Many more names (perhaps thirty or forty) could be added—singers who were not quite in their league, but close enough to sing regularly in Italian and other European houses. It was a hard life. Traveling was a necessity, and that meant long, uncomfortable, and sometimes dangerous stagecoach journeys across Europe. The health of the voice was a constant worry: drafts and diseases were difficult to avoid. And there was always the audience to worry about— would it be friendly or hostile? Would it be noisy or attentive? Would it be dominated by hostile factions? Yet, when all was said and done, this was a

Giovanni Carestini (1705–1760). "Tall, beautiful and majestic,"
Dr. Burney called him: "He was a very animated and intelligent actor."
(Royal College of Music, London.)

wonderful time to be a singer. A leading soprano, male or female, could normally expect to sing six or eight separate arias during an evening, all of them da capo, with multiple opportunities to ornament, improvise, and show off. With all their years of training, and the assured techniques it had given them, the castrati were in their element.

The end of the castrati supremacy was signaled by the premiere of Gluck's *Orfeo ed Euridice* in Vienna in 1762. It was the first of his "reform operas." One of his purposes, as he later declared in the preface to *Alceste,* was to "divest [opera] entirely of all those abuses, introduced into it either by the mistaken vanity of singers or by the too great complaisance of composers, which have so long disfigured Italian opera and made of the most splendid and beautiful of spectacles the most ridiculous and wearisome." [22] *Orfeo* had no da capo arias, no strict alternation of recitative and aria, no "dry recitative" accompanied only by continuo. Instead, it was written as a dramatic whole, with fully orchestrated recitatives containing much passion and color, and strategically placed arias that were essential parts of the drama, rather than the customary "exit arias" in which singers halted the action while they contemplated the beauties of nature and often gave gratuitous demonstrations of their virtuosity. In Gluck's later operas the chorus, and to some extent the ballet, assumed roles almost as important as those of the principal singers.

Gluck's intention was certainly not to put the castrati out of business—his reforms were aimed at all singers, not just some of them—and one of the many interesting things about *Orfeo* was that its initial success owed a great deal to Gaetano Guadagni, the alto castrato who sang the title role at the first performance (indeed, he would go on singing it, or versions of it, for the rest of his professional life). In 1762 he was thirty-two years old and his credentials for the part of Orfeo could not be denied. He had just come from an extended period of singing at the enlightened court of Parma, where Tommasso Traetta was maestro di capella. In many ways, Traetta had as much right as Gluck to be called the prophet of reform: he disliked the vainglorious attitudes of opera seria and he had begun to merge features of French *tragédie lyrique* with the more aria-centered tradition of Italian opera. Caterina Gabrielli, then the most celebrated prima donna in Italy, and one with whom Guadagni was widely suspected of having more than just a professional relationship, was Traetta's principal muse.

Guadagni's training, or what we know of it, was unorthodox—indeed, he may have had very little formal instruction. He joined the choir of San Antonio in Padua when he was sixteen but was sacked a year later (for absenteeism—he was away in Venice singing minor parts in opera houses). At nineteen, he went to England as *primo amoroso* (male lead) in a comic opera company, and it was while he was there that he found favor with Handel—not as an opera singer (by that time Handel had left all that behind him), but in oratorio. Burney, who knew Guadagni well in London, said he was "more noticed for his singing in English than Italian,"[23] and claimed to have helped the young man study parts in *Samson* and the *Messiah*, which Handel had originally written for Susanna Cibber, a female soprano, and now adapted for Guadagni. Handel also wrote a completely new part for him—Didymus in *Theodora*. Just as important, perhaps, was the fact that Guadagni came under the influence of the greatest actor of the age, David Garrick, who coached him in acting and directed him at Drury Lane in a production of *The Fairies,* a musical version of *A Midsummer Night's Dream.*

By the time he arrived in Vienna to sing for Gluck, Guadagni was thus singularly well equipped to provide the composer with both the musical and dramatic performance he was looking for. Much of the contemporary evidence suggests that the opera's initial reception was moderate, but Guadagni's performance caused a sensation. His alto voice was a thing of beauty, and his impressive acting was a revelation to the Viennese audience, especially in an opera whose every note was intended to convey a development of the action.

No one who heard them ever compared Guadagni with Farinelli or Caffarelli. True, they were all castrati, but Guadagni was a different kind of singer. If he had the technique and breath control to perform the brilliant cadenzas and high-flying ornamentations for which his peers were famous, then he rarely displayed them. His skill in comic opera, his Handelian training, and, most of all, the virtues he was taught by Traetta and Gluck disposed him to be a dignified, dramatic singer who thought it preferable to make his audiences laugh or cry than to have them standing on their chairs hollering for an encore. Indeed, he often infuriated people by declining to sing encores at all—on the grounds that they interrupted the flow of the drama. Burney, hearing him again in his post-Orfeo phase, marveled at the way he used suggestive pauses in extemporary solo passages to create meaning and emotion. "I frequently tried to analyze the pleasure he communicated to the audience, and found that it chiefly arose from his artful manner of diminishing the tones of his voice like the dying notes of an Aeolian harp. Most other singers captivate a swell or messa di voce; but Guadagni, after beginning a note or passage with all the force he could safely exert, fined it off to a thread, and gave it all the effect of extreme distance."[24]

None of this is to say that Guadagni was not a highly effective interpreter of opera seria, but *Orfeo* was a Rubicon from which he could never retreat. When Gluck adapted and enlarged the opera for Paris in 1774, the title role had to be rewritten for an *haute contre* (high tenor)—castrati were still not acceptable in France—but Guadagni was almost always in demand to sing the Italian version, and he himself reworked the aria "Men tiranne" and often used it in *pasticcio* evenings (pasticcio literally means "jumble" or "hodge podge": a very popular practice in the eighteenth century was to plaster together a number of different musical excerpts, generally chosen by the singers, and commission a rough and ready libretto to link them: the story of Orpheus was a frequent victim of this practice. Guadagni himself compiled a complete pasticcio of *Orfeo,* based on Gluck but using additions and alterations by Bertoni, J. C. Bach, and himself). Guadagni may have come across to his colleagues, and even to audiences, as more than a little pompous, but he was a genuine and good man, and in his last years a mystical one. He amassed a fortune, gave it all away, and died impoverished in Padua just a few weeks before Mozart suffered the same fate in Vienna.

There were many other reasons for the decline of the castrati besides the reforms of Gluck. Many things were questioned during the Age of Enlightenment, and since many of the era's leading philosophes—Voltaire, Rousseau, Diderot, d'Alembert—were as interested in music and the arts as they were in politics and the rights of man, it was inevitable that opera should come under fire. The rigid, formalized structures of Italian opera seria and French tragédie lyrique were disparaged as "moribund," "antidramatic," and "repetitive"; they were compared unfavorably with the lively, bubbling genres of opera buffa and *opéra-comique* that had become popular all across Europe. A little piece by Pergolesi, *La serva padrona,* composed in Naples in 1733 for two singers and a nonsinging actor, had taken Italy by storm and moved on to France. In the 1750s it precipitated the *guerre des bouffons*—a Parisian pamphlet war in which the philosophes, the court, and even the public took sides for and against the competing styles. An increasing number of people agreed with Gluck that the singers were out of control and that it was time to call for order.

Societal changes also played a part. The economic depression in which most of Italy had been sunk for more than a century came to an end in the 1730s, and with it came a steady decrease in the number of young boys being castrated. This was partly because the monastic orders began a long period of retrenchment, but it was also because it became fashionable to question the practice of castration. Many of the most influential writers of the mid-century—Burney, de Brosses, Brydone, Grimm—were either skeptical or downright opposed. While it was true that most of these writers were non-Italians, it was also true that Italy was peculiarly susceptible to foreign opinion—it was not a unified country, any more than Germany was: it had Spanish, Austrian, and French rulers, not to mention the papacy, and only its geographical position prevented it from being the almost constant battlefield the German territories had become.

All these factors were at work in the late eighteenth century, but they did not stop the castrati from having a last and rather brilliant fling. The greatest of them were Gasparo Pacchierotti, Luigi Marchesi, and Girolamo Crescentini. Increasingly, they found themselves singing with tenors—Crescentini had a famous partnership in Naples with Giovanni David, one of the first of the great virtuoso tenors—and they found, too, that many of the parts that might once have been written for castrati were now being assigned to female sopranos. Their rivalries were not so much among themselves as they were with prime donne—Pacchierotti with Anna Lucia De Amicis in Naples; Marchesi with the Portuguese mezzo-soprano Luisa Todi in Venice (he once discovered he had been contracted to sing in a season that was officially publicized as "anno Todi"); and Crescentini with Josephina Grassini, the Italian contralto who, like Crescentini, was a favorite of Napoleon.

Most composers—among them Gluck, Salieri, Sarti, Martín y Soler, Mozart, Zingarelli, and Cimarosa—continued to write occasionally for castrati, but they were as often writing *opere buffe* as they were *opere serie,* and castrati were virtually excluded from the former. Nevertheless, the vast majority of theaters were still under royal or aristocratic patronage, and as the Age of Enlightenment ended in flames in Paris and in terrifying declarations of democracy in other places, conservative patrons often preferred to hand a composer an opera seria libretto by dear old Metastasio (he died in 1782) than to run the risk of commissioning an opera buffa in which all sorts of subversive doctrines might surface. That was certainly why Mozart, in the last year of his life, was given Metastasio's *La clemenza di Tito* to set for the Emperor Leopold II's coronation in Prague, and why he wrote the role of Sesto for a castrato.

Comparing singers of one generation with those of another was a fruitless but popular game in the twentieth century, made possible by the existence of recordings. It was just as popular in the eighteenth century when there were no recordings. Burney was too young to have heard Farinelli sing (though he met him in Bologna in his retirement), yet he did not hesitate to say: "Such execution as many of Farinelli's songs contain, and which excited such astonishment in 1734, could be hardly thought sufficiently brilliant in 1788 for a third-rate singer at the opera."[25] When he wrote this, Burney was doubtless under the spell of Pacchierotti, whom he said unequivocally was the greatest singer he had ever heard. Another good judge, Lord Mount Edgcumbe, agreed: "Pacchierotti's voice was an extensive soprano, full and sweet in the highest degree: his powers of execution were great, but he had far too good taste and good sense to make a display of them where it would have been misapplied. Such was his genius in his embellishments and cadences, that their variety was inexhaustible. He could not sing a song twice in exactly the same way; yet never did he introduce an ornament that was not judicious and appropriate to the composition. His shake (then considered an indispensable requisite, without which no one could be esteemed a perfect singer) was the very best that could be heard in every form in which that grace could be executed."[26]

Whether or not Pacchierotti was the greatest singer of them all, his performance onstage was handicapped by his appearance—he was very tall and thin, and renowned for his clumsiness. His range was reputed to be almost three octaves, not as high as Farinelli's but remarkable for its low notes. Burney said he could sing tenor arias made famous by David in their original pitch, and he could go down "sometimes as low as B-flat or the second line in the bass."[27] Not surprisingly with this sort of range, Pacchierotti was particularly famous for what was called "the pathetic style" of singing. Patrick Brydone, who heard him in Palermo as early as 1770 (when Pacchierotti was already thirty but only four years into his late-starting stage career), commented that "he speaks truly to the heart, while nearly all those who sing today intend merely to divert the imagination." Brydone also heard him sing with Caterina Gabrielli, "the greatest singer in the world," and described how Pacchierotti, the most modest and diffident of men, was so intimidated by her virtuosity that he fled the stage in tears. Persuaded to return, he won over both the audience and the prima donna with the tenderness and expressiveness of his singing.[28]

Great artist though he was, Pacchierotti could not compete with Luigi Marchesi when it came to audience appeal. Marchesi was fifteen years younger, a matinee idol with a voice and range almost as great as Farinelli's, but with very little interest in the tender and pathetic arias that were the hallmark of Guadagni and Pacchierotti. His opinion of himself was summed up by the way he invariably made his first entrance, here described by Patrick Barbier, a modern historian of the castrati: "He insisted that the impresarios and composers should allow him to make his first appearance, whatever the opera, at the top of a hill, carrying a sword, a gleaming lance and wearing a helmet crowned with white and red plumes 'at least six feet high,' as Stendahl described it. Marchesi insisted too on beginning with the words *Dove son io?* (where am I?) and then after an inevitable trumpet fanfare he would sing loudly *Odi lo squillo della tromba guerriera!* (Hear the sound of the warlike trumpets!); after that he invariably sang his 'portmanteau aria,' *Mia speranza pur vorrei,* composed by Sarti and later included in *Achille in Sciro.* Slowly the singer would descend the steps to the stage, his weapons gleaming and the plumes on his helmet nodding, and come down to the footlights to receive the ovations of the jubilant spectators."[29]

Marchesi could get away with this sort of behavior because of the extraordinary effect he had on audiences, and particularly on women. His youthful beauty ("beauty" was a word often used in descriptions of him), his bravura approach to every part he played, and the wonderful agility of his voice appear to have sent quite staid and respectable matrons into ecstasies. Stendahl reported that female members of the Viennese court wore medallions bearing his portrait around their necks, on their arms, and sewn into their shoes.[30] In Milan, a group of wealthy ladies formed a society, the insignia of which was a sash worn round the waist with the initials LM embroidered on it.[31] And everywhere he went Marchesi played to the audience: "He relished ornamenting a melody in a hundred different ways, . . . his specialty being *passagi* with sixteen double crotchets to a bar, adding vibration to the first in each group of four and expressive nuances to the remaining three."[32] Nothing like him had been seen since the young Farinelli had arrived on the scene sixty years before.

Aside from his voice, Marchesi probably had more in common with

Caffarelli than he did with Farinelli. His behavior may never have been quite as outrageous, but their beginnings and their endings had remarkable similarities. As young boys, both of them were apparently castrated on their own insistence (in Marchesi's case, with the help of his teacher and against the wishes of his father, who was a professional trumpeter), and in retirement they both appear to have used their enormous fortunes in philanthropic ways—Caffarelli for the Church, Marchesi to establish the Pio Istituto Filarmonico to support the widows and orphans of musicians.

If anyone could have competed with Marchesi as a popular hero, it would probably have been Girolamo Crescentini, the handsome young soprano from the Marches around Urbino (though, unlike Marchesi, Crescentini did not age well: by the time he was forty he was decidedly portly and heavily jowled). He had a high soprano voice, pure and sweet, with slightly less range than Marchesi's but with much greater expressiveness. Although he did not finally retire until 1812, his most productive period was between his debut in 1782 and his arrival in Paris in 1806. These were the last years in which opera houses regularly used castrati. After about 1807 cast lists show a sudden falling off in the number being employed, even in Italy.[33] Crescentini was probably not thought of as an oddity (as Velutti, eighteen years younger, certainly was), and there were still just enough composers writing opere serie to ensure a fairly constant supply of new roles—Cherubini, Cimarosa, and Zingarelli all wrote for Crescentini—but it was clear to most observers that he was a representative, albeit a very fine representative, of a dying breed.

Crescentini was a musician first and foremost: he specialized in the expressive *patetico* style of singing that was generally much more fashionable at the turn of the century than Marchesi's constant bravura. Artur Schopenhauer, the German philosopher, heard Crescentini sing in Vienna in 1805 and wrote in his diary: "His supernaturally beautiful voice cannot be compared with that of any woman: there can be no fuller and more beautiful tone, and in its silver purity he yet achieves indescribable power."[34]

Schopenhauer was not the only listener to be enthralled by Crescentini in Vienna. Napoleon Bonaparte was another, and it was not long before the castrato was installed in Paris as singing teacher to the imperial family and the emperor's favorite performer. Napoleon's attitude toward castrati was somewhat paradoxical. On the one hand, he had done much to erase the practice of castration by dictating new legal codes for the regions of Italy his armies had conquered; on the other hand, he was literally moved to tears by Crescentini's singing, and never more so than when he performed Romeo in Zingarelli's *Giuletta e Romeo,* with the contralto Josephina Grassini as Giuletta. These were roles the two singers had created together at La Scala on the eve of the French army's first invasion of Milan in 1796. (Grassini was singing there again in 1800 when Napoleon entered the city after his victory at Marengo: she sang the *Marseillaise* at a concert that night and so bewitched Napoleon that she spent the night with him and was soon installed in her own house in Paris: long after the affair had ended, Napoleon would invite Grassini to sing at the Tuilleries, and especially with Crescentini). Romeo became Crescentini's most famous role, his calling card wherever he went. Within it, he inserted an aria allegedly written by himself—"Ombra adorata aspetta." It began with a messa di voce that allowed the castrato to float a note of extraordinary purity—very quietly at first, then swelling it to a great volume, then diminishing it again to pianissimo. This aria almost always made Napoleon cry, and he loved to hear it, even if most of his courtiers were bored out of their minds (their boredom turned to fury when Napoleon awarded Crescentini the Iron Cross of Lombardy, a decoration previously reserved for military heroes).

The uncertainty of the castrati's hold on opera at the beginning of the nineteenth century is graphically illustrated by the role of Romeo in Zingarelli's opera. Within a few years of Crescentini's retirement from Paris in 1812 there were two equally famous Romeos in Europe, Giuditta Pasta and María Malibran. The great female sopranos moved swiftly and ruthlessly to colonize the territory that was being vacated.

Crescentini himself spent the last thirty-four years of his life as a celebrated teacher, first in Bologna, then in Naples, where Isabella Colbran was one of his pupils. He was not the last great castrato—that was the fate of Giovanni Battista Velluti—but it is probably accurate to say that Crescentini was the last that truly lit up the world of opera. Velluti's career, by contrast, though it began well, became increasingly lonely, and by the time he retired in 1830, an anomaly.

In 1807, Rossini, then a fifteen-year-old student at the Accademia Filar-
monica in Bologna, heard Velluti sing. He was highly impressed (though
maybe not quite so impressed as he was by another singer he heard that same
season—Isabella Colbran, who would become one of his most important
muses, and his wife).[35] Six years later, when he was already an established
composer with the likes of *Tancredi* and *L'Italiana in Algeri* under his belt,
he was given the libretto of *Aureliano in Palmira* to set for La Scala, and he
was required, against all the custom of the time, to set the role of Arsace for
a castrato. It was an experience Rossini came to regret, since Velluti, exercising the traditional freedom of his predecessors, insisted on providing his
own ornaments and embellishments to the composer's score. Rossini was
furious, and he never again allowed a singer to improvise on his work: what
ornamentation was needed he wrote into the score himself. It wasn't that he
was against the use of ornamentations—he frequently devised them for his
favorite singers, and not just for his own operas but quite often for those
of other composers too! Where his own operas were concerned, though, he
was determined to keep control.

Despite his experience with Velutti, Rossini was a great admirer of the
castrati. He thought their passing had done irreparable damage to the art
of singing, and as late as 1863, when he wrote his *Petite messe solennelle*, he
listed its requirements as "twelve singers of three sexes, men, women and
castrati" (which wasn't what he got, of course).[36] He spoke about castrati as
"the bravest of the brave," and he had good reason to empathize with them.
He once told the Belgian musicologist Edmond Michotte that there had been
a terrifying moment in his own boyhood when one of his uncles, a barber,
had suggested that his fine treble voice might profitably be perpetuated if the
necessary operation was speedily performed. "My brave mother would not
consent at any price," he recalled.[37] But Rossini, like Mozart, had more profound reasons for admiring the contribution the castrati had made. Neither
of them could be described as a revolutionary where opera was concerned:
they saw themselves as part of a continuum that stretched back at least a
century (of the century before that they were mainly ignorant: it is probable
that neither of them knew much, if anything, about Monteverdi). They took
the traditions of the eighteenth century—opera seria, opera buffa and, in

Mozart's case, German *Singspiel*—and changed them radically by the force of their genius, but they always recognized the debt they owed to their predecessors, and that included the extraordinary contribution of the castrati. That they both wrote for castrati, though neither much enjoyed the experience, was an important part of their own development and a vital step in the evolution of opera.

The same might be said of Meyerbeer, who had the distinction of writing the last substantial role for a castrato, in 1824. *Il crociato in Egitto,* with Velutti as Armando, the crusader knight, preceded Meyerbeer's *grand opéra* period in Paris, but not by much. It was the last and most successful of the operas he composed during his eight-year residence in Italy. "The composer," writes Patrick Barbier, "whose curiosity extended to everything, was trying out a vocal experiment which he knew would have no future."[38] Originating at La Fenice in Venice, *Il crociato* was restaged in Florence, Trieste, Padua, Parma, and London in little more than a year, providing Velutti with a triumphal tour and a last platform for the castrato voice in opera. But when it got to Paris in 1825, the role of Armando was rewritten for Giuditta Pasta, and a great age in the story of opera came to an end.

Velutti's fame was largely dependent on his being The Last Castrato. By the time he made his debut in 1801, Marchesi and Crescentini were fast approaching retirement (in 1805 and 1812 respectively, though Crescentini's last six years were spent in Paris singing almost exclusively for Napoleon). Velluti was lucky that there was still at least one significant Neapolitan composer, Giuseppe Nicolini, writing opere serie, and he had a busy career in Naples, Rome, Milan, Venice, and other Italian cities. But the end was near. By 1815, when Rossini was contracted as resident composer in Naples, Velluti found himself with fewer engagements, and many of those were abroad. At the end, between 1825 and 1830, he was in London (the first castrato to sing there in a quarter of a century) as an outright curiosity, singing only occasionally but managing the opera house with some success. He finally left when he lost a court case brought against him by members of the chorus, from which, it was claimed, he had tried to exclude women.[39]

After that, if you wanted to hear a castrato sing, the only place was in a church—and after 1870, when the Church lost all sovereignty over temporal affairs in Italy, it was only the Sistine Chapel in the Vatican. That, too, finally ended in the early years of the twentieth century, following Pope Leo XIII's 1902 edict banning the use of castrati in church music.

For two hundred years—half the span of opera's history—the castrati had been a hugely influential presence. Their ascendancy may be dated within a somewhat smaller period between 1660 and 1780. Their actual dominance (when they were quite simply indispensable) was even shorter—perhaps 1700 to 1750—and that, not surprisingly, was when opera seria was at its zenith. This was a form of opera that was basically artificial, much more so than the original concept of dramma per musica that had been developed in Caccini's day. Caccini and his peers had wanted to do little more than augment the words by setting them in a form of "dry recitative" with very basic instrumental accompaniment. A century later, opera seria not only gave the music as much importance as the words, but it gave the singers a great amount of latitude within the written score. It made a virtue of virtuosity, and it was tailor-made for the greatest virtuosi of them all, the castrati.

At this distance of time, when we cannot know what they really sounded like and when we find the idea of castration abhorrent, it is easy to dismiss the whole era as an aberration, something we neither want nor need to know about. But it is not as easy as that—and not just because the castrati were an undeniable historical phenomenon: they also did much to form and define the art form that has come down to us today. They created a standard—a standard to which female singers of their own day aspired, and one that was implicit in the vocal teaching of the nineteenth century.

The castrati were intensely musical: their training from boyhood and their concentration on music at the expense of all other disciplines equipped them with the sort of technique and understanding that we might normally associate with prodigies (which is exactly what many of them were). Moreover, so much is made of the excitement and audacity of their vocal acrobatics that it is easy to forget that they were also the most expressive and evocative of singers, capable of moving audiences to rapture, sadness, ecstasy, and even horror—in short, they could *involve* the audience in the action of a drama. That is a rare gift among opera singers. We think of them, too, as deformed or ugly: in fact, some of them were striking and impressive men, and some of them were tolerably good actors—but what they excelled at was vocal acting, the ability to use their voices to express emotion. Carestini's Xerxes, or Guadagni's Orfeo, or Crescentini's Romeo were characterizations that swept audiences along with them. Just as important, it was the voices of Carestini, Guadagni, and Crecentini that had inspired Handel, Gluck, and Zingarelli to write the roles in the first place, and the same was true of countless other operas.

Not many of these operas have survived, and fewer still can be heard in the modern repertory. That is partly because there were so many of them, mostly written to order and at high speed—the average time lapse between delivery of a libretto to a composer and his deadline for completing the score was rarely more than four weeks, so many of them were not very good, and there was a regular industry in recycling music from one opera to another. But it is also because the vocal forces for which they were written no longer exist. As the castrati departed the scene in the early nineteenth century, their places were largely taken by female contraltos "in breeches," occasionally by high tenors like Adolphe Nourrit and Gilbert-Louis Duprez.

The nineteenth century made its own music: it had little need, and very little inclination, to revive the operas of a forgotten era. Mozart, of course, was recognized for what he was—a genius (but *Idomeneo,* arguably the greatest opera seria ever written, was almost never heard throughout the century); and Gluck was much admired, especially among musicians. But Handel, Hasse, Porpora, Vinci, Pergolesi . . . all forgotten, at any rate so far as their operas were concerned. When, eventually, the twentieth century began to rediscover them, the castrato roles were generally filled by female contraltos, though sometimes they were reset for tenors, and very occasionally they were given to countertenors. Only at the very end of the century, when a number of talented countertenors began to appear, was it possible to hear an echo (still a very faint echo) of the original castrato sound. If, on the other hand, it was not the exact sound you wanted, but the agility, expressiveness, and purity of technique, then it was still possible to hear it in performances by female singers like Marilyn Horne and Cecilia Bartoli and male singers like David Daniels.

In truth, though, the castrati had no successors.

CHAPTER FIVE

Après Gluck and the Time of Mozart

One of the reasons the castrati had no successors was because opera changed radically in the years following Gluck's reforms, not necessarily as a direct result of those reforms, but certainly in response to musical and theatrical changes that Gluck had prefigured. Opera seria and French tragédie lyrique withered and died because of their own internal limitations: they were representative of an era that had passed. Their artificiality was replaced by a new emphasis on realism, or something approaching realism, and this eventually blossomed into Romantic melodrama. At the same time, composers began writing for much larger orchestras whose thicker textures the singers were required to penetrate: they had to sing louder. The finest voices of the eighteenth century had often been likened to instruments of the orchestra—Farinelli's surviving cadenzas read like parts from violin concertos[1]—but now the superb accuracy and expressiveness of those vocal instruments was replaced by more forceful, attacking voices that could make themselves heard above a large orchestra. The total effect was often more exciting and dramatic, but some of the artistry was lost. It did not mean that the singing was worse—but it was certainly different.

All of that lay ahead in the nineteenth century, but it was preceded by a period of redefinition. Gluck reformed opera, harking back to its original roots in dramma per musica. Mozart humanized it: he wrote about people and emotions that were immediately recognizable to his audiences, and he did it with so much skill that the music and the drama were more intimately linked than they had ever been before. Eventually, Rossini changed it forever: he ushered in the Romantic Age with a superfluity of melody, a facility for musical characterization, and a dual requirement of his singers—that they should possess the virtuosity of their predecessors, yet also be able to meld into extended ensembles that united their voices with the augmented orchestra.

The Gluckian reforms of the 1760s and 1770s, besides involving castrati like Guadagni, had had a great effect on the female singers. Porpora's pupils Regina Mingotti and Caterina Gabrielli were too early to be closely involved in them. Gabrielli sang for Gluck, but she was much more closely involved with Tommaso Traetta, whose work in combining French and Italian influences was almost as radical as that of Gluck. Mozart, who heard Gabrielli near the end of her career (she never sang for him) was scornful of her technique: "She was no more than a virtuoso in runs and roulades; these she executed in a manner so remarkable that she aroused admiration, which did not, however, survive a fourth time of hearing . . . she was unfortunate in being unable to *sing*."[2]

There were other famous singers who simply managed to bypass the reforms. Gertrud Elisabeth Mara (normally known as Mme Mara, though she was German) was one of them. As a violinist, she had been a child prodigy, touring Europe with her father from the age of six. In her early twenties, with great difficulty, she got herself accepted by Frederick the Great as prima donna in Berlin. Frederick detested German singers: he thought only the French and Italians could sing acceptably, but he admitted that Mara proved him wrong. She had a major stage career between 1770 and 1803, but she was handicapped by her inability to act, probably because she had suffered from rickets as a child, and consequently moved about the stage with difficulty. The voice, however, was extraordinary—more than three octaves "save one single note,"[3] and she was renowned in London and Paris as a performer of favorite works that were going out of fashion—Cleopatra in Handel's *Giulio Cesare* was one of her biggest hits.

Most of the other great female singers of the late eighteenth century did come under the influence of Gluck, and many of them had the good fortune to encounter Mozart as well. Anna Lucia De Amicis was one of them. She concluded her career by singing the title role in the Italian premiere of Gluck's *Alceste* in Bologna in 1778, but six years before that she had created Giunia in *Lucio Silla* for the sixteen-year-old Mozart. "Wolfgang has

Gertrud Elisabeth Mara (1749–1833) in the title role of Mortellari's
Armida. After eight years as a member of Frederick the Great's court
opera in Berlin, Mara moved (via Paris, Turin, and Venice)
to London, where she sang for almost two decades.
(Royal College of Music, London.)

put passages in it which are new and quite especially and astonishingly difficult," wrote his father Leopold; "she sings them to amaze you and we are
on the best of terms with her."[4] He was referring to the long coloratura sections of Giunia's awesome aria "Ah se il crudel periglio," in which Mozart
was doubtless testing De Amicis's reputation: she was said (by Burney) "to
go up to E flat in altissimo, with true, clear and powerful *real* voice."[5] She
was also said (by Metastasio) to be one of the best actresses ever seen on the
opera stage.

Five years earlier, the eleven-year-old Mozart and his father had been
in Vienna to see the original production of Gluck's *Alceste*. This was the
second of his "reform" operas, following *Orfeo*, and it may be the gloomi-

est opera ever written (perhaps intentionally, since it was written while the Viennese court was still in mourning for the Empress Maria Theresa's husband). The reason the Mozarts were in Vienna was to persuade the new emperor, Joseph II, to commission an opera from Wolfgang—which he did: he gave him a hundred ducats, a Goldoni libretto, and "the best singers in Vienna." Mozart duly composed *La finta semplice* within three months, and he wrote the role of Ninetta for Antonia Bernasconi, the singer he had just heard in the title role of *Alceste*. Despite her name she was German, and she had specialized up to that time in opera buffa—in fact, in one of Gluck's most radical departures from the tradition of opera seria, *Alceste* was given its premiere by an opera buffa company rather than the usual amalgam of international star singers (it was also the first of his major Italian operas not to have a castrato role). But court politics and intrigue, with which Mozart was to become very familiar later in his life, held up the production of *La finta semplice,* and Bernasconi was not available when it was finally given its first performance in Salzburg a year later. She was absent but not forgotten: three years later, when Mozart wrote *Mitridate,* his first opera for Milan, Bernasconi created the role of Aspasia to great acclaim. He criticized her for her very German declamation, but he had enough respect for her vocal and dramatic abilities to write the great "Pallid'ombre" section for her, in which Aspasia receives the poisoned chalice from King Mitridate.

The young Mozart, like the much older Gluck, was writing his operas for specific singers, and he generally delayed writing the arias until the singers were assembled and he could hear their voices. Recitatives, and even ensembles, were customarily handed in much earlier so that they could be copied, but arias were tailor-made to specific voices. For *Mitridate* that meant he had barely more than a month to compose all the principal music—and to rewrite parts of it after he heard it in rehearsal. The original version of the duet between Aspasia and her lover Sifare (a castrato role) was apparently too difficult for the singers and had to be substantially revised. Not the least of the singers' problems was that Mozart was writing in Milan for a much larger orchestra than was usual—twenty-eight violins, compared to the twelve that were available in the great court theaters of Vienna, and only six that would be available for the premiere of *Die Zauberflöte* at the Freihaus in 1791.⁶

Perhaps the most amazing soprano the Mozarts met during their Italian travels was Lucrezia Aguiari. She sang for them in 1770 in her own home at Parma, where she was *virtuosa di camera*. Leopold "could not believe that she was able to reach C *sopra acuto*" without any evident difficulty, but, he wrote, "my ears convinced me,"⁷ and fourteen-year-old Wolfgang notated a series of bravura passages she had sung for them.⁸ Gluck had also been mightily impressed. In 1769, the year before the Mozarts called on her, he had been in Parma to produce *Le feste d'Apollo* for a wedding celebration. It was a pasticcio in which several of his previous works were recycled, including a shortened version of *Orfeo*. It was very successful, but the star attraction was Aguiari, not Gluck.

As Aguiari's fame spread, so did the number of invitations she received to sing all over Europe, yet she rarely left Parma. One reason, no doubt, was her nickname: she was publicly known as La Bastardella because of her origins as a foundling (that was how the Mozarts referred to her in their letters home from Parma). Another reason was that she walked with a pronounced limp, a result of being badly bitten (some said partly eaten) by a dog in infancy. But the most important reason was her attachment to Giuseppe Colla, maestro di cappella at the court of Parma. For most of her career, even on her visits to Paris and London, she sang very little other than his music, and that was a misfortune because Colla was not a great composer. Burney, who was able to make comparisons better than anyone, said she was "a truly wonderful performer. The lower part of her voice was full, round, of an excellent quality, and its compass . . . beyond anyone who had [then] been heard . . . Her shake was open and perfect . . . her execution marked and rapid; and her style of singing . . . grand and majestic."⁹ All the evidence suggests that Lucrezia Aguiari was one of the truly great singers of the eighteenth century.

France also produced its share of outstanding singers, and none more so than Sophie Arnould. She was a pupil of Marie Fel, the principal soprano at the Paris Opéra between 1734 and 1757, and the most important creator of roles for Rameau. Arnould succeeded her in 1757, when she was only seventeen, and held on to her prestigious position for more than twenty years. Rameau died in 1764, but his operas and those of Lully, who had been dead for more than seventy years, were an almost constant diet at the Opéra: Arnould was a famous interpreter of them. She was, in most ways, the ideal French dessus—her voice was not large, but sweet and expressive, and she was a very fine actress who was much admired by Garrick. In other ways, she was a fairly typical dessus—generally immersed in affairs of the heart that threatened to explode into her professional life, and sometimes did. She had a long-standing liaison with the Comte de Lauraguais, the father of her three sons, which was occasionally interrupted by the comte's excursions with young ballerinas, and, once or twice, by fidelity to his real wife. Nor was Arnould's life made any easier by her gift for *bons mots,* mostly at the expense of her colleagues at the Opéra. But when Gluck arrived in Paris in 1774 it was natural that he should want her to take the lead in the first of his new operas, *Iphigénie en Aulide.* Together, they had a huge success, but the French version of *Orfeo* that followed was not received so well: Arnould's Eurydice was much criticized, and when Gluck came to cast *Alceste* the principal female part went to Rosalie Levasseur. Arnould was mortified and was convinced that Levasseur had got the part only because she was mistress to the Austrian ambassador. Her public acceptance of the blow was phrased with typical Arnould sarcasm: "Rosalie ought to have the part— she has the voice of the people" (a none too subtle reference to Levasseur's humble origins).[10]

Gluck's greatest champion in Paris was Marie Antoinette, and as popular anger at the monarchy increased, so did resentment of anyone too closely associated with it. Singing Gluck's operas was thus quite a dangerous activity. When Arnould appeared in a revival of *Iphigénie* she was persistently booed by the audiences; they quieted down when Marie Antoinette attended three successive performances (there was still some respect for the monarchy), but on subsequent nights the hissing was so loud that Arnould could hardly be heard. By 1777, her voice was in disrepair and her career in tatters —one critic remarked that she had "the finest asthma" he had ever heard.[11] Nevertheless, like Mlle de Maupin before her, she had become something of a legend: it served to protect her through the bloodletting of the Revolu-

Sophie Arnould (1740–1802). Voltaire, Rousseau, and Benjamin Franklin were among those who attended Arnould's salon. "I am eighty-four years old, mademoiselle," Voltaire told her, "and I have committed eighty-four follies." "I am not yet forty," replied Arnould, "and I have committed more than a thousand." (Beinecke Rare Book and Manuscript Library, Yale University.)

tion, and it eventually spawned a literature of its own, including a twentieth-century comic opera by Gabriel Pierné (*Sophie Arnould*, 1927).

In February 1786, in the orangery of Vienna's Schönbrunn Palace, the imperial court witnessed an embarrassing scene. The Emperor Joseph was entertaining the governor-general of the Netherlands while two female sopranos, separated by a tenor who was trying to keep them apart, indulged in a scene worthy of Cuzzoni and Bordoni at their worst. *"Ich bin die erste Sängerin,"* they screamed at each other. Only one of them could be the "first singer," or prima donna, but apparently they both felt entitled to it.

The ladies in question were Caterina Cavalieri and Aloysia Lange. They probably didn't much like each other, though they were hardly competitors since no one in Vienna doubted that Cavalieri was the more accomplished of the two. Luckily, the emperor and his guests were amused. The emperor's court composer was not quite so amused (he was, after all, Cavalieri's teacher and "protector"), and the young man who had orchestrated this entire scene (it was Mozart, of course) was downright anxious — he wished to ingratiate himself with the emperor; he needed the patronage of the court composer; and Frau Lange was actually his sister-in-law. Mozart had composed this little Singspiel (an opera with spoken dialogue) on a commission from the court, and it was one of the few opportunities he had had to show what he could do. *Der Schauspieldirektor* (The Impresario) did, in fact, please, but not as much as the companion piece written for the occasion by the court composer, Antonio Salieri. In the end, all parties were reasonably satisfied. The emperor and his guests had been entertained; Salieri's position at court had been in no way eroded and he could continue his very successful run of operas for Paris without having to spend too much time looking over his shoulder; and Mozart had reminded the people who mattered that he was around. They probably did not know it, but he had already begun his great collaboration with Lorenzo Da Ponte.

Mozart had settled in Vienna five years earlier. He had gone there after the successful production in Munich of his opera seria *Idomeneo*. He had immediately been dismissed from the service of the archbishop of Salzburg, partly because he had overstayed his time in Munich, partly because he finally told the archbishop what he thought of him. Opera commissions, which were what he craved, had been slow to come in Vienna. *Der Schauspieldirektor* had been only the second, and that was partly a reflection of a change of policy by the emperor. In the late 1770s, in an effort to encourage German opera, Joseph had set up a national Singspiel company in the court theaters, to the virtual exclusion of French and Italian operas. Mozart had quickly endeared himself to the emperor by making a magnificent contribution to Singspiel — *Die Entführung aus dem Serail* (The Abduction from the Seraglio) — but it was virtually the dying breath of Joseph's initiative. Italian opera had almost as long a pedigree in Vienna as it had in Venice, and the Viennese wanted it back. It was not long before composers of Italian opera were once more in the ascendant. Did he but know it, the emperor had the best of them sitting on his doorstep, begging for work, but there were many more established composers in Vienna at that time—Martín y Soler, Paisiello, Sarti, Salieri, Cimarosa—and they had pride of place. Mozart had to wait impatiently until Da Ponte was appointed librettist to the imperial theaters; it was Da Ponte who came up with the idea of *Figaro* in 1785. In the short time that remained to him (almost exactly six years), Mozart wrote the three Da Ponte operas—*Figaro, Don Giovanni,* and *Così fan tutte*—as well as another opera seria, *La clemenza di Tito,* and the most popular of all Singspiele, *Die Zauberflöte.*

The music Mozart wrote for his singers generally lies well for the voice. Some of it is exceptionally testing and makes great demands on a singer's technique, but it never puts undue strain on the voice. There are undoubtedly virtuosic passages, but the most obvious requirement of a Mozart singer is the ability to sustain a melodic line. There is a premium on exact intonation and the observation of strict tempi. "Purity" is a word often applied to it, and several great Mozartians have talked about a run of Mozart performances as an admirable way to "refresh" the voice.[12] But the most important thing about it is characterization. Mozart achieved what great composers like Handel and Gluck had sought before him—the precise expression of human personality in music. His predecessors had been handicapped by the formulas in which they had had to write: Gluck tried hard to break out of them, but it was Mozart who threw off the straitjacket, not by abandoning the traditional forms of opera—he still wrote opera seria and opera buffa and Singspiele—but by overcoming their restraints. Every role he ever wrote is unique: it is tailored to the dramatic situation and it portrays a personality, a real person. That is one reason his operas were never as successful with Viennese audiences as they were with the people of Prague. The Viennese, comfortable in the artificial make-believe world of eighteenth-century opera, were unwilling to suspend their disbelief—they did not wish to think of the people on stage as real people, certainly not as people like themselves—whereas the Czech people, for so long in thrall to the Habsburg empire, were all too ready to see Figaro and his friends as the sort of people they would like to be. Mozart did not caricature: he wrote about life and people as he knew them, and that was as true of the fairy-tale characters of *Die Zauberflöte* as it was of the occupants of the Almaviva estate.

So the singers for whom he wrote these parts have an important place in the history of opera and of singing, not because they were the greatest virtuosi of the day but because it is around their personalities and their vocal abilities that some of the seminal roles of opera were created. Even when his operas were revived, with different singers in principal roles, Mozart would frequently add new music to suit new personalities and new techniques.

Mozart's singers during his Viennese years were a tight-knit group. With the exception of Adriana Ferrarese, who did not arrive in Vienna until 1788 and did not sing for Mozart until the 1789 revival of *Figaro*, none of his female singers were great international prime donne. Several of them—Luisa Laschi, the first Countess, and Nancy Storace, the first Susanna—might have disputed that statement, but they were certainly not the equals of the great Italian singers Mozart had heard in his youth—Lucrezia Aguiari or Anna Lucia De Amicis, for example. Nevertheless, they were very accomplished singers. Mozart knew them well and heard them often: he would not have written the exacting music he did unless he knew they could perform it. The Queen of the Night's bravura arias were written for another of his sisters-in-law, Josepha Hofer: he would not have written that fearsome coloratura for any ordinary soprano. The Italian singer Luisa Laschi, whose life was to be even shorter than Mozart's, had been singing in Vienna for more than two years when she created the Countess: he would not have written taxing arias like "Porgi amor" and "Dove sono" for any journeyman soprano.

No more would he have written Konstanze's "Martern aller Arten" in *Die Entführung* unless he had known that Caterina Cavalieri could sing it. It is constructed rather like a concerto for the voice, with four accompanying solo instruments—flute, oboe, violin, and cello—and it was clearly written as a showpiece for Cavalieri, with her famous upper register. Dramatically, it is highly questionable; musically, it is a masterpiece. Cavalieri was twenty-two years old when she first sang it, a young Austrian singer who was a protégée of Salieri, and there is every reason to believe that the music Mozart wrote for her was intended to please the powerful court composer as much

Luigi Marchesi (1759–1829) and Caterina Cavalieri (1760–1801) in Sarti's
Giulio Sabino, Vienna, 1785. Marchesi was the most flamboyant, the most
handsome, and one of the most successful castrati of opera seria.
Cavalieri, who created Konstanze for Mozart in 1782,
was Salieri's pupil and mistress. (Index Firenze.)

as anyone. In a letter to his father, Mozart admitted he had accommodated
another aria, "Ach ich liebte," "to the flexible throat of Mlle Cavalieri."[13]

Cavalieri was Vienna's very own prima donna (she may never have
performed outside Austria) and she was equally adept at comic and serious
roles. When Vienna was treated to Sarti's *Giulio Sabino* in 1785, perhaps the
most popular opera seria of the time, she made a sensational appearance as
Epponina opposite the Sabinus of Luigi Marchesi, the handsome castrato.
Both musically and dramatically they seemed perfectly matched. Composers
vied with each other to show off Cavalieri's voice, often adding new arias to
existing works: Salieri and Cimarosa were both adept at it, but Mozart was
the champion. After Konstanze came Mme Silberklang in *Der Schauspiel-*

direktor (evidence that Cavalieri had enough sense of humor to send herself up in front of the court), and when *Don Giovanni* had its Vienna premiere in 1788 her Donna Elvira was given a new aria, "Mi tradi," to make the role as substantial as that of Donna Anna. "Mi tradi" is an astonishing demonstration of vocal fluidity—"a piece of vertiginous emotion embodied in perpetual-motion quavers"[14]—and every subsequent Donna Elvira has had reason to be grateful to Cavalieri for inspiring it. The following year, when she sang the Countess for the first time in the revival of *Figaro,* Mozart rewrote "Dove sono" for her, adding bravura ornamentation to the faster section. But the subdued range of these later pieces suggests that Cavalieri no longer possessed the spectacular high notes of *Die Entführung*. She had a crowded, high-flying career, but a short one: there is little evidence of her performing much after Mozart's death in 1791, and she died ten years later at the age of forty-one.

Aside from the occasional inclusion of Cavalieri and Ferrarese (mistresses respectively to Salieri and Da Ponte), there was a friendly, and sometimes even a family, connection between Mozart's singers. They were not often singing for him, of course—there were appallingly few performances of his operas in his lifetime—but he clearly kept in touch with most of them, heard them in works by other composers, and often accompanied them at recitals. Therese Teyber, for instance, who was the first Blonde in *Die Entführung,* was also the "Mad:elle täuber" Mozart played for in public concerts.[15] She came from a famous Viennese family of musicians: her father, Matthäus, was a violinist at the imperial court, and her brother Franz (referred to by Leopold Mozart as "my very good acquaintance from Vienna; a thorough, excellent musician, good composer, organist and violoncellist")[16] was a member of Schikaneder's traveling troupe, though he had left it by the time of *Zauberflöte*. Mozart probably knew the family quite well, and he certainly made good use of Therese. She was not much more than twenty when she created Blonde, the pert and pretty soubrette of *Entführung,* and she returned to sing Zerlina, another artless and charming young girl, in the later performances of *Don Giovanni* in Vienna. Indeed, she was generally typecast in such roles and was much admired by the reviewers.

Another musical family Mozart had gotten to know somewhat earlier was the Wendling family of Munich. The elderly Herr Wendling was often his generous host and boisterous companion during visits to that city, and it was Wendling's two daughters-in-law who provided Mozart with his female leads for *Idomeneo*. Dorothea was forty-five when she created Ilia. She had had a distinguished career as prima donna at the Mannheim court, and Mozart had great admiration for her voice: in 1778 he wrote a concert aria especially for her. Ilia certainly has the most beautiful arias in *Idomeneo,* but not necessarily the most dramatic. Elisabeth, the younger of the sisters-in-law by ten years, was accustomed to singing *seconda donna* to Dorothea's prima, so it might have been expected that Elettra would be a somewhat easier role: in fact, it is one of the most demanding Mozart ever wrote, both musically and dramatically. Aside from two magnificent arias about her love for Idamante, her other arias are full of fury, and even madness—the last one, "D'Oreste," which concludes the opera, ends in a manic laugh. Mozart was forced to cut it from the first performances in order to shorten and tighten the opera, which must have been agonizing for both him and Elisabeth Wendling, but she made good use of what she was given: the very next year, promoted to prima donna, she was singing the title role at the premiere of Salieri's *Semiramide*.

One family, of course, played a bigger role than any other in Mozart's life. He first met the Webers in Mannheim in 1777, and Papa Leopold devoutly wished he hadn't. Fridolin Weber was a prompter and music copyist at the court theater, and an occasional bass singer. The family was not very well off: they lived a somewhat bohemian life, and Leopold was aware that they had a litigious streak. Fridolin and his wife, Cäcilia, had six children, one son and five daughters.[17] Mozart promptly fell in love with the middle daughter, Aloysia, who was not yet eighteen and was embarked on a promising career as a singer. He gave her lessons and wrote several concert arias for her, and although she jilted him the following year, he never quite got over her ("she is still not a matter of indifference to me," he told his father four years later, by which time she was married to the court painter, Joseph Lange);[18] he continued to involve her in his work long after he had married her sister. Mozart's writing for Aloysia generally has small orchestration and high tessitura, so we can assume a voice that was not large but had a fairly remarkable upper register. She took over the role of Konstanze in revivals of *Die Entführung* when Cavalieri was no longer available, and the role of Mme Herz in *Der Schauspieldirektor* was written for her. She was also the Donna Anna of the first Vienna performances of *Don Giovanni* (it had been given its premiere in Prague), and only three weeks after the death of her brother-in-law she sang Sextus (originally a castrato role in Prague) in the Viennese premiere of *La clemenza di Tito*. There is nothing to suggest that Aloysia was in the class of Cavalieri—a paler version, perhaps, with many of the same attributes—but she was a popular singer in Vienna between 1785 and 1795 and might have had a more considerable role in the Italian repertoire if she had not had an inflated idea of the salary she was worth. By the time she was engaged to sing opera seria at the Burgtheater in 1790, it was as seconda donna, not prima.

Aloysia's older sister was Josepha. Her chief claim to fame is that Mozart wrote the Queen of the Night for her in *Die Zauberflöte*. Anyone expected to cope with the terrifying coloratura of that role must have possessed outstanding technique and a very high tessitura. Josepha Hofer (she was married to a court musician) certainly had those qualities, and Mozart had already tested them in the bravura aria he wrote for her to insert into the German version of Paisiello's *Il barbiere di Siviglia,* but most accounts agree that she had a fairly rough edge to her voice and very poor stage presence. She did not sing at the court theaters in Vienna; instead, she made her living at the suburban Theater auf der Wieden and in other Austrian cities, notably Graz. When Franz Hofer died in 1796, she married Sebastian Mayer, who created Pizzaro in Beethoven's *Fidelio.*

Constanze, the Weber sister whom Mozart married in 1782, was five years younger than Josepha, almost two years younger than Aloysia. Their father had died in 1779, and Cäcilia had promptly moved the family to Vienna. It was there, in 1781, that Mozart became their lodger. The three unmarried girls—Josepha, Constanze, and young Sophie—were part of the household, and Leopold Mozart had reason to worry about their proximity to his son. He had always distrusted the Webers. He knew Cäcilia to be a grasping woman who had already extorted a large settlement from Joseph Lange, who had made the mistake of getting Aloysia pregnant before marrying her. Leopold's worst fears were realized in December 1781, when Wolfgang wrote to tell him he was planning to marry Constanze: "She is not ugly, but by no means a beauty. Her whole beauty consists in two small black eyes and a winsome figure. She is not witty but she has enough sound common sense to enable her to fulfill her duties as a wife and mother."[19]

In many ways, Leopold was right to be fearful. Constanze was a terrible manager, she was often ill, and she offered Mozart very little help in his career—yet he came to love her deeply, and that was what mattered. As a Weber, she could not be unmusical: she often copied parts for him and he must have tried out many of his ideas on her, but it was only after his death that she became active as more than just his wife. In 1795 she took *La clemenza di Tito* on a tour of Graz, Leipzig, and Berlin, singing the role of Vitellia herself (with Aloysia as Sextus), and she never ceased to champion his work throughout the fifty years by which she survived him.

Aside from the Wendlings and Webers, there were other family connections among Mozart's singers. Stefano and Maria Mandini, who created the Count and Marcellina in *Figaro,* were a married couple; so were Francesco and Dorotea Bussani, who created Bartolo and Cherubino. Dorotea was making her opera debut in *Figaro,* and the "breeches role" of Cherubino asked a great deal of her—not because there was anything new about women portraying boys on the stage, but because Cherubino is much more than an incidental character: he is pivotal to both the comedy and the dramatic action. Something of Dorotea's own personality can probably be heard in the youthful charm of Cherubino's two most famous arias, "Non so più cosa son" and "Voi che sapete," and it is no surprise to know that she went on to create Despina in *Così fan tutte* four years later. She specialized in these ingenue roles and was clearly a favorite of Viennese audiences—but not of Da Ponte: he thought she and her husband had intrigued against Mozart and himself during the *Figaro* rehearsals and he wrote of her that "by dint of grimaces and clowning and perhaps by means even more theatrical, she built up a large following among cooks, grooms, servants, lackeys and wigmakers, and in consequence was considered a gem."[20] In defense of Dorotea, it should be said that Da Ponte's reminiscences have frequently proved unreliable.

If Dorotea Bussani was an interesting bit of casting as Cherubino, then Anna Gottlieb was an even more interesting one as Barbarina. She was only twelve years old, and there she was with her own last act aria. Actually, she was already something of a veteran of the opera stage: her parents were both members of the German National Theater company and she had been appearing in small parts since she was five. Mozart later wrote the important part of Pamina for her in *Die Zauberflöte* (by which time she was a respectable eighteen), and she went on to have a long career at the Leopoldstädter Theater, where she graduated to playing comic old women. She was eventually dismissed without a pension in 1828 and lived in considerable poverty until her death in 1856, the centenary year of Mozart's birth. There is a charming story of how, in 1842, determined to get to Salzburg for the unveiling of the Mozart monument, she introduced herself to the editor of a music magazine as "the first Pamina and the last living friend of Mozart." The magazine raised a fund to take her to Salzburg.[21]

Not all Mozart's singers were unknown outside Austria. Nancy Storace, the first Susanna, was an Englishwoman who had studied and performed successfully in Italy before spending four years in Vienna. Luisa Laschi, the first Countess and the first Zerlina (an interesting combination), had a short but brilliant career between Naples and Vienna and was much in demand as an interpreter of Sarti, Cimarosa, Paisiello, and Salieri. Adriana Ferrarese arrived in Vienna in 1788 with a considerable reputation as a singer of opera seria in Venice, Florence, and London. These three ladies all had a part to play in the creation of Mozart's operas, but Storace was his favorite.

She was that rare thing, an English singer good enough to be acclaimed in Italy. Elizabeth Billington would follow in her footsteps, but Billington went to Italy in order to escape the scurrilous English press rather than because she had any great ambition to conquer the mother country of opera (though she did that too). Like Billington, Storace had had the good fortune to be taught in England by one of the great castrati, Venanzio Rauzzini. He had moved to London in 1774 in order to concentrate on teaching and composing, both of which he did with great success, but he must also have provided Storace with an introduction to Mozart, who had heard him sing Hasse's *Partenope* in Vienna in 1772 and had so admired his voice

Nancy Storace (1765–1817). As a ten-year-old prodigy in England, Storace sang alongside Caterina Gabrielli in the premiere of *L'ali d'amore,* by her teacher Venanzio Rauzzini. One thing that Rauzzini (a castrato) and Storace eventually had in common was that Mozart composed for both of them. (Lebrecht Collection.)

that he had written for him the most brilliant of all his motets, *Exsultate, jubilate.*

Nancy Storace was also a rare thing in another sense: she was the creator of Lilla in Martín y Soler's *Una cosa rara,* the opera that caused the greatest sensation of all during Mozart's time in Vienna. It replaced *Figaro* at the Burgtheater (after only nine performances) and, in the words of the Irishman Michael Kelly, who also sang in it, "almost threw the city into a frenzy."[22] It had a libretto by Da Ponte, and its leading singers were almost all from the *Figaro* cast, including Dorotea Bussani and Luisa Laschi. If Mozart resented it, he also admired it, even to the extent of quoting from it in the supper scene of *Don Giovanni*.

In *Una cosa rara*, Storace had some of the most beautiful and moving love music composed for the stage during the eighteenth century: Count Zinzendorf, who was present at the premiere, thought it was "too erotic for young people."[23] She also had to dance—a seguidilla in the opening scene and the famous waltz at the end. This was no problem to her because she was renowned as a vivacious and charming actress, and reports of the time indicate that she had demonstrated an equal facility with Susanna in *Figaro*. She was clearly regarded as a star in Vienna, and that was reflected in the size of her fees, but it was also a reflection of the size of her reputation when she arrived from Italy. She had gone there in 1778, following in the footsteps of her older brother, Stephen, who was a budding composer. By 1782, she was singing important roles in Milan, Turin, Parma, Rome, and Venice; and composers of the stature of Sarti and Salieri were writing for her. Her first great success in Vienna was as the Countess in *La scuola dei gelosi* (The School of Jealousy), which Salieri had written for her in Venice. By then, she was experienced in both "serious" and comic opera, but her greatest gift was for comedy. Her voice clearly had limitations: its range was not great, and most of the music written for her was relatively simple and tuneful rather than bravura, but her precise intonation and stylishness were qualities that composers loved to exploit. When Mozart was composing *Figaro* he began by writing Susanna's music below that of the Countess (which would have been the natural order of things), but he evidently changed his mind, because in the final version Susanna was given the top line in most of the great vocal ensembles. That was probably a response to the purity and precision of Storace's singing.

Figaro and *Una cosa rara* were the highlights of Storace's four seasons in Vienna, but she had also made her presence felt in operas by Paisiello, Salieri, and her brother, Stephen. Early in 1787, with praise for Susanna and Lilla ringing in her ears, she returned home to England and pursued her career there for more than twenty years—successfully, but never again at the fever pitch of invention that it had been her good fortune to be a part of in Italy and Austria. Mozart adored her, and for her farewell concert he wrote an aria, "Chi'io mi scordi di te," which is marked in his composition book "Für Mselle Storace und mich." Before they left Vienna the Storaces invited him to London, where he had been as a young boy with his father. He never did revisit that city, of course, and Nancy never again sang Susanna—*Figaro* was not given its premiere in London until 1812, four years after her retirement from the stage and twenty-six years after she had created Susanna in Vienna.

While Nancy Storace's life is fairly well documented, Luisa Laschi's is as little known as it was short. It apparently began in Florence in 1760, and it appears to have ended in Vienna in 1789, sometime after her last recorded appearance in February. She had arrived in Vienna in 1784, presumably from Italy, and quickly made a name for herself. "She has a beautiful clear voice, which in time will become rounder and fuller," wrote a reviewer in the *Wiener Kronik;* "she is very musical, sings with more expression than the usual opera singers and has a beautiful figure."[24] With the exception of the 1785 season, when she sang in Naples (and probably met her husband, the tenor Domenico Mombelli), she spent the rest of her career in Vienna, singing with great success for all the principal composers. Like Storace, she was in the first casts of *Figaro* (the Countess) and *Una cosa rara* (Queen Isabella), but unlike Storace she was still around in 1788, when *Don Giovanni* had its Viennese premiere. One would naturally expect a *Figaro* Countess to be cast as Donna Anna, or possibly Donna Elvira, but Laschi sang the young village girl Zerlina. One explanation is that Mozart had an embarrassment of riches—Cavalieri as Elvira, Aloysia Lange as Anna—but it may also help to explain why, in *Figaro,* Storace's Susanna had been given the top line over Laschi's Countess: perhaps her voice had *not* become "rounder and fuller," as the reviewer in *Wiener Kronik* had foretold it would. That is pure speculation, but it is certainly true that her appearance as Zerlina, the young virgin, was more than a little incongruous since she was seven months pregnant at the time. She sang up until the day before her confinement, and she was back onstage four weeks later (Therese Teyber took over during her absence). Whether or not this experience had anything to do with Laschi's death, probably less than a year later, is not known, but she appeared in several operas in the intervening months, including Salieri's *Il talismano,* in which she created Carolina.

Adriana Ferrarese presented Mozart with altogether different problems. Unlike most of his other singers, she was neither a friend nor an artist he particularly admired. That she was Da Ponte's mistress is almost certainly the reason he used her to create the role of Fiordiligi in *Così fan tutte* and to take over Susanna in the 1789 revival of *Figaro* (in Nancy Storace's absence). She was frankly unsuited to Susanna, and the musical characterization of Fiordiligi is curiously, and rather effectively, at odds with the rest of *Così*. It was more like that of an opera seria heroine, which was precisely what Ferrarese was for most of the time, both onstage and off—vain and beautiful, not someone to whom acting or characterization had any importance whatever. She had trained at the Mendicante in Venice, eloped to Florence, sung in London for two years and then in Florence again before moving to Vienna in 1788, where she very soon teamed up with Da Ponte. Mozart needed Da Ponte, and liked him enormously, so he cannot have had much doubt that he would have to make use of her. For her Susanna he wrote new music to suit her voice—a rondo in seria style to replace Susanna's lovely aria "Deh vieni, non tardar" in the final scene, and an entirely new aria to replace "Venite inginocchiatevi," when Susanna dresses Cherubino as a girl. Of the latter Mozart wrote: "The little aria I have made for Ferrarese I believe will please if she is capable of singing it in an artless manner, which I very much doubt."[25] At all events, the revival of *Figaro* was a success: it ran for twenty-six performances.

Unlike Susanna, Fiordiligi was created for Ferrarese from first to last. She is "a rigid *seria* character who is the object of comic intrigue,"[26] and Mozart did not hesitate to make use of Ferrarese's strengths. He gave her huge intervals to negotiate (elevenths and thirteenths) as well as a series of enormous leaps alternating with sustained low notes. The premiere of *Così* came only two months after Ferrarese had created Eurilla in Salieri's *La cifra* (The Cipher), and it has long been suspected that Mozart was parodying Salieri, who had given her even greater intervals, including a fifteenth. At all events, Ferrarese had a fine success as Fiordiligi, as did her stage sister, Dorabella, who was created by Louise Villeneuve. She was another Italian soprano who had recently arrived in Vienna, and whom Mozart knew well enough to have composed several arias for her to insert into operas by other composers (a common practice at the time). Villeneuve's great success, first in Milan, then in Vienna, had been as Amore in Martín y Soler's *L'arbore di Diana,* and it is typical of Mozart that he makes musical allusion to it in Dorabella's second act aria "Amore un ladroncello" (Love is a little thief).

Così had only five performances in Vienna before the theaters were closed due to the death of Emperor Joseph, and only another five when they were reopened. Its record of performance after that was abysmal—there were a number of "improved" adaptations in German that generally played fast and loose with the music and the plot—and it was not until the twentieth century that it was joyfully rediscovered and given its rightful place in the pantheon. It may be that the subject matter offended nineteenth-century taste (its full title could be translated "All Women Do the Same, or The School for Lovers"); it may be that it just got lost in the plethora of Romantic opera that was about to engulf Europe. So far as its principal creators were concerned, history was even crueler: Mozart was dead within two years; Da Ponte and Ferrarese were quickly dismissed by the new emperor and left Vienna; and neither Ferrarese nor Villeneuve seems to have had much success back in Italy.

Even when Mozart was not composing for his Viennese singers, it is probable that, in a sense, he was. Two of his mature operas, *Don Giovanni* and *La clemenza di Tito,* were written for Prague, but Mozart knew that it was in Vienna, not Prague, that his career must prosper. After the successful premiere of *Don Giovanni* he wrote wistfully to a friend: "Perhaps it will yet be performed in Vienna? I hope so."[27]

The Italian opera company in Prague was run by Pasquale Bondini and Domenico Guardasoni at the Nosticke Theater (now the Tyl Theater). We know very little about the singers in this company—neither Mozart nor Da Ponte had much to say about them in their writings. They were clearly not as good as the Viennese singers, with the possible exceptions of Luigi Bassi, the first Don Giovanni, and Teresa Saporiti, the first Donna Anna, who went on to have a substantial career in Italy. Essentially, they were members of a repertory company, an outpost of Italian opera that alternated between Prague and Leipzig, but Mozart had every reason to be grateful to them for their two commissions, and for putting on productions of his operas that were enormously popular in Prague and that made him a genuine celebrity in that city, which he never was in Vienna. Despite somewhat chaotic first nights (often the case in Vienna as well), they seem to have coped very creditably — but it seems clear that Mozart was always writing with his Viennese singers in mind.

One can speculate on how different Mozart's operas might have been if he had been writing for the greatest virtuosi of his time — for De Amicis, or Aguiari, or even Mme Mara — and the likelihood is that they would not have been very different at all. It is true that he invariably tailored parts to his own singers, and made revisions for new singers like Ferrarese, but it is also true that he was essentially a dramatic composer: he wrote music that worked on the stage, that fitted the often intricate directions of Da Ponte's or Schikaneder's plots, and that characterized in music the personalities of the fictional people he portrayed. Mozart singers do not need to be great virtuosi, but they do need to be excellent technicians; they need to be able to carry and interpret the melodic line with exact intonation and precise execution; and they need to put as much effort into ensemble and recitative as they put into their great arias. No composer ever gave his singers more opportunities, and few provided greater pitfalls for the unwary and the inadequate.

Yet most singers of Mozart's time had hardly heard of him. Some, like De Amicis and Aguiari, met him when he was very young, others might have heard tell of him on the grapevine, but for the vast majority he was a phenomenon that took twenty years or more to percolate to the non-German centers of European opera. A few bastardized versions of *Figaro* were heard in Italy and France in what remained of the eighteenth century, generally with spoken dialogue and including music by other composers. *Don Giovanni* was not staged in Italy at all until 1811, and the London public remained ignorant of Mozart until *La clemenza di Tito* was presented in 1806. So most leading singers of the time missed out. Brigida Banti, an Italian soprano from Cremona who had a great international career between 1776 and 1802, was unlucky: her only season in Vienna was in 1780, the year before Mozart moved to that city. Josephina Grassini, Napoleon's favorite female singer, sang everywhere and did everything between 1789 and 1823, but never, so far as is known, performed in a Mozart opera. The greatest of them all, Angelica Catalani, *did* get to sing Mozart: she sang Vitellia in *La clemenza di Tito* when it reached England, and she was London's first Susanna in 1812. The idea of that flamboyant, tasteless, and extraordinary lady taking over the role created by Nancy Storace (who may well have been in the audience at the King's Theatre) is mind-boggling, yet it has to be said that Catalani's Susanna was deemed very successful by the London critics. But then everything Catalani did was successful — in the sense that it was unfailingly sensational — and that included her appropriation of violin variations by Rode and her rearrangement of Figaro's "Non più andrai," written for the bass voice of Francesco Benucci, as a concert aria for herself.

There may never have been, before or since, a prima donna who so perfectly encapsulated the angel/monster dichotomy, so Catalani serves as a bridge between the pre-Gluckian world of opera seria and the post-Mozart world of Romantic opera — a reminder that there was much else going on in the world of singing than what was happening in the very confined circles of Mozart's Vienna.

Catalani was, in many ways, an angel. She was exceedingly generous throughout her life, giving away a large proportion of the massive fortune she earned and, in her retirement, endowing a school for aspiring female singers. She was a woman of great charm and great beauty, whose private life appears to have been beyond reproach. And her voice was amazing. As one contemporary observer wrote: "The first notes of Madame Catalani's voice can never be forgotten by those who have heard it burst upon the astonished ear. With this voice, extending in its most perfect state from G (below the soprano staff) to F in altissimo, full, rich and grand in its quality beyond previous conception, capable of being attenuated or expanded into a volume of sound that pierced the loudest chorus, she bore down by force the barriers of criticism, and commanded the admiration of Europe. Nevertheless, it is, we think, incontestable that Madame Catalani is a singer of execution rather than expression."[28]

And there's the rub. Catalani had no taste whatsoever. She was in love with the sound of her own voice and intensely aware of the amazement it invariably induced in her listeners. Her husband expressed her philosophy

Angelica Catalani (1780–1849). Catalani's 1826 contract with the King's Theatre, London, included the following: "Madame Catalani shall choose and direct the operas in which she is to sing; she shall likewise have the choice of performers in them; she will have no orders to receive from anyone . . . Madame Catalani and her husband shall have a right to superintend the receipts . . . [she] shall receive the half-part of the amount of all the receipts which shall be made in the course of the season . . . free from every kind of deduction." (Royal College of Music, London.)

crudely but truly when he told Parisians that all that was needed to put on an opera was "my wife and four or five puppets."[29] A British observer, Lord Mount Edgcumbe, whose greatest admiration was reserved for Brigida Banti, agreed that Catalani's voice "is of a most uncommon quality, and capable of exertions almost supernatural," but, he added: "It were to be wished she was less lavish in the display of these wonderful powers, and sought to please more than to surprise; but her taste is vicious, her excessive love of ornament spoiling every simple air, and her greatest delight (indeed, her chief merit) being in songs of a bold and spirited character, where much is left to her discretion (or indiscretion) without being confined by accompaniment, but in which she can indulge in *ad libitum* passages, with a luxuriance and redundancy no other singer ever possessed, ever practiced, and which she carries to a fantastical excess."[30]

Catalani seems to have had very little education and very little musical training, though it was said that she took some lessons from the castrato Marchesi. She made her debut in Venice in 1797 at the age of seventeen and sang in Italy for the next six or seven years—enough time to make a sizable reputation that was faithfully reflected in the enormous fees her husband negotiated for her, first in Lisbon, then in London. In England, between 1806 and 1814, she simultaneously enchanted the public with her vocal powers and abused the art of opera. Then she went on to make an unholy mess of the Théâtre Italien in Paris, where she was both prima donna and director for three horrific years. Aside from her merciful aversion to Mozart after the 1812 *Figaro,* she was extremely catholic in the number and variety of composers whose works she sang—Portogallo, Nasolini, and Nicolini were particular favorites, but Cimarosa, Paisiello, Piccinni, Paer, and Mayr all got the Catalani treatment in varying degrees of tastelessness. Yet there was still much to admire. A listener as critical as the young German composer Louis Spohr was lost in wonder at "the perfection of every kind of figuration and embellishment and the individuality of her interpretive style," and he noted that "her trill is especially beautiful whether in whole or in half tones."[31] The French critic Castil-Blaze, writing in 1820, described her voice as "an admirable soprano of prodigious compass, from *la* to the upper *sol,* marvelous in point of agility, and producing a sensation difficult to describe."[32]

Catalani was both before and after her time. Had she been twenty years older she would almost certainly have been the queen of opera seria. Had she been twenty years younger she might very well have occupied the position that was eventually Giuditta Pasta's—as *prima donna assoluta* of the Romantic Age.

That she came when she did—as an isolated phenomenon between two eras—is something for which we should probably be grateful. But it would have been fun to have heard her—at least once.

CHAPTER SIX

Prime Donne Assolute

There is a seismic divide between eighteenth- and nineteenth-century opera. That much is obvious in retrospect—indeed, it was obvious by 1820—but the division did not come about overnight: it was a process of evolution rather than revolution. It happened during the most turbulent period of social and political change Europe had witnessed since the end of the Dark Ages—a period epitomized by the French Revolution, though that was only the most spectacular manifestation of what was truly a continentwide phenomenon, and one that even crossed the ocean to the British colonies in America.

One of the most striking consequences of this change was a profound alteration in the intellectual and cultural climate. For a large part of the eighteenth century the so-called Enlightenment had offered "solutions," based on science and reason, to Europe's problems, but the Age of Enlightenment had now ended catastrophically in violence and revolution. What had been done could not be undone, and in any case the monarchists and the landowning aristocracy were probably the only people who actually wished to undo it, but there was a widespread feeling of revulsion against the methods by which it had been done, and an even more widespread desire for an age of peace and stability.

The intellectual template for this new age was not really a philosophy at all: it was more like a faith. It relied on instinct rather than science, on emotion rather than reason; it believed that what was natural was moral, and what was intellectualized or rationalized was suspect. The cultural identity assumed by these beliefs came to be known as the Romantic movement. For most of the nineteenth century, and even beyond, it dominated the literary, artistic, and musical taste of Europe, and its impact on opera was enormous and lasting.

To begin with, the business of opera went on as it had for almost two hundred years. Composers continued to write for specific singers and specific occasions. They churned out operas as fast as ever to feed hungry opera houses and ambitious impresarios. Revivals of earlier works, though by no means infrequent, were not the principal order of business: audiences expected to hear new works. But what they were hearing was different—less formalized, less artificial, less decorative, less unreal. A few Italian houses, like the San Carlo in Naples and La Fenice in Venice, continued to present opere serie on a regular basis, but they were exceptional. Milan, as the seat of Austrian (and later, Napoleonic) occupation, was much more open to the new ideas blowing through Europe and was rapidly becoming the most influential center of opera in Italy. Singers of the old school, like Mme Catalani, battled on, but they must have known they were almost as anachronistic as their old colleagues the castrati, who were literally disappearing from the stage.

Ever since the 1750s, old formats like opera seria and Lullian tragédie lyrique had been struggling. Even though their twilight existence was long and not undistinguished, propped up by the reforms of Gluck and a generation of composers who took their cue from him, it was clear that audiences wanted something different, something more dramatic. Opera buffa had shown the way, never more so than in the works of Mozart and Da Ponte, but it did not mean that serious opera was dead: it simply had to be rethought. History, and sometimes quite recent history, was now more acceptable than mythology. Grétry's *Pierre le Grand* and *Guillaume Tell* and Spontini's *Fernand Cortez* all met with significant success. The new genre of "rescue opera" was suddenly very popular—Cherubini wrote *Les deux journées* and *Lodoïska,* Gaveaux wrote *Léonore,* and Beethoven chipped in with *Fidelio* (which was based on a story that had already been used by Paer and Mayr, as well as Gaveaux). Most of these developments took place in Paris before, during, and after the Revolution, and were bizarrely mixed up with a series of proselytizing and best-forgotten productions promoted by leaders like Robespierre and Napoleon, who were acutely aware of opera's potential for propaganda. So even as the ancien régime perished in violence, Paris was busy establishing itself as the cosmopolitan capital of the opera world, the place where singers and composers of the nineteenth century, whatever their nationality, would most need to be seen and heard.

Rossini, Bellini, and Donizetti would all converge on Paris in the 1820s and 1830s, but to begin with they were isolated from the developments taking place there, just as they were largely isolated from the developments in symphonic music taking place in Germany and Central Europe. Their inheritance came directly from the bel canto world of Italian opera they had grown up with. Like their predecessors, they called for florid and expressive singing, but almost always in more dramatic contexts than had been the case in the static, "stand-there-and-sing" world of pre-Mozartian opera. The da capo tradition of improvisation was largely gone, the orchestration was bigger and more brilliant, and the singers frequently had to meld into large ensembles. More powerful voices were required, but voices that were still capable of conveying a whole palette of emotions, from the pathetic to the bravura, and could do so in many of the same ways the castrati had pioneered.

While these new Romantic composers were clearly part of the classical Italian opera tradition, they were also responsible for reining in the singers. They were less willing to put up with improvisations, more determined that what they wrote was what should be performed. Freed from the formalized structures of opera seria, they became increasingly preoccupied with dramatic situations, with insisting that the singers must sustain and amplify those situations by entering fully into them. Among other things, that meant fewer pauses while the action was interrupted to showcase a singer's virtuosity. So, even if Rossini, Bellini, and Donizetti could be said to have represented the greatest flowering of the classical Italian tradition, they also presaged its end. Their immediate successor, Giuseppe Verdi, would be the apostle of a much more dramatic form of opera, and therefore of singing.

Rossini began this process. Though he was only five years older than Donizetti and nine years older than Bellini, he was way out in front of them. His thirty-nine operas were all completed by the time he was thirty-seven, and most of them were written in Italy between 1813 and 1823, by which time the other two were only just starting out. Like Mozart, whom he so greatly admired, Rossini was not so much a revolutionary as he was a musical genius whose understanding of the capabilities of the human voice enabled him to challenge singers and to lead them into new forms and structures. Yes, he was part of the continuum of Italian opera—"a Classical, not to say Baroque, survival into the Romantic age," Julian Budden has suggested[1]—but by the time he was through, Italian opera was changed, if not out of recognition, then certainly in fundamental ways that had a profound effect on the art of singing.

The demise of the castrati affected opera in many ways: musically, it was a loss, but dramatically it was a gain. Opera continued to be ambivalent about gender—in some ways more so, with women *en travesti* very often taking the place once occupied by castrati—but now, for the first time, tenors came into their own as *prime uomine*. The San Carlo in Naples boasted a remarkable roster of them between 1815 and 1825—Giovanni David, Manuel García, Andrea Nozzari, and the one who would eventually be the greatest Italian tenor of the age, Giam-Battista Rubini. Rossini, who was under contract to compose for Naples for much of this period, was often required to get as many as three of them onstage at the same time (in *Otello*, for instance). This greatly influenced the way female singers went about their business, and the way composers wrote for them: the musical and dramatic tension that could be generated between a female soprano and a male tenor was altogether different from the interplay of two soprano voices, even if one of them was male.

The castrati might be gone from the stage, but their influence lived on in other ways. Because of their peculiar physiognomy, they had always produced their greatest power from the chest. Soprano castrati like Farinelli and Caffarelli had brilliant head registers as well, but contemporary accounts agree that most of their divisions and passage-work were generated from the chest. Not surprisingly, female sopranos had worked hard to emulate these chest registers, and at the end of the eighteenth century the lower mezzo-soprano and contralto voices were more in vogue than the high soprano. (Classifications are difficult because there was a built-in tradition of transposition: singers were expected to be able to tackle almost any music that confronted them by transposing it up or down to suit their own voices. Composers like Handel, Gluck, and Mozart were not the slightest bit affronted by this practice: they only wanted the singers to find keys that would be comfortable for their voices). But there is no doubt that Rossini, and to some extent Bellini and Donizetti in their early days, were writing principally for female singers we would describe as either mezzo-sopranos or contraltos. Isabella Colbran, Geltrude Righetti, Marietta Marcolini, Giuditta Pasta, and María Malibran—all the greatest Rossinians up to about 1830—had markedly low voices. Thereafter, as the Romantic mood engulfed the opera world, female leads generally had higher voices, no less agile and flexible, and able to soar above the orchestra at moments of great emotional drama. Henriette Sontag, Giulia Grisi, Fanny Persiani, and Jenny Lind (and later, Patti and Melba) were outstanding examples.

Rossini's first inspiration was Marietta Marcolini. Between 1811 and 1814 she created five roles for him, not all of which were successful. In the first of them, *L'equivoco stravagante*, the "curious misunderstanding" of the title was that Marcolini's character, Ernestina, disguised herself as a boy in order to avoid the unwanted attentions of a suitor. The Bologna police banned the opera after only three performances, not because Ernestina was pretending to be a castrato (nothing wrong in that) but because she was also pretending to be an army deserter—and one getting away with it. That was a controversial matter in a country as divided as Italy in 1811, and it might have been a problem for Rossini personally had not another of his operas for Marcolini, *La pietra del paragone* (The Touchstone), had such a rousing success at La Scala in 1812 that he was exempted from military service.

It was Rossini's good fortune in his apprentice years that he was able to work with two magnificent singers. Marcolini and Filippo Galli, a bass, had both been singing seria and buffa roles with great success for almost a decade before Rossini came on the scene. He rejoiced in their voices and learned, very early, to make full use of them. Galli had a long career—he was still singing at La Scala as late as 1840, a famous interpreter of Mozart (Don Giovanni, Guglielmo) as well as Donizetti (Henry VIII in *Anna Bolena*) and Rossini, of course. But it was Marcolini who was Rossini's muse in the early years—and probably more than just his muse: Stendahl reported that, "not wanting to be in arrears with Rossini, [she] sacrificed Prince Lucien Bonaparte to him."[2] It was for her distinctive contralto voice, with its considerable compass and great agility, that he wrote King Cyrus in *Ciro in Babilonia*, Marchesa Clarice in *La pietra del paragone*, Isabella in *L'Italiana in Algeri*, and the title role in *Sigismondo*. Of these, Isabella was the greatest success, and that success owed not a little to Marcolini's gifts as a comic actress, but it is not the role for which she is best remembered. That is Tancredi.

Marcolini did not create Tancredi at La Fenice in 1813 because she was not under contract to that theater, but it was certainly composed with her in mind and it eventually became her most famous portrayal. She must have sat through the triumphant premiere with very mixed feelings, knowing the part was really hers, and knowing that Adelaide Malanotte, who was a pupil of the castrato Crescentini, had scored a phenomenal success with it. But four months later, having already revised *Tancredi* for Ferrara (with a tragic ending replacing the original happy ending), Rossini sat down and wrote *L'Italiana* in twenty-seven days for Marcolini, Galli, and the San Benedetto theater. In an entirely different genre—buffa as opposed to seria—it, too, was a huge success, and Marcolini, despite the fact that she was said to be unwell on opening night (subsequent performances had to be postponed), had the greatest triumph of her career up to that point.

These two Venetian operas of 1813—*L'Italiana* and *Tancredi*—illustrate the range of Marcolini's talents and the inspiration that she was to Rossini. "It was at *her* side," wrote Stendhal, "upon *her* piano, and within the walls of *her* country house at Bologna" that he wrote much of his music in those early years.[3] The two operas, so different in form and structure, both carry the stamp of her talent and Rossini's refusal to trap that talent within the confines of any single format. Tancredi's entrance aria, "Tu che accendi," with its even more famous cabaletta, "Di tanti palpiti," might be termed archetypal opera seria, but it is not: it owes just as much to opera buffa's refusal to let the action stand still while a character emotes. The same might be said in reverse of Isabella's patriotic aria in *L'Italiana*, "Pensa alla patria": it would have had no place in an eighteenth-century opera buffa, but it sits perfectly well among the sentimental and often farcical elements of a Rossinian comedy. In large part, that is because they are both tailored to the voice and personality of the singer Rossini had in mind—Marcolini. Perhaps the best way to imagine this is by recalling the voice and personality of one of the few twentieth-century singers able to do justice to both parts, Marilyn Horne. Her remarkable technique, her great range and flexibility (from stentorian chest registers to a brilliant top), and the very distinctive timbre of her voice, so beautifully projected, are hallmarks of a style and effect that Rossini created for Marcolini—to which Horne, like Marcolini, was able to add a genuine talent for comedy and an innate ability to provide vocal characterization.

Marietta Marcolini disappeared from the opera scene somewhere around 1818, when she was still in her late thirties. Whether she died, or simply retired into obscurity, is not known. Her last collaboration with Rossini—*Sigismondo,* an opera seria for Venice in 1814 in which she sang the travesti title role—was not a success, but she certainly continued to sing Tancredi to much acclaim. So did another contralto, Teresa Belloc-Giorgi. In 1812 she had created the role of Isabella in one of Rossini's early successes in Venice, *L'inganno felice* (The Fortunate Deception), and five years later she was the first Ninetta in *La gazza ladra,* the very successful semiseria piece Rossini wrote for La Scala (based on the true story of a girl accused of a theft which had in fact been committed by "the thieving magpie"). But Belloc-Giorgi's greatest success was in the Rossinian roles she had not herself created—Tancredi, Isabella in *L'Italiana,* Rosina in *Il barbiere* and Angelina in *La Cenerentola*—all of which she sang in Italy and London. She was one of the first singers to make a career out of Rossini's early infatuation with the low soprano voice.

Whether either Marcolini or Belloc-Giorgi was available for *Il barbiere di Siviglia* in 1816 is also unknown. It may be that they were engaged elsewhere; it may be that Rossini wanted someone younger and different. What is certain is that he specifically requested Duke Sforza Cesarini, the impresario who commissioned *Il barbiere,* to engage the twenty-three-year-old Geltrude Righetti-Giorgi (no relation to Belloc-Giorgi) to create the role of Rosina. Signorina Righetti was well known to Rossini: they had grown up together in Bologna and he must have known that she had made successful debuts in Rome and Bologna in 1814. He may also have known that she had then promptly retired from the stage in order to marry Luigi Giorgi, a lawyer. It was to be a short retirement.

Rossini had probably had Beaumarchais's Figaro stories in mind for some time. *Le mariage de Figaro* was off limits because Mozart had made it his own, but the "prequel," *Le barbier de Séville,* was a reasonable target, even though Paisiello had already had a popular success with it—and maybe Rossini had always thought of it with his childhood friend in mind. At all events, she answered his call and came to Rome to be his Rosina—and the following year his Angelina in *La Cenerentola* as well. Her voice was low, but not as low as Marcolini's (mezzo-soprano rather than contralto), and she had a very wide range—two and a half octaves, according to Ludwig Spohr, the German composer, who heard her in Florence in 1816.[4] She was an excellent actress, and she had something else that Rossini clearly valued: very clear and precise enunciation. Much of Rosina's character is defined by the way words and music are rhythmically related, sometimes even counterpointed. Her character assessment of herself ("Una voce poco fa") is full of it: "Io sono docile," she sings (I am docile), but a moment later "sarò una vipera" (I can be a viper) if crossed in love. Words and music are inextricably intertwined, even in the huge finales that climax the two acts. At bottom, Rosina is a calculating woman: she is going to get her own way (Figaro calls her a mistress of cunning), and what she is thinking is as important as what she is doing.

Geltrude Righetti's interrupted career turned out to be a short one: she suffered from ill health and retired from the stage for good by 1822, when she was still not thirty. But even while Rossini was working with her in Rome in 1816–17, he was already beginning his long collaboration with a much more famous singer, Isabella Colbran. In Naples, where Rossini and Colbran were both under contract, he was required to write operas to fairly precise specifications: they had to be serious rather than comic because that was the prevailing taste in Naples (though "serious" no longer meant opera seria in the old-fashioned sense), and they had to provide roles for Colbran and for at least some members of Naples's battery of tenors. Provided he fulfilled the terms of this contract, Rossini was allowed to moonlight elsewhere. That is what he was doing in Rome, and would do later in Milan and Venice, writing mainly in the comic and semiseria genres that he clearly enjoyed so much. In all these places he had to write for singers already under contract—with the single exception, it seems, of Geltrude Righetti. There were other female singers he came to admire very much (Colbran being the foremost), but Righetti, however young and inexperienced, appears to have had both the vivacity and the discipline Rossini wished for. She certainly ornamented her music—too much, according to Ludwig Spohr—but she used the same ornamentations in each performance. For the composer, ever fearful of singers interpolating meaningless and inappropriate ornaments of their own devising, this would have been welcome (and maybe even a requirement, since Rossini probably devised the ornamentations for her in the first place); but for audiences of the time, often attending several performances of an opera in the same season, it was unusual and irritating. "I am told," wrote Spohr, "that [Righetti] contributes nothing of her own, but rather accepts what is drilled into her, with the result that her ornaments which are precisely the same, note for note, every night, soon become tiresome."[5]

For almost two hundred years, ornamentation had been a very personalized art form for singers. Ever since Vittoria Archilei had ornamented Jacopo Peri's music in Florence at the end of the sixteenth century ("those charms and graces that cannot be notated and, if notated, cannot be deciphered," Peri wrote)[6] singers had been using the device to great effect. The castrati, most of them well educated in composition, and the prime donne who shared center stage with them, were all interior decorators of music. Generally, they came with their ornamentations prepared and practiced; sometimes they improvised them on the night, but they were always aware that their ornaments would be the critical focus of a performance, often much more so than the production, the drama, or even the main body of the music. Gluck had reined them in; Mozart had often rendered improvisation impossible; but for Italian singers of Rossini's time it was still an expectation—one that he gradually whittled away by the brilliance of his own writing. Righetti's repetitive ornaments certainly had his approval, even if he didn't write them himself, while Colbran's, cleverly devised to show off the good parts of her voice and hide the less good, were definitely written by Rossini.

He had first heard Isabella Colbran sing in Bologna in 1807, when he was fifteen and she, just arrived from her native Spain, was twenty-two. He was impressed, but it was not until he went to Naples, eight years later, that he began to write for her. In theatrical terms, she was a tragedian, not a comedian: Rosina, Angelina, and the Isabella of *L'Italiana in Algeri* were not for her, even though she could have coped with them musically. Her voice is probably best described as a low soprano rather than a mezzo-soprano, but it had enormous range, right down to G below the stave and up to E-flat *in alt*. She was very beautiful, and very grand—"a beauty in the most queenly tradition," wrote Stendahl, who was not a great admirer: "Off-stage, she possessed about as much dignity as the average milliner's assistant; but the moment she stepped on to the boards, her brow encircled with a royal diadem, she inspired involuntary respect."[7]

Stendahl, whose hero was Rossini, often paid tribute to Colbran's acting ability—a "wealth of exquisitely observed detail could be read into the statuesque calm of her every gesture"—but he was disdainful of her singing, certainly after 1816. The journalist and librettist Giuseppe Carpani, on the other hand, who knew Rossini and Colbran much better, was full of praise for her voice as late as 1822, when she was singing Rossini's *Zelmira* in Vienna: "She has a very sweet, full, sonorous quality of voice, particularly in the middle and lower notes; a finished, pure, insinuating style. She has no outbursts, but a fine *portamento,* perfect intonation, and an accomplished method. The graces seem to have sprinkled with nectar each of her syllables, her *fioriture,* her *volate,* her shakes. She sings with one breath a series of semitones, extending to nearly two octaves, in a clear, pearly manner. Her acting is noble and dignified, as becomes her imposing and majestic beauty."[8]

Rossini and Colbran were lovers for several years before they finally got married in 1822, and one of the advantages Colbran certainly derived from their relationship was Rossini's ongoing knowledge of the strengths and weaknesses of her voice, and his willingness to write accordingly. In personal terms, their partnership was not to stand the test of time—after 1830 he lived in Paris, she in Bologna, and they were formally separated in 1837 so that Rossini could marry Olympe Pélissier—but in opera the partnership was historic. From *Elisabetta, regina d'Inghilterra* in 1815 to *Semiramide* in 1823, he composed ten roles for her that began to define a new and much more dramatic form of opera. In all of them she was singing opposite fine tenors (the high voices of David and Rubini, the much more baritonal sound of Nozzari), and increasingly there were substantial roles for basses and female contraltos as well. There were always solo arias, but not as many as would have been the case twenty years earlier. Often their place was taken by duets and trios and the great ensembles that became a feature of Rossini's work. It was heavy duty for Colbran's voice, and there is no need to doubt Stendahl's opinion that it suffered in consequence. She was singing against bigger and louder orchestration than any of her predecessors had, with timpani and brass much in evidence—the trombones of *Otello,* the horns of *Semiramide.* Rossini occasionally augmented the orchestra with stage bands as well (as Mozart had in *Don Giovanni*). Reaching for the great climaxes was exhausting work and may often have been an inexact science (Colbran had "a marked tendency," Stendahl remarked, "to sing either above or below the required pitch").[9]

Nevertheless, Rossini was writing for a woman he loved, and he would not have subjected her to music he thought was beyond her. Elena in *La donna del lago,* written in 1819, has a final aria that is so taxing it has sometimes been omitted altogether in subsequent productions; and *Semiramide,* his final opera for Colbran in 1823, has soprano and contralto parts so difficult to cast that it was almost never performed in the twentieth century until Sutherland and Simionato teamed up for it in 1962, followed by Caballé and Horne. Most of Colbran's characters were royal or semiroyal, and much of the music correspondingly grand, but there were also moments of great pathos (Desdemona's "Willow Song"; Zelmira handing over her child to Emma) as well as tender and touching love music (never more so than in *Armida*). To accomplish all that Rossini required of her, she must have been an extraordinary artiste, and that is certainly how Neapolitans thought of her—as a queen among singers. But after Naples there was nothing left. Hearing her in London in 1824, Lord Mount Edgcumbe wrote: "Her powers are so diminished that she is unable to produce any effect on the stage."[10]

In contrast to the brilliant and very dramatic music he wrote for Colbran, Rossini sometimes found himself in need of what, in former times, would have been a low castrato. With no such person readily available, even in Naples, he turned to female contraltos, and he was lucky enough to find a remarkable and very brave lady named Benedetta Rosmunda Pisaroni. Originally, she had been a soprano of phenomenal range, more than three octaves, but an illness in 1813 deprived her of her top notes and she concentrated instead on expanding her lower register. She thus enabled Rossini to write the first great seconda roles for contraltos that were to become such a feature of Italian opera, culminating in Verdi's Ulrica, Azucena, and Mistress Quickly. Pisaroni was Zomira in *Ricciardo e Zoraide*, Andromache in *Ermione*, and Malcolm Graeme in *La donna del lago*. Later, although she did not create the role, she was a famous Arsace in *Semiramide*. Two of these characters were female, two male, but in each case it was the vocal characterization that Rossini was looking for, and he found it in Pisaroni's low and exceptionally powerful voice. First Marietta Brambilla, then Marietta Alboni (who was a pupil of Rossini's) would follow in Pisaroni's footsteps as great exponents of these roles—by which time Bellini, Donizetti, Meyerbeer, and others would have added substantially to the contralto repertory.

Pisaroni's courage was legendary. She was grossly deformed. For a woman such as her to appear on the opera stage in the eighteenth century would have been unthinkable, and it says much for the advances made by female singers that she not only did appear regularly in the first quarter of the nineteenth century but that she made a great international career for herself. With the disappearance of the castrati, and with the ascendancy of tenors still in its infancy, women had come to dominate opera. They were no longer thought of almost automatically as courtesans or women of low repute; they no longer had to be physically beautiful (though it cannot be denied that that was still an advantage). It was their vocal ability and their acting skills that counted most, and Pisaroni was living proof that this was so—as was her principal rival, Rosa Mariani, who created Arsace in *Semiramide*. Lady Granville, wife of the British ambassador to France, heard Pisaroni sing in Paris and reported on the audience's reaction: "Hideous, distorted, deformed, dwarflike Pisaroni. She has an immense head, a remarkably ugly face . . . With all this, she had not sung ten minutes before a Paris audience was in ecstasies . . . Every word is felt, every sound an expression . . . I came home quite enchanted."[11]

Not all female singers had Pisaroni's courage and independence. When Rossini arrived in Naples in 1815, Colbran still found it necessary to have "protectors" in high places—she was *favorita* of the King of Naples, and probably mistress to the impresario Barbaia before she joined forces with Rossini. But opera *was* growing up: independent women like Righetti-Giorgi and Pisaroni were ensuring that it did. Karoline Unger was another of them. She was Austrian, one of the first German-language singers to make a great career in Italy. She was only eighteen when she sang Tancredi in Vienna, and twenty when she sang for Beethoven at the first performance of his Choral Symphony, but soon after that she moved permanently to Italy and rejoiced in a series of roles written specially for her by Donizetti, including the title roles in *Parisina* and *Maria di Rudenz*. It was when she was at the Théâtre Italien in Paris in 1833 that Rossini memorably described her as possessing "the ardor of the south, the energy of the north, brazen lungs, a silver voice and golden talent."[12] Unger was a highly intelligent woman, tall and striking in appearance, with a big voice. She was also a highly independent woman— and that description could equally be applied to Giuditta Pasta and María Malibran.

If any singers of the nineteenth century could be compared to Maria Callas, it would probably be Pasta and Malibran. Unquestionably, all three were endowed with superb natural instruments, but those instruments certainly had their faults: they were not always beautiful; sometimes they were even ugly, and sometimes this ugliness was a calculated effect. People complained of Callas that her singing could be guttural or metallic, and much the same complaints were made of Pasta and Malibran, yet all three could sing with surpassing beauty. The talent they shared was an ability to color and project their voices in ways that did more than just hint at the emotions and motivations of the characters they portrayed. For their respective audiences, they were not just singers in the title role of *Norma*—they *were* Norma. They knew that anger, fear, and desperation were not best illustrated by a stream of beautiful, sensuous sounds, and they had the talent and courage to sweep their audiences into the real drama of the stage, however horrifying and ugly it might be.

While they sang much of the same repertory, their voices were by no means similar. Callas was a natural soprano—she reached the high F of Rossini's Armida with no apparent difficulty—yet in hours of hard work and exercising she schooled herself to reach down into the mezzo range, even to A-natural below the stave, which would have been much more natural for Pasta and Malibran.[13] They, conversely, were mezzos with more difficulty at the top of the range. Stendahl reported that Pasta could "achieve perfect resonance on a note as low as bottom A and can rise as high as C-sharp or D," but while the bottom A was probably natural, the top notes were almost certainly forced.[14] Malibran was born with a contralto voice, very deep, but her father, Manuel García, the tenor who created Count Almaviva for Rossini in *Il barbiere,* trained her voice with frightening rigor so that it would extend at the top into the soprano range. Between the natural voice and the extension there was said to be an interval of dead notes she had to be careful to avoid in performance.[15] What all three—Callas, Pasta, and Malibran—had in common were years of exhausting work to ensure that their voices could cover the huge compass of range and coloring necessary for portrayals as diverse as Rosina, Norma, Anna Bolena, and the sleepwalking Amina. What this implies, of course, is that they all had remarkable techniques—as remarkable in their way as the techniques of the great castrati—and it was these techniques that gave them the range, flexibility, agility, and lightness to sing the music written by the composer, and then to add to it the texture and coloring the drama demanded.

Like Callas, both Pasta and Malibran were good actresses—Pasta more intense, Malibran sometimes prone to going over the top. Both were highly intelligent, erudite women who loved nothing more than to be at the center of their salons. But Malibran was intuitive and fun-loving, a graceful, beautiful woman who commanded devotion and rejoiced in little wickednesses, whereas Pasta was more homely, somewhat straitlaced, and physically striking only when she was immersed in a performance. Malibran was loved and revered, Pasta was hugely admired—and by no one more so than Rossini. The only role he actually wrote for her was Corinna in *Il viaggio a Reims* in

Giuditta Pasta (1797–1865) in the title role of Rossini's *Tancredi*. Rossini, Bellini, and Donizetti were three of Pasta's greatest admirers. In the space of twelve months in 1830–31, she created Anna Bolena for Donizetti, and Norma and Amina *(La sonnambula)* for Bellini. (Royal College of Music, London.)

1825, but by then she had superseded Colbran as the most important ambassador of his work.

Only a year after her debut in Milan as an eighteen-year-old in 1816, Pasta was on the international circuit, first in Paris, then in London. She sang her share of "trouser" roles—Zingarelli's Romeo, Mozart's Cherubino, Telemachus in Cimarosa's *Penelope*—but then, almost as quickly as Righetti-Giorgi and Colbran created new Rossinian characters, she was introducing them to French and British audiences, and often to opera houses in northern Italy as well. *Cenerentola* was one of her early successes, but it was at the

Théâtre Italien in Paris that she became an international star. There, in 1821–22, she sang Angelina, Desdemona, Queen Elizabeth, and Tancredi, and it was not long before she was adding Zelmira and Semiramide as well. In London, in 1824, she signed a huge contract for fourteen thousand pounds, effectively bankrupting the theater, and the following year she was back in Paris to showcase her Rossinian roles at the Théâtre Italien, now under the direction of Rossini himself.

Although she often sang in Italy, and occasionally in London, it was in Paris that Pasta became the ultimate star, often in partnership with Giam-Battista Rubini, who had made the leap from being a fairly ordinary tenor to being quite extraordinary. The 1825 season was entirely devoted to Ros-sini's operas, with the sole exception of Meyerbeer's *Il crociato in Egitto,* in which Pasta took over the role of Armando, originally written in Italy for the castrato Velluti. Rossini certainly regarded her as his greatest interpreter (he was quite dazzled by her and she was devoted to him), but she was careful to maintain her interest in other composers, alive and dead—she performed Zingarelli's Romeo, Mayr's Medea, Paisiello's Nina, and Pacino's Niobe—and it was not long before two more Italian composers were competing to make her their muse.

Gaetano Donizetti was the first of them. For him she created Anna Bo-lena in Milan in 1830, in his first great international success. It was a role that would reenter the modern repertory when Callas revived it in 1957. The long final scene is for Anna alone—unhinged, sometimes aware of her des-perate situation, sometimes daydreaming of happier times when she was in love with Percy. No one, not even Rossini, had written anything as power-ful as this for the opera stage, and for Donizetti, whose thirtieth opera it was, it was the inspiration of Pasta that made it possible. But where Doni-zetti was, Vincenzo Bellini would not be far behind, and within weeks, at the same theater, Pasta was creating Amina in *La sonnambula* (The Sleep-walker)—another role that Callas would assume in 1957. In contrast to *Anna Bolena,* this was a rustic opera semiseria (though it was now given the more Romantic description of *melodramma*), and Amina, like Anna, was given a hugely dramatic final scene in which she was found sleepwalking on the eaves of the millhouse roof, apparently quite mad. Like *Anna Bolena, La sonnam-*

bula was written not just for Pasta but also for the tenor Rubini: much of the music is pitched extremely high, even including a high E-flat for Pasta. Her first act cabaletta, "Sovra il sen la man mi posa," is extraordinary for its brilliance and its length, and her final cantabile, in which she addresses the dead flowers originally given her by her lover ("Ah! Non credea mirarti") is a wonderful example of what Verdi would later call Bellini's "long, long, long melodies"—thirty-six bars of slow tempo with no form of reprise.

Bellini had originally favored a fine French soprano, Henriette Méric-Lalande. Between 1826 and 1829 she had created four major roles for him, including Imogene in *Il pirata* (Bellini's first undisputed success in 1827), and she would later create the magnificent title role of Donizetti's *Lucrezia Borgia* (1833). But from the time that Pasta first sang Imogene in an 1830 revival of *Il pirata* in Vienna, Pasta was the singer for whom Bellini wanted, and needed, to compose. First *La sonnambula,* then *Norma,* and finally *Beatrice di Tenda* were the fruits of their collaboration.

Norma, the druid priestess, is the peak to which many sopranos have aspired, but which few—a very few—have reached unscathed. When Bellini first told Pasta about the role early in 1831, he wrote that it contained an "encyclopedic" range of expression, ideally suited to her voice. Pasta was not sure. She first asked for "Casta diva" to be rewritten; only later, when she had spent several weeks studying it, did she acknowledge she could sing it. It comes at the very beginning of the evening, a great coloratura set piece, but with the added complication of spacious, long lines of melody that have to be sustained and molded over acres of bars. Norma is the only well-defined character in the opera; she bears the full weight of the drama and the music. She needs power and endurance, but grace and finesse as well. She has scenes of great tenderness and moments of great rage. At the end, she goes to the pyre with astonishing dignity, something approaching grandeur. Pasta never had any doubt about the dramatic aspects of the role: it had an intensity, and ultimately a nobility, that was ideally suited to her own character, as it was to Malibran's when she took it over at La Scala during the 1834 season. But musically and vocally there is no more demanding role in the soprano repertoire, and that explains its rarity. Giulia Grisi, who as a twenty-year-old sang the lesser role of Adalgisa at the premiere, became a

Maria Callas (1923–1977) as Norma at the Rome Opera House, 1958.
(UPI/Corbis Bettmann.)

great Norma. So, later on, did Therese Tietjens, Rosa Ponselle, Joan Sutherland, and Montserrat Caballé, and it is notable that one or two fine Wagnerians, of whom Lilli Lehmann is the most important, have tackled the role
with impressive results, but its most famous exponent after Pasta and Malibran was the only one who ever equaled their dramatic power as a singer—
Maria Callas (herself a former Brünnhilde of some distinction).

Callas was also known for her revival of Cherubini's *Médée*, a work
of the late eighteenth century described as an opéra comique because it contained spoken dialogue (though its quotient of comedy is nil: it chronicles
one horror after another). Cherubini required vocal gymnastics from his
Medea, and great dramatic ability, but it was not the Medea that Pasta knew

and loved. Hers was *Medea in Corinto*, written for Naples in 1813 by Simon Mayr, who was later Donizetti's teacher. *Medea* shared the same librettist with *Norma*, Felice Romani, and it is not difficult to see why it appealed so much to Pasta and her audiences. Without approaching the musical heights of *Norma* (though it had been written for Colbran and therefore displayed the soprano voice to great effect), it had the wide variety of mood swings and emotions that Pasta was supremely capable of portraying, and her performances of it in Paris, London, and Milan were as famous in their day as was her Norma.

Not yet forty, Pasta retired from the stage in 1835—and probably not a moment too soon. She had used her voice unsparingly for most of her career and it was no longer in good repair. By 1833, the critics were complaining that she had real problems with pitch—she simply could not be relied upon to sing in tune—and her last years were marred by a number of excruciating evenings that were best forgotten. Her natural successor was the young Giulia Grisi, who had been Adalgisa to her Norma in 1831, and whose precocious voice and stage presence were already preferred by many of Pasta's former champions—including Rossini, who was partly responsible for contracting Grisi to sing at the Théâtre Italien in Paris during the 1835 season, thereby ensuring that it was Grisi, not Pasta, who became the prima donna of the great *Puritani* quartet that created Bellini's last opera. Grisi was young, attractive, and very talented, whereas Pasta was clearly fighting a losing battle with her own legend. And anyway, there was still Malibran, who was eleven years younger than Pasta and in most ways her equal, if not, as many people thought, her superior.

But 1835 turned out to be a twilight hour. Within a year, both Bellini and Malibran were dead.

María Malibran was the scion of one of opera's few real dynasties. Her father, Manuel García, Spanish by birth, was one of those tenors in Naples for whom Rossini had written—he had also been the original Almaviva in *Il barbiere* and had later sung Otello to Pasta's Desdemona. His two daughters, María and Pauline (like María, she was generally known by her married name, Viardot), were two of the greatest singers of the century, and their brother, Manuel García Jr., was a singing teacher and voice doctor of enormous influence: he died in 1906 at the age of 101. María's teacher was her father—her adored father who beat her black and blue as he drilled her spirit and her voice into submission. That she spent the rest of her life frenetically trying to be loved is hardly surprising. She wrote hysterical adolescent letters to Pasta—"Love me, love me as I love you, and if you have the chance, *for the love of God!* write to me even though it be only two lines."[16] Pasta never did write. When María found a man she wanted to marry, her independence came at a price: Eugène Malibran had to compensate her father for the loss of María to the "family company." Alas, Eugène quickly lost his money, and María, after several months of scratching out a living in New York (she sang in the choir of Grace Church), returned to Europe alone: the marriage was eventually annulled.

With this background, Malibran's short life had the tragic momentum of the Romantic heroines she depicted on the stage. Its chronology was busy and compact—her debut in London as Rosina at the age of seventeen (as a last minute substitute for Pasta); two years in North America, singing Rossini and Mozart in New York with her father's company and making her bid for independence in marriage; back to Europe and a stream of uninterrupted successes in Paris, London, and Italy, capped by her 1834 La Scala debut as Norma; her marriage to the Belgian violinist Charles de Bériot; and her death as a result of a riding accident when she was pregnant at the age of twenty-eight.

She led a life of perpetual motion—she simply could not sit still. Her favorite exercise was horseback riding, which she did almost every day. She painted, she wrote long exuberant letters to her friends, she embroidered. She practiced, she rehearsed, she performed—and then she almost always went on to make appearances at parties and soirées until daybreak. In Naples, she climbed Mount Vesuvius, bathed in the sea in the heat of the day, and spent evenings rowing on the bay. For her farewell performance in London at the end of the 1835 season she performed Amina in *La sonnambula* and Leonore in Beethoven's *Fidelio*, both of them *in full*—and then she caught a late night ferry from the Thames to begin a journey to Italy. Everything she did she entered into with total commitment. There were those who found

María Malibran (1808–1836). Just as Malibran was a Romantic
heroine on the stage, so she was in her short life and tragic death.
(Royal College of Music, London.)

her irritating and were irked by her overacting and overreaching, but most
people were simply enchanted. She had a gift for friendship and for binding
people to her in tight emotional bonds. She enslaved Bellini, Mendelssohn,
and Chopin; she made lasting friendships with competitors like the German
soprano Henriette Sontag (after several years of spectacular bitchiness), and
with colleagues like the huge Italian bass Luigi Lablache. Wherever she performed, however lukewarm the initial reception, she always won over the
audience. At La Scala, where Pasta herself was in the theater for her first
Norma, and the claque came ready to boo her, even the *Pastists* stayed to
cheer. "Other singers may captivate by their art," wrote the pianist Ignaz
Moscheles, "but Malibran had magic power to lead us captives, body and
soul."[17] Whether face to face or across the footlights, she was always able to
communicate the special joy that surrounded her. Only those closest to her
understood that it might contain a destructive streak as well.

One of the saddest facts about Malibran's life is that no composer ever wrote a major role for her, and she may be the first really great prima donna in the story of opera about whom that can be said. There were two fairly minor roles written for her, Balfe's *Maid of Artois* and Persiani's *Ines de Castro*. The latter, it is true, had such a successful first night in Naples that the city government was moved to pass a law limiting the number of bows a solo artist could take at the end of a performance, but Malibran had always had doubts about the piece and never sang it again: it became a vehicle for Persiani's wife, Fanny, and disappeared from the repertory within fifteen years of its premiere, not to be revived in Italy until 1999. So Malibran was basically a reinterpreter of roles created for other singers—yet Rossini and Donizetti adored her, and Bellini worshiped her (on his cravat he often wore a gold locket with two miniature portraits inside it, one of himself, one of Malibran, both of them painted by her). In many ways, her range was greater than Pasta's—the voice, even if it did contain some dead notes, spanned three octaves, and it had great power both above and below. She could sing Beethoven's Leonore as well as Mozart's Zerlina, Rossini's Tancredi as well as Donizetti's Maria Stuarda. "The word 'limit' was unbearable to her," wrote the French playwright Ernest Legouvé; "she found it impossible to grasp the fact that she could not do what anybody else in her profession could do. She spent her life in trying to mount as high as Sontag and as low as Pisaroni." In the same passage, Legouvé compared her with Sontag: "When Sontag sang, her notes were so limpid and brilliant that one might have compared them to a flood of light. Malibran's voice was like gold, but like gold it had to be dug from the bowels of the earth; it had to be separated from the ore; it had to be forged and beaten, and made pliable like the metal under the hammer. One day in Rome when she was to play Rosina, I heard her study the shakes [trills] of her *cavatina*. Every now and then she stopped short to scold her own voice, saying 'Obey me, I'll make you obey me!'"[18]

The nearest Malibran came to having a great opera composed for her was Bellini's *I puritani*. Malibran was not in Paris for that brilliant 1835 season, and it was always intended that Giulia Grisi would create Elvira, but Bellini was also under contract to write a new opera for Naples later in the year. He decided that this should be a revised version of *I puritani,* and he therefore adapted it into what is known as the "Malibran version," with much of Elvira's music transposed down to the mezzo range. But the new version did not arrive in Naples in time, and Bellini died his lonely death a few weeks after the Paris triumph. The Malibran version remained unperformed until it was done by Katia Ricciarelli in Bari in 1986 (though Joan Sutherland used some of the music for her 1975 recording).

When news reached her of Bellini's death, Malibran was in Milan. Her second series of *Norma* performances at La Scala had begun with sixteen curtain calls at the end of the first act—the city's principal magistrate had had to be summoned to restore order before the curtain could finally be brought down. As she wept over the totally unexpected message from Paris, she said, "I feel I shall soon follow him." She died on the first anniversary of Bellini's death.

Aside from the two Henriettes (Sontag and Méric-Lalande, for both of whom Bellini and Donizetti had considerable admiration), the only soprano to challenge the hegemony of Malibran and Pasta was an Italian named Giuseppina Ronzi De Begnis. Like them, she had begun her career in the years when Rossini was at his peak and Mozart was finally being discovered by European opera houses outside the German world; and like them, she had become a great star at the Théâtre Italien in Paris. But it was in 1825, when she returned to Naples, where her husband Giuseppe De Begnis was a well-known bass, that she began creating new roles. After Mercadante's *Zaira* in 1831, there followed five separate roles for Donizetti, including the title role in *Maria Stuarda* and Queen Elizabeth in *Roberto Devereux*. She was known as a fine actress with a voice of great facility and power, low enough for Bellini's Romeo and Norma but easily able to encompass the coloratura of Rossini's Rosina or Donizetti's Queen Elizabeths. She went on singing until 1849, more than a decade after Pasta and Malibran had passed from the scene.

Ronzi De Begnis was also known to be a sworn enemy of one of her rival sopranos in Naples, Anna Del Sere. Unfortunately, they were both cast in the premiere of *Maria Stuarda* in 1834—Ronzi De Begnis in the title role, Del Sere as Queen Elizabeth. When they came to rehearse the great confrontation between the two queens at the end of the first act, Del Sere took personally the words of the curse Mary Stuart pronounces ("Obscene and unworthy prostitute, may my curse fall on you"), and she launched an unscripted physical assault on her rival. It was a one-sided contest, as it turned out, because Ronzi De Begnis was a large and heavy woman, more than able to return punch for punch. Del Sere was carried from the theater in a swoon.[19]

That was by no means the end of the calamities visited upon *Maria Stuarda*. A real-life queen, Maria Cristina of Naples, attended the dress rehearsal and was so upset by the sadness of the ending (it was said that she fainted) that her husband, the King of Naples, announced he would ban the opera altogether unless major changes were made to the plot. Donizetti, ever adept at tinkering with his own work, delivered the same music with a different story line and a happy ending. It was called *Buondelmonte*. But even when the original title and plot were restored for the La Scala production a few months later, with María Malibran now in the title role, there was more trouble. Malibran was not well and sang poorly, and when the local censors ordered the removal of the words *vil bastarda* (vile bastard) from the confrontation scene, Malibran simply went on using them and the production was closed after only six performances.

In the meantime, Giulia Grisi's success in Paris had made it possible for her to be thought of as Pasta's eventual successor. She had gone there in 1832 at the age of twenty-one, having already made a name for herself in Italy and Vienna. The year before, in Milan, she had created Adalgisa opposite Pasta's Norma and she had also sung in the successful premiere of *Ullà di Bassora* by Feliciano Strepponi, the father of Verdi's second wife. One of the least attractive sides of Grisi was her ability to spot the main chance, and then to seize it. This is what she did when she broke her contract with La Scala—on the grounds that she had been a minor when she signed it—and moved to Paris to sign a much more lucrative contract with the Théâtre Italien. Other than a brief visit after her retirement in 1861, she never again set foot in Italy.

Like Malibran, Grisi was part of a theatrical dynasty. Her aunt was Josephina Grassini, creator of Zingarelli's Giulietta, sometime mistress of Napoleon and more recently Pasta's teacher. Her father, a Napoleonic general who lived to be over a hundred, sired two gifted daughters: Giuditta, a fine mezzo who created Romeo in Bellini's *I Capuleti e I Montecchi,* and Giulia, the younger by six years. Their cousin, Carlotta Grisi, was one of the most talented ballerinas of the century, the first Giselle. In those days, it was quite normal for female singers to begin their careers while still in their teens (Pasta at nineteen, Malibran at seventeen—more than a hundred years later Callas was only nineteen when she first sang Tosca), and Giulia Grisi was no exception: she was seventeen when she made her debut in Bologna. Nor did these early beginnings necessarily mean they would have short careers—in a time before jet travel, voices had more time to recover between performances. Grisi went on singing into her fiftieth year, which was certainly longer than was wise. The state of her voice suggested she should have stopped much earlier (she actually gave her first "farewell performance" in 1849, twelve years before her actual retirement!), but it was hard to stop when Giovanni Mario, the most celebrated tenor of the age and Grisi's partner and companion of more than thirty years, was still singing to considerable acclaim. Grisi and Mario were the most romantic couple of the Romantic Age; theirs was a fairytale partnership that had no equal before the arrival of movies.

Grisi's voice had none of the flaws of Pasta's and Malibran's. It was said to be perfectly placed and perfectly even over a range of two octaves— and it was powerful, for Grisi's career spanned an astonishing era in the development of opera, from Rossini, Bellini, and Donizetti, through the *grands opéras* of Meyerbeer, to the middle period of Verdi (one of Grisi's last assumptions was the Leonora of *Il trovatore*). She sang Mozart's Donna Anna, Rossini's Semiramide, Bellini's Norma, and Donizetti's Queen Elizabeth in *Roberto Devereux.* Eight years apart, she created Elvira in *I puritani* and Norina in *Don Pasquale,* each time as a member of a legendary quartet. She took up the challenge of grand opéra in Meyerbeer's Paris—Alice in *Robert le diable,* Valentin in *Les Huguenots,* even Fidès in *Le prophète* (though that was unwise)—and she had sufficient attack and forcefulness in her voice to make successful ventures into Verdi—Giselda in *I Lombardi,* Lucrezia in *I due Foscari,* and that final Leonora. Yet these operas represented only a small part of her total repertory. She was busy, very talented, and a perfect partner to the handsome Mario, with whom she often sang. She was a professional to her fingertips, a monster for managements to deal with, an angel before the public—but she was never a Malibran, nor even a Pasta.

There was something hard about Giulia Grisi. One cannot blame her for being a good businesswoman: she was the leader of the quartet of singers who created *Don Pasquale* in 1843 (Mario, Lablache, and the baritone Antonio Tamburini were the others), undoubtedly the most important box-office attractions of the time, and they had a right to be well paid. But Grisi turned them into a rather unpleasant cabal ("all of us or none of us") for whom she negotiated with a ruthlessness that would have done credit to a modern Hollywood agent. Clearly she was in the right place at the right time—a fine singer with no obvious competitors—but she was not an original. As Henry Chorley, the English critic of *The Athenaeum,* put it: "Madame Grisi has been remarkable for her cleverness in adopting the effects and ideas of others more thoughtful and originally inventive than herself."[20] The hardness was most visible in her attitude toward Pauline Viardot, Malibran's younger sister. Viardot was hardly a direct competitor—she had a much lower, mezzo voice—and though their repertories sometime intersected (they both sang Norma and the *Sonnambula* Amina, for instance) they had no reason to be afraid of each other. But Grisi did not want Malibran's little sister treading on her turf, and for the best part of a decade she used her negotiating muscle to keep her out of London. When she did come, in 1848, when Grisi's voice was well past its best, Mario was used as the instrument of torture. At very short notice, he withdrew from performances of *La sonnambula* and *Les Huguenots,* leaving Viardot to sing with lesser and unrehearsed tenors. The same tactics were applied to a performance of *La juive* in 1850. Since Viardot and the substitute tenors scored considerable triumphs, the only losers in this battle were Grisi and Mario. A later attempt to upstage Viardot by singing Fidès in *Le prophète* at Covent Garden (it was a role Viardot had created for Meyerbeer in Paris) was a disaster for Grisi. At the end, her career deteriorated into something approaching farce, and at the very end (a "coming out of retirement by public demand" to sing *Lucrezia Borgia* at Covent Garden in 1866) it was pure farce. Taking a bow at the end of act one, she was knocked down by the curtain and was unable to rise without the help of an army of stage attendants.

If Grisi sometimes belittled herself by her behavior, it should not be allowed to detract from the importance of her career as a whole. Among sopranos, she was the bridge that took them from the enchanted world of bel canto into the altogether more dramatic form of singing required by Verdi and his younger contemporaries. Grisi's immediate successor, the much loved Therese Tietjens, went both deeper into this territory and further back: she sang Gluck's Iphigénie, Cherubini's Medea, and Mozart's Konstanze as well as the powerful ladies of Rossini, Bellini, and Donizetti (Semiramide, Norma, Lucrezia Borgia), and she went forward into the Verdian repertory—Hélène in *Les vêpres siciliennes,* Elvira in *Ernani,* the two Leonoras of *Il trovatore* and *La forza del destino.* Tietjens's career was cut short by the cancer that killed her in 1877 when she was still only forty-four, but it illustrated the vast range of roles now available to a versatile soprano willing to sing in French, Italian, and German. Gounod's sweetly tuneful Marguerite and Wagner's angry Ortrud were two of Tietjens' most successful impersonations in the 1860s.

Something else had changed in the world of sopranos. Most of the great female singers of the first half of the nineteenth century, from Colbran to Grisi, had been low sopranos. They possessed upper registers of considerable reach and brilliance, but it was their middle and chest registers that defined their voices, that enabled them to give such dramatic vocal characterizations to women like Norma, Lucrezia Borgia, and Anna Bolena. But another group of singers had grown up alongside them. These were emphatically high sopranos—singers like Fanny Persiani, Henriette Sontag, and Jenny Lind. They had the beautiful, limpid, precise top notes that went with coloratura techniques that were (apparently) quite natural and easy. They had power, too—they could soar above large orchestras and huge ensembles—but, most of all, they seemed to have more feminine voices, more fitting to the pathetic heroines that inhabited so much of Romantic drama—women like Donizetti's Lucia di Lammermoor and Bellini's Elvira in *I puritani.* Eventually this type of voice, given the much more dramatic dimensions that Grisi had had to add late in her career, would become the dominant female voice of Italian opera. Adelina Patti, Christine Nilsson, Marcella Sembrich, and Nellie Melba were all sopranos, as opposed to mezzos. Some of them might still sing Semiramide, or even Norma (generally transposed up a bit), but they lacked the chest registers to characterize such women in the way their predecessors had.

So, for all the excitement these dramatic sopranos added to opera, there was also a loss: low soprano voices with enormous range, like Colbran's and Pasta's and Malibran's, became rare to the point of extinction. Contraltos and mezzos certainly had a part to play in opera, but from now on they would generally, and far too often, be confined to seconda roles.

Seventeenth- and eighteenth-century voice teachers had made a fetish of birdsong.[21] Sopranos, male and female, were taught to listen to birds and to practice imitating them—their exact intonation, their rapid trills through a series of detached notes. Reproducing these trills accurately was an exercise that countless singers had endured countless times: it was thought to be the purest form of vocalise. Certainly, it was a spectacular effect—the first time—but it was also anodyne and bland when repeated again and again. Opera singers were portraying *people* on the stage: they were expected to characterize them, both in their physical acting and in their voices, so color and texture were equally important ingredients—sometimes (as Pasta and Malibran, and later Callas, were not afraid to demonstrate) to the point of ugliness.

It was no accident that the high sopranos of the mid-nineteenth century were often likened to songbirds—Jenny Lind was "the Swedish Nightingale"; Henriette Sontag was "the lark at heaven's gate," according to Berlioz. They were capable of executing the most florid and difficult arpeggio passages with extraordinary accuracy—"with the neatness of a good finger on the pianoforte," as one reviewer wrote of Sontag.[22] This is not to say there was no heart in their performance, but many of the characters they were called upon to portray were sweet, virginal, unhappy, and fairly one-dimensional. Even if they went mad (and several of them did), they remained innocents—caged birds singing along to their predestined ends.

Purity of character was conveyed by the purity of the singing. However high the coloratura, it had to be precise—not thin but bold, never scooping or swooping. The inexact singer, the one whose breath control or intonation let her down, was inevitably found out. Keeping the voice pure meant keeping all forms of ugliness out of it, and that included vibrato. No one can speak or sing without vibrating the vocal cords—that is how sound is produced—but vibrato implies much more than that: it is the deliberate oscillation or undulation of the voice so that it produces fluctuations in pitch. Occasionally, it is a useful effect, but it can easily become a very bad habit (one that was already becoming common among tenors like Rubini and would become distressingly common among all singers as the music they performed became ever more dramatic). Tremolo is much the same—literally, a trembling in the voice—but when properly used, as a rapid repeat or alternation of notes, it can be a valuable tool, and certainly one well suited to the pathetic nature of Romantic heroines. For female singers on the crest of the bel canto wave, circa 1840, tremolo, in moderation, was a talent; vibrato, on the other hand, was almost always unacceptable: it was thought of as a form of impurity.

Lucy, Sir Walter Scott's *Bride of Lammermoor,* was the ultimate Romantic heroine, and she was created on the opera stage by Fanny Tacchinardi-Persiani. She was known as *la piccola Pasta,* "the little Pasta," but it was a misleading name because Persiani's voice was of the utmost purity and unbelievable accuracy—it was often likened to a flute. It had none of the grand tones or dramatic passions of Pasta's voice, but it had a wonderful agility in the stratosphere and went perfectly with Persiani's much more fragile presence on stage—tremolo, yes; vibrato, no. She was not, by nature or physique, a graceful woman ("pale, plain and anxious," wrote Chorley), nor was she an actress of any renown, but in 1835, when she created Lucia at the age of twenty-two, she was petite and girlish, just the sort of frail and delicate creature Scott and Donizetti had imagined. In modern times, when the role has frequently been appropriated by much more dramatic sopranos (Callas was one of them), it has sometimes been difficult to see this quality clearly, but it was certainly what Donizetti wanted. Persiani went on to sing the role all over Europe, most of all in Paris and London, where she was pretty well anchored for most of her career, right up to 1850. She had a wide repertoire, even broadening into Verdi at the end, but it was chiefly as an interpreter of Mozart, Rossini, Bellini, and Donizetti that she was known—and as a faith-

Henriette Sontag (1806–1854). Even during the nineteen-year intermission in her stage career (1830–49), Sontag was not forgotten by the opera world. She was clearly the inspiration for Scribe's libretto *L'ambassadrice*, which was set to music by Auber and produced at the Opéra-Comique in Paris in 1836. (Royal College of Music, London.)

ful champion of her husband's operas, many of which might never have made it to the stage without her.

Henriette Sontag was vocally the equal of Persiani—and her superior in almost every other way—but Sontag went missing for nineteen years right in the middle of her career. Beginning in Prague in 1821 as a highly precocious fifteen-year-old, she moved to Vienna, where Weber invited her to create the title role in *Euryanthe*. Shortly after her eighteenth birthday, she and her friend Karoline Unger charmed Beethoven into allowing them to originate the female solo parts of the *Missa solemnis* and the Choral Symphony. Everywhere she went in the German world Sontag was the darling of audiences and critics. She was sweet, adorable, very beautiful—and she could sing. She arrived in Paris in 1826 and immediately conquered the Théâtre

Italien (which, for a twenty-year-old German singer who had never before sung in the Italian language, was quite an achievement). This was where she found herself in competition with Pasta and Malibran, who had just returned from her adventures in New York. Sontag could hold her own in any such company, but this was not so much a rivalry as an embarrassment of riches. As the French critic Castil-Blaze put it: "Pasta, Malibran and Sontag were so different that rivalry was absurd. Thanks to the three, I have heard Desdemona sung to perfection. The Roman Empire was not conquered by one general!"[23] But in 1830, still only twenty-four, Sontag retired from the stage on the announcement of her marriage to a Sardinian diplomat, Count Rossi (they claimed to have been secretly married since 1827). For the next twenty years, Sontag was an ambassador's wife and mother to seven children: her only performances were at private parties.

Those twenty years, of course, witnessed the retirement of Pasta in 1835, the death of Malibran in 1836, the end of Persiani's career, and the entirely unexpected withdrawal from the stage of Jenny Lind in 1849. Only Grisi was left standing. Around them all (and of peculiar importance to Countess Rossi in her diplomatic life at The Hague), Europe was once again falling apart, culminating in a series of widespread upheavals and conflicts in 1848–49. One of the most unequal of these conflicts was that between Sardinia and Austria. The Austrian victory at Novara led to Charles Albert's abdication in favor of his son, and the end of Count Rossi's career. So, at the age of forty-four, Sontag once again became the family breadwinner. She traveled to London to take the place of Jenny Lind, who was about to sail the Atlantic to become P. T. Barnum's newest novelty.

To resume a stage career after such an interval was unprecedented. To do so on the basis of her old repertory of Rosinas and Isabellas would have been understandable, but that was not Sontag's way. She learned a whole new repertory of Bellini and Donizetti works composed during her absence, beginning with *Linda di Chamounix* and going on to *La sonnambula*, *La fille du régiment*, and even *Lucrezia Borgia*. She performed in London, Paris, and Germany; she went on concert tours of England, Scotland, and (following in Lind's footsteps) the United States. Her health suffered, but still she went on, until finally, in 1854, she was caught in a cholera epidemic in Mexico City and died there. No one who heard her ever doubted her artistry or her magnetism on the stage. Her voice appears to have retained its two-and-a-half octave range from first to last, and her marvelous technique and flexibility never deserted her. If there was a criticism, it was that she was unemotional, that she lacked the passion of a Pasta or a Malibran. But for most people, Sontag was beyond criticism: she had, wrote Hector Berlioz, "all the gifts of art and nature: voice, musical feeling, dramatic instinct, style, exquisite taste, passion, reflectiveness, grace—everything and still something more."[24]

Many people thought Jenny Lind had everything—but maybe she lacked the "something more." Her stage career was spectacular, brief, and erratic. Yet she, more than any other singer of the nineteenth century (other, perhaps, than Malibran), had the ability to captivate her audiences. Whether she was singing for the Queen of England, or composers like Mendelssohn and Meyerbeer, or the patrons of the upper circle, they were enchanted by her. Petite, almost waiflike, she *was* the Romantic heroine. At the end of the mad scene in *Lucia di Lammermoor,* instead of making a dignified exit as most singers did so that they could return for curtain calls, she fell senseless on the stage—which, as the London *Times* soberly pointed out, "brought the situation to a more pointed conclusion." In *La sonnambula,* instead of allowing the customary substitute to perform the dangerous sleepwalking escapade, she did it herself, her sightless eyes staring out ahead of her as she crossed the rickety mill bridge (not even Lind did her sleepwalking on the eaves of the millhouse roof as prescribed by the libretto). And it was not just her acting that distinguished her. Mainly, it was her voice.

Jenny Lind's voice was an object of wonder in an age that was supremely aware of the vocal art, but it was not always there for her—and that, perhaps, was a result of having started too young. She entered the Royal Opera School in Stockholm at the age of nine, at least five years before the normal entry age. She was performing in major concerts at twelve and became a prima donna of the Stockholm Royal Opera at eighteen, singing enormous roles like Agathe in Weber's *Der Freischütz,* Alice in Meyerbeer's *Robert le diable,* Mozart's Donna Anna, Bellini's Norma, Donizetti's Lucia, and the hugely demanding role of Julia in Spontini's *La vestale* (another Callas role of the 1950s). It quickly took its toll. In 1841, when she was twenty-one, her middle register began to fray and then to disappear. In Paris, she consulted Malibran's brother, Manuel García Jr., and after six weeks of enforced silence he began to bring her voice back to life. The middle register would always be somewhat veiled, but the rest of her voice was better than ever, extending now over two and three-quarter octaves, right up to G above high C. It had the silvery sheen of Sontag's, the astonishing strength and accuracy of Persiani's, and (more than either of them) a truly dramatic quality. She returned to Sweden, and then to Germany, and took on more roles.

She was a nervous lady. "I possess neither the personal advantages, the assurance, nor the charlatanism of other *prime donne*," she wrote primly to a London impresario in 1845.[25] She was also immensely generous, puritanical, and more than a little prudish: she had a lot in common with her number-one fan, the young Queen Victoria. Once she left Sweden and ventured into Germany and England, she found the adulation and the expectations hard to deal with—and theater managements found her hard to deal with. "Jenny Lind fever" was a phenomenon: tickets were traded on the black market at inflated prices; everyone seemed to be in love with her; and she herself was increasingly confused by her celebrity. She came under the influence of evangelical Christians in England who persuaded her that a respectable woman should not be appearing on the stage. Such advice was probably a relief to her. In the summer of 1848, amid the triumph of her appearances in her newest role (as Elvira in Bellini's *I puritani*) and with Mendelssohn's devastating death six months earlier still hanging over her, she sang her last operatic performance on the stage. She was twenty-eight—the same age as Malibran had been at her death.

Of all the great sopranos, Lind may have been the most scrupulous musician. Her voice was God-given to an extent, but she was always aware of its deficiencies, its creaks and frailties. No one has ever worked harder to iron them out, to achieve absolute purity. Norma may not have been her most famous role, nor even the wisest, but no one who ever heard the bell-like clarity of her repeated top As in "Casta diva" forgot them in a hurry. For Mendelssohn, it was the quality of her F-sharp that caused him to write "Hear ye, Israel" in his oratorio *Elijah* (written for her and performed by

Jenny Lind (1820–1887) as Vielka in *Ein Feldlager in Schlesien* (A Camp in Silesia). Friedrich Wilhelm IV commissioned the opera from his director-general of music, Meyerbeer, to mark the reopening of the Berlin Hofoper after a fire. Prussian officials insisted it must appear to be an all-Prussian effort, so the libretto (by the Frenchman Eugène Scribe) was attributed to its translator, Ludwig Rellstab, and Lind, for whom Meyerbeer wrote the leading role, did not appear in the production until seven days after its opening night. (Royal College of Music, London.)

her on the first anniversary of his death). For *I puritani*, she wrote her own cadenza to "Qui la voce" at the beginning of Elvira's mad scene—"showering her trills and roulades like sparkling diamonds," one witness wrote. The two major operas written for her proved somewhat disappointing: Amalia in Verdi's *I masnadieri* (The Bandits) was an ungrateful role in an opera that never really worked, and the gypsy Vielka in Meyerbeer's *Ein Feldlager in Schlesien* (A Camp in Silesia), though it was immensely popular in Berlin and Vienna, was never a great vehicle for a soprano of Lind's talents.

Jenny Lind's brief career on the international stage (just five years from the time she first sang outside Sweden to the day of her retirement) was proof of the extraordinary power of opera in the mid-nineteenth century—and the ultimate proof that the female opera singer was now someone who could take her place in the highest reaches of society. Pasta and Malibran had made the same point in their own way (though never quite to their satisfaction), but it was Sontag and Lind who established what we would now recognize as the "film star" status of the greatest singers, hobnobbing with kings and princes while they received the accolades of rich and poor alike. Their hit tunes were played on barrel organs at street corners; their lives were chronicled in the newspapers and broadsheets; they were recognized wherever they went.

They were also beginning to make an awful lot of money. There was nothing particularly new about that, except that now they were hanging on to it: it was comparatively rare to hear stories of great prime donne of yesteryear dying in poverty. They had managers (very often their husbands) and they negotiated with opera houses from positions of strength. But impresarios were increasingly aware that these ladies did not necessarily need a large cast and an opera house around them. Once they had made their reputations in the opera houses, their biggest box-office potential was very often on the concert platform. Giving occasional concerts was one thing—even short tours of regions of Britain and Germany—but Jenny Lind was the first to do it on the grand scale. In 1851–52, shortly after her retirement from the stage, she made an exhausting nine-month tour of the United States (before the age of railways) under the management of Phineas T. Barnum. Even after she had given a part of her earnings to charity, as she almost always did, she returned to Europe a very wealthy woman.

Had Jenny Lind wandered down to the Bowery during her visit to New York in 1851, she might have come across an eight-year-old Italian girl named Adelina Patti. She had just made her concert debut singing Eckart's Echo Song (which Lind herself had made famous) and "I Am a Bayadère."

By the time she died in 1887, Lind would be thoroughly familiar with the name of Adelina Patti, because Patti's career was the greatest of any female singer of the nineteenth century, and the most lucrative. "There is only one Niagara," Lind wrote admiringly, "and there is only one Patti."[26] Verdi, who heard all the best singers of the century with the exception of

Colbran, thought Patti stood head and shoulders above them all—"her artistic nature is so complete that perhaps there has never been anyone to equal her."[27] But it is always the praise of one's peers that is most gratifying, and had she been able to read it (it was published eight years after her death in 1919) Patti would doubtless have enjoyed the assessment of Emma Eames, a fine American soprano twenty years her junior but old enough to have heard her many times: "[Patti's] was the most perfect technic imaginable, with a scale, both chromatic and diatonic, of absolute accuracy and evenness, a tone of perfect purity and of the most melting quality, a trill impeccable in intonation, whether major or minor, and such as one hears really only in nightingales, liquid, round and soft. Her crescendo was matchless and her vocal charm was infinite. I cannot imagine more beautiful sounds than issued from that exquisite throat, nor more faultless phrasing, nor more wonderful economy of breath. Her phrases were interminable."[28]

Patti would have been gratified by such praise, but she would hardly have understood it. Few singers have been less concerned with technique. To her, it was something natural, something that had been taught her by her brother-in-law Maurice Strakosch when she was very young, before the age of twelve. Strakosch was a former singing pupil of Giuditta Pasta's; in New York he had started a new career as an impresario in partnership with Patti's father. In young Adelina he saw a child prodigy who could be a touring phenomenon as successful as anyone in the Barnum stable (except, perhaps, Jenny Lind herself, though he carefully billed Adelina as "La Petite Jenny Lind"). That is how Patti spent much of her time between the ages of eight and fifteen, touring with Strakosch and her parents (and sometimes with Louis Gottschalk and Ole Bull, the violin virtuoso) from New Orleans to Minneapolis, from Cuba to Toronto. At sixteen, she began to sing in opera houses—*Lucia di Lammermoor*, *La sonnambula*, *Don Giovanni*, *Il barbiere*, *I puritani*, even Flotow's *Martha* and Verdi's *Rigoletto*. Finally, in 1861, when she was eighteen, Strakosch took her to London and started her on her great career. She would sing at Covent Garden in twenty-five consecutive seasons.

If she was not overly concerned with her technique, Patti was nevertheless obsessed with her health. She lived on a strict diet allied to an equally strict daily routine. She never took alcohol or caffeine; she had lunch at precisely eleven o'clock every morning (eggs and white meat); she always had a siesta and a short walk in the afternoon, followed by some vocal exercises and consommé.[29] Then she was ready to perform—unless she had noticed the slightest sign of stress or vocal discomfort, in which case she would cancel without compunction. She demanded, and got, terms that no other singer could dream of. She frequently sent a stand-in (generally her maid) to attend rehearsals on her behalf; her name had to be billed one-third bigger than anyone else's; and she invented a fee scale for herself that was eventually a great deal more than one-third bigger than anyone else's. Late in her career, while on a concert tour of the United States, she insisted on payment of the dollar equivalent of one thousand pounds sterling for each performance, to be delivered by 2 p.m. on the day of performance—or no performance. The impresario, Colonel J. H. Mapleson, would stand anxiously beside the box office praying there would be enough in the till to make the payment on time. There generally was, because everyone wanted to hear Patti.

She was never a creator. Her repertory was quite large (forty roles), but it was basically the repertory of a great bel canto singer—Rossini, Bellini (but never Norma), and Donizetti, with early and middle-period Verdi up to Violetta, Gilda, and the Leonora of *Il trovatore*. There was Meyerbeer and the new French composers—Gounod's *Faust, Mireille,* and *Roméo et Juliette,* Thomas's *Mignon,* and Delibes's *Lakmé* (the French roles were invariably sung in Italian). Her two greatest adventures were both at Covent Garden—Aida in 1876 and Carmen (in Italian) in 1885. The Carmen was an unrepeatable mistake, but the Aida was a huge success, and she went on to perform it at La Scala. *The Athenaeum*'s review of the London performance gives some idea of Patti's abilities as a tragedienne: "Her bearing [was] shrinking and retiring as the slave, but dignified and forcible as the royal maiden; it was interesting to watch her facile expression, so well did it indicate the passing action. Her voice, so equal in its *timbre* throughout her register, came out with electric force at times, towering above the *fortissimo* of her colleagues, band, and chorus."[30]

Late in her career, when she was giving an interminable series of "farewell" concerts, Patti occasionally included some Wagner—the song called "Träume" that had originally been a sketch for *Tristan und Isolde,* and Elisabeth's Prayer from *Tannhäuser*. George Bernard Shaw, arch Wagnerian and strict constructionist of the composer's intentions, wrote that she performed the Prayer "with the single aim of making it sound as beautiful as possible . . . thus making her German rivals not only appear in comparison clumsy as singers, but actually obtuse as to Wagner's meaning."[31]

The meaning of composers (almost all of them) is clear: they want beautiful singing, bel canto, and Patti's art was directed at nothing less. She did not have a large voice—most people described it as light—but it was certainly powerful and it extended easily to high F. She may have thought of her technique as natural, but it was nonetheless amazing for its apparent ease and spontaneity. And to it she added, according to the character she was portraying, a great range of vocal coloring and expressiveness. Some of this can be heard in her recordings, but she was over sixty by the time she made them and they cannot be reckoned as anything like a true representation of her powers. Michael Scott, the modern historian of vocal recording, puts it like this: "Much of the brilliance, the command of ornamentation . . . was a thing of the past by the time she came to make recordings. Still her singing remains more affecting in itself than anyone else's on records. In her recordings, we can hear so many of the ancient graces of singing; here are the real portamento style, the elegant turns and mordents, the trill free of any suggestion of mechanical contrivance. Behind the singing we can almost see the face."[32]

The face was sweet, expressive, and full of character. She was a small woman, not much above five feet tall with a trim figure. The portraits of the 1860s and 1870s—by Frossard, Winterhalter, and Gustav Doré (who was infatuated with her)—show her sometimes as a Romantic heroine, innocent and appealing, sometimes as a great lady of Parisian society in the Second Empire (dressed à l'Impératrice Eugénie), but the image is always that of Patti. Just as she could color her voice to assume a new character, so she could change her demeanor, her deportment, and her facial expressions to portray the character in the flesh. That is a rare combination of gifts.

Patti was certainly a great actress, but she was also a prima donna to her fingertips. Applause was the fuel that kept her going (and going and going, through nearly twenty years of farewell appearances). George Bernard

Adelina Patti (1843–1919) made her European debut at Covent Garden in 1861, just as the United States, where she had spent all her early life, was being consumed by civil war. Her last appearances, more than fifty years later, took place at patriotic World War I rallies in London.
(Royal College of Music, London.)

Shaw once admitted he was petrified of dropping his cane during one of her death scenes in case she would get up and bow to him. Even in 1914, at the age of seventy-one, she could bring down the house at a patriotic wartime concert by singing, once again, the great ballad with which the British public had always associated her, "Home, Sweet Home."

For Patti, home was now a long way removed from the Bowery. It was a large estate in Wales called Craig-y-Nos ("Rock of the Night" in English).

What she had bought in 1878 was a large square building, but she converted it, at enormous expense, into a grand French-style chateau with a magnificent 150-seat theater where she could entertain and perform on her own terms. For forty years, it was what she called her "anchorage"—a totally private place for a woman who was a celebrity wherever she went.

She had competitors, of course, but probably no one she actually thought of as a peer. The Canadian soprano Emma Albani sang much of her repertory and was even married to Ernest Gye, the director of Covent Garden, but Patti chose to ignore the threat. Albani wisely moved into the Wagnerian roles that Patti eschewed—Elsa, Elisabeth, and Eva—and ended her career in 1896 with an astounding success as Isolde to Jean de Reszke's Tristan. The Swedish singer Christine Nilsson might also have been a competitor. She was the same age as Patti and sang a lot of the same roles, but her specialty was French opera and she sang more in Paris than in London. When she did go to London, it was generally to Drury Lane or Her Majesty's rather than Covent Garden, and Patti did not sing at New York's new Metropolitan Opera until four years after Nilsson had opened it as Marguerite in Gounod's *Faust*. When the two singers both appeared in Russia in 1872 their performances were carefully synchronized so that Patti was singing in St. Petersburg when Nilsson was in Moscow, and vice versa. What rivalry there was was conducted by press releases from their respective agents announcing the astronomic number of curtain calls each singer had received. The Austrian soprano Pauline Lucca might have been another competitor, but she made most of her career at the Vienna Hofoper and sang only infrequently on Patti's turf. And the Eastern European coloratura sopranos, Etelka Gerster and Ilma di Murska (both of them somewhat eccentric and unreliable), made their careers almost entirely in Patti's shadow.

None of these ladies were rivals to Patti. Nellie Melba, had she been twenty years older, might have been. But Melba did not make her European debut until 1887, and by then Patti's operatic career was over—at any rate, the part of it that did not involve "farewells."

Patti and Melba were both, first and foremost, bel canto singers (indeed, Patti was the first singer to whom that term was generally applied), but Melba's repertory was broader: it included some of the more dramatic roles that became available at the end of the century, including Verdi's Desdemona and Puccini's Mimi. In one sense, however, Patti could be seen as the more "modern" of the two: she was much the better actress (Melba simply couldn't be bothered with it), and altogether a more complete performer of opera. Surprisingly, Melba never sang Mozart or Bellini, nor very much in the way of Rossini or Meyerbeer, and Lucia was her only major Donizetti role. That was because, between Patti and Melba, the emphasis of European opera had shifted once again: French opera was in the ascendant, and Italian opera, epitomized by late Verdi and early Puccini, was becoming a platform for the *lirico spinto* voice—the "pushed" lyrical voice that was basically alien to the bel canto style of Adelina Patti and her great predecessors.

CHAPTER SEVEN

The World's Showcase

Paris 1800–1871

All the various strands of opera met and mingled in nineteenth-century Paris. If you were a singer with any kind of pretension to international stardom (except, perhaps, a German specialist) you needed to be seen and heard in the square mile that centered on the Boulevard des Italiens. Here you would find the Opéra, the Opéra-Comique, the Théâtre Italien, and the Bouffes-Parisiens, and an afternoon stroll might involve rubbing shoulders with Rossini, Berlioz, Donizetti, Bellini, Meyerbeer, Offenbach, and any number of famous singers and musicians. It was the showcase of Europe.

Paris was a dangerous city in the nineteenth century. Its dirty, narrow streets with rank and festering sewage all about them were not recommended for nighttime, or even daytime, strolls. The Boulevard des Italiens, with its cafés and restaurants and ice cream parlors, was one of the few places you could comfortably walk three or four abreast, but even there you had to beware of being splashed by a passing coach. Nor was it politically stable. From the disaster of the Revolution to the catastrophe of Sedan and the German occupation of 1871, it was one thing after another—multiple revolutions, coups and rumors of coups; one year an empire, the next a monarchy, the next a benevolent bourgeoisie, and then an empire again—even, for a brief period in 1871, rule by commune. Yet, through it all, the cultural life of Paris remained constant, glittering, and creatively very interesting.

For almost two hundred years it had been fashionable to debate the rival merits of French and Italian singing, and nowhere more so than in Paris, where there had been many examples of such discussions developing into fisticuffs, or worse. Italian opera had been built around the ornamentations and embellishments of opera seria and the glorious reign of the castrati. French opera was altogether more formal, more courtly, and more theatrical—in the sense that it was drama set to music rather than music set to drama (which might be a crude definition of Italian opera before Gluck). But at the end of the eighteenth century something had gone seriously wrong with French singing. It had deteriorated into barking. Visiting the Opéra in 1778, Mozart found the singers "did not sing, they yelled and howled through their noses and throats with all the force of their lungs."[1]

La mode de l'aboiement (the barking style) was a product of the emphasis on "sung theater" rather than the free-flowing melodies of Italian opera. It could be seen in the teaching of François-Joseph Gossec, a Walloon composer who was appointed first director of the *Ecole royale de chant*, established at the Opéra in 1784. Gossec's long and undistinguished line of compositions culminated in the 1790s in some of the most regrettable works to be staged at the Opéra in the name of revolution—*Le triomphe de la République* was the best known and most successful of them—and all this time he was teaching young singers to destroy their voices by learning what the Italians derisively called *urlo francese* (French howling).

There were honorable exceptions, and one of them was Louise-Rosalie Dugazon. She had begun her career in 1767 as a dancer at the Opéra, but she soon graduated to singing when Grétry discovered that her light soprano voice was ideal for soubrette roles. He took her to the Opéra-Comique and she performed there for more than a quarter of a century, with such success that the term *jeune Dugazon* became a common description for the light voice and expressive style she used in romantic roles (such as Nina in Dalayrac's opera of that name, which was one of the sixty—sixty!—roles she created at the Comique). As she grew older, she switched to more matronly characters, and *mère Dugazon* joined the vocabulary. She was undoubtedly exceptional as a singer and an actress, but she was also exceptional in managing to avoid the barking disease.

This affliction could be seen with distressing clarity in the career of Marie-Thérèse Davoux Maillard. She had succeeded Mme Saint-Huberty as first lady of the Opéra in 1790, when that great singer had had to flee the country with her husband, the Comte d'Antraigues. Saint-Huberty had created roles for Piccinni, Salieri, and Sacchini in the 1780s and would normally have had at least another ten years at the Opéra if politics had not intervened (she and her husband were eventually assassinated by a servant while in exile in London). But Saint-Huberty's hurried departure was a heaven-sent opportunity for Mme Maillard. Her voice quickly became the operatic voice of the Revolution and the Directory: its once beautiful sheen became hectoring and declamatory—not unsuited to the temper of the times, perhaps, but decidedly unmusical to the Italianate ear. The same could be said of Etienne Lainez and François Lays and other leading singers of the Opéra, and the trend was even more pronounced at the Opéra-Comique, where spoken dialogue was a necessary part of every opera, whether it was a comedy or a tragedy or a piece of thinly veiled propaganda. Napoleon, who was not particularly musical but had a great fondness for Italian opera, abominated French singing—"yelling," he called it—and he had a lot of support from the professional critics. By the time Spontini staged the premiere of *La vestale* in 1807, with Lainez, Lays, and Maillard all barking away, it was painfully evident that French singing was not capable of doing justice to the new kinds of opera being created in Paris, very often by Italian composers, like Spontini and Cherubini, who chose to reside in France.

The most notable performance at the premiere of *La vestale* was Caroline Branchu's creation of the magnificent role of Julia. Branchu was a significant figure in Napoleonic Paris, not least because she had once been Napoleon's mistress. She had been one of the first pupils of the Conservatoire nationale de musique and its leading voice teacher, Pierre Garat. The Conservatoire had quietly come into existence in 1795, in the first year of the Directory, when it had absorbed Gossec and his *école de chant*: Garat had gone to teach there the following year. He had been a court-singer in the last years of the monarchy, a great favorite of Marie Antoinette, and he had suffered accordingly during the Terror, but he now established himself as the leading voice teacher of France. He believed in clear enunciation of words and syllables (an article of faith in France since Lully's time), but he also believed that the fluency and expressiveness of the Italian style was preferable to the staccato barking he found all around him in Paris. His own voice was remarkable: it encompassed a full three octaves and enabled him to sing arias originally intended for a wide variety of voices, from bass to soprano, often with the most brilliant ornamentations (although he adamantly refused to

Caroline Branchu (1780-1850) as Julia in Spontini's *La vestale,* a role she
created in 1807. Although she was described by Lucien Bonaparte as
"devilishly ugly," and although she was a victim of the barking disease
that disfigured French singing in the first decades of the nineteenth
century, Branchu was indisputably a great actress and an outstanding
exponent of tragédie lyrique, the peculiarly French form of opera
that had dominated the Paris Opéra since the time of Lully.
(Bibliothèque Nationale de France.)

ornament the music of Gluck, whom he revered). But Garat could not overcome the prevailing style at the Opéra—what the critic Paul Scudo described
as "that bombastic and degenerate declamation which belongs neither to
tragedy nor to music"[2]—and the urlo francese continued to disfigure French
singing right up to 1820 and beyond. Sadly, Caroline Branchu, whose gifts
as an actress made her a commanding presence on the stage, became as
bad as any of them. She had major successes—not least in the spectacular
stagings of Spontini's three great Paris operas, *La vestale* (1807), *Fernand
Cortez* (1809), and *Olympie* (1819)—but these were the successes of a phenomenal actress, not a great singer. As Alphonse Royer, the historian of the

Paris Opéra, wrote of her and her colleagues: "The least vocalization baffled them."[3]

But rescue was at hand. It came in the form of an Italian migration that changed the taste of Parisian audiences and eventually forced French singers to cease their barking and join their Italian colleagues in one of the greatest and longest-running festivals of opera any city has ever enjoyed.

French opera had been established by Lully and Louis XIV on the premise that it would be exactly that—French, not Italian. Yet it had always been hard to exclude Italian influences, and at the time of the guerre des bouffons in the 1750s, when the competing virtues of French tragédie lyrique and Italian opera buffa were widely debated, it was clear that France could no longer ignore the Italian invention. The last years of the eighteenth century witnessed a distinguished line of Italian composers setting up shop in Paris and writing French operas that were often Italian in style. Duni, Piccini, Salieri, and Sacchini all had great success in the French capital, and the line was extended at the end of the century by Spontini and Cherubini, who were to be the most important "French" composers for the next two decades.

Cherubini's influence was the greater, partly because of the success of his own operas, but mainly because he occupied an influential position at the Conservatoire for more than forty years—the last twenty of them, right up to his death in 1842, as its famously irascible director. Much earlier, during the revolutionary years, he had been music director of the Théâtre Feydeau, and that was where his best operas were written, from *Lodoïska* in 1791 to *Les deux journées* in 1800. They were categorized as *opéras comiques* for the very French reason that they all contained spoken dialogue, but in most other ways they eradicated the traditional differences between tragédie lyrique and opéra comique, and several of them prefigured the advent of grand opéra only three decades later. *Les deux journées* (known as *The Watercarrier* in English) was successful all over Europe in the early nineteenth century, and *Médée*, which was not very successful at its premiere in 1797, became in the twentieth century the work by which Cherubini was best remembered, and a famous vehicle for Maria Callas.

The Feydeau had originally been established to perform Italian opera

—not a good idea in Paris in the 1790s. It had quickly switched to opera in French, and that was the tradition it continued to develop until it was merged with the Opéra-Comique in 1801. But the demand for Italian opera had never gone away, and it resurfaced immediately when order was restored. With Napoleon's blessing, the Théâtre Italien was formally established in 1801. Thenceforward, for eighty years, through all manner of vicissitudes—bankruptcies, fires, twenty-two different managements, and no fewer than ten changes of location—it remained a jewel in the operatic life of Paris.

What happened at the Théâtre Italien was unapologetic red-blooded singing. All the greatest bel canto singers of the age appeared there, most of them frequently, and most of them with great success. Production standards were execrable; costumes were odd to the point of eccentricity; lighting was generally crude; acting was not greatly prized as a virtue. No one appeared to know, or care, whether the orchestra and chorus were particularly good or particularly bad (at various times they were both). All that really mattered was the singing.

There were three performances a week during the winter season, generally Tuesday, Thursday, and Saturday so as not to overlap with the Opéra's schedule. For a time, a Monday performance was added to accommodate the less fashionable sections of society (and, frankly, to keep them separate from the wealthy crowd). Unlike the Opéra, where evenings were long, with one or more ballets on the bill as well as an opera, the Théâtre Italien performed only one work in an evening—always in Italian, most often a complete opera, but sometime a pasticcio in which bits and pieces of several operas by one or more composers were stuck together as an evening's entertainment. So long as it provided great singing, who cared?

The audience of the Bouffes (which was how the Théâtre Italien was affectionately known) was immensely knowledgeable. It was notably aristocratic—it was *the* place to be—and it was dominated by the dilettanti, the army of devotees who went week after week and very often attended rehearsals as well. They recognized every subtlety, every nuance, in every performance. They were as quiet as church mice while singers were performing, but the end of an aria or a set piece was invariably greeted by raucous demonstrations of approval or disapproval (mainly the former). Whether the company was currently performing at the Odéon, the Louvois, the Favart, or the Ventadour (it was never at one place for long), the theater's lobbies and salons were always decorated with style and taste—appearances were second only to the singing.

Gossip, back-stabbing, and internal politics were an integral part of the Bouffes, and the singers were as responsible as anyone for making sure it was so. Unlike the Opéra, where there was an official claque, the Bouffes was one enormous collection of claques. You rooted for your favorite singers, you made snide remarks about your least favorite. And there were gods—*divas* and *divos*—each with their own fanatical following. Pasta and Rubini, Sontag and Lablache, Malibran and Tamburini, Grisi and Mario . . . these were the great singers of bel canto, and the Théâtre Italien was the place Parisians went to worship them.

In the early years of the century, they went to the Bouffes to hear eighteenth-century works—as far back as Pergolesi, as far forward as Cimarosa, Paisiello, Mayr, and Paer. Spontini ran the company for a time and put on some of his own works. Then Mme Catalani ran it and put on herself. She was undoubtedly the greatest virtuosa of the time, but her tastelessness, rapaciousness, and egotism were ill-suited to the directorial role. She almost ran the theater into the ground, and would have done so had she not had the wit to introduce Rossini's operas for the first time. Eventually, Rossini himself arrived, and from that time forward, right up to its final demise in 1881, Rossini and the Théâtre Italien were inextricably linked.

Rossini was like a magnet to singers. Even though his two-year directorship of the Théâtre Italien was almost as chaotic as Catalani's, it was his presence in Paris that attracted so many great Italian singers. In fairness, the company he found in residence when he arrived in 1823 was not at all bad. Its leading prime donne were Francesca Festa and Caterina Barilli. Festa was well known to Rossini: she had created the role of Fiorilla for him in *Il turco in Italia* in 1814—not a great success at the time because it came less than a year after the very similar *L'Italiana in Algeri* and was (unfairly) thought to be a pale imitation. Festa's low soprano was typical of the female voices favored by Rossini at the time and she was extremely popular in Paris. So was Barilli, who was married to one of the leading male singers in the company (she later married yet another singer, Salvatore Patti, and gave birth to their daughter, Adelina, just a few hours after singing Norma in Madrid in 1843).

But once Rossini was established in Paris these capable singers were replaced by much more starry names. Not all of them were Italians: there were many performances in which half the cast was made up of non-Italians—Austrians and Germans like Henriette Sontag and Karoline Unger; Spaniards like Manuel García and his daughters Malibran and Viardot; Russians like the tenor Nicolay Ivanoff; and a number of outstanding French singers, of whom Laure Cinti-Damoreau was the most important. And although they always sang in the Italian language at the Bouffes, they were not necessarily singing Italian operas: Mozart had finally been discovered by the French, Beethoven's *Fidelio* was immensely popular, and works by the Spaniard Martín y Soler, the Bohemian Gluck, and the German Meyerbeer were well represented. Nevertheless, Italian opera was always the focus, and in most seasons that meant a large dose of Rossini. There were some years in the 1820s when 75 percent of the schedule was Rossinian, and even when he had to share the space with Bellini, Donizetti, and Verdi (who conducted *Nabucco* in 1845), not to mention more venerable names like Zingarelli, Paisiello, and Salieri, Rossini was always the king.

If the Théâtre Italien was about singing, then the Opéra was about spectacle. It, too, moved around a bit, coming to rest at the Salle Le Peletier in 1821 and remaining there until it burned down in 1873. It was always a ballet house as well as an opera house—the stage on which Marie Taglione, Fanny Elssler, and Carlotta Grisi gave their great performances—and dance was a necessary ingredient of any opera performed there. When Wagner staged his *Tannhäuser* at the Opéra in 1861, the performances were loudly disrupted by the blades of the Jockey Club, who had no interest whatever in opera or music and came only for the second act during which they could ogle the ballerinas. Wagner was prepared to include a ballet, but only in the Venusberg scene in act one. The Jockey Club saw him off with their hunting horns and tin whistles. Other composers, whether they were Meyerbeer, Verdi, or Donizetti, were more accommodating and therefore better received.

The barking epidemic maintained its hold on the Opéra for the first two decades of the century, but advances were made in other ways. The theater's orchestra, averaging eighty-five players, was exceptional. Led by great conductors like Rodolphe Kreutzer and François-Antoine Haberneck, it established new standards for the playing of ballet and opera scores and became a favorite accompanist for the instrumental virtuosi who were beginning to make their presence felt in Europe. Gas lighting was introduced in 1822, and electric lighting in 1849, when it was used to project arcs of light between carbon poles to simulate the rising sun in *Le prophète*. But the most important improvement was in production values. The mise-en-scène, once a priority at the Opéra, had fallen into disrepute, and it remained so until Edmond Duponchel became *metteur-en-scène* in the late 1820s. Between Auber's *La muette de Portici* in 1828 and Meyerbeer's *Le prophète* in 1849, he staged a series of dazzling productions that promoted *spectacles d'optique* to prime importance. Working with his more famous assistant, Pierre-Luc-Charles Cicéri, Duponchel blew up Vesuvius at the end of *La muette;* he scared the audience rigid in the cloister scene of *Robert le diable;* he vividly recalled the St. Bartholomew's Day massacre for *Les Huguenots;* and he provided enormous and colorful productions for grands opéras as varied as Rossini's *Guillaume Tell,* Auber's *Gustave III,* and Halévy's *La juive.* The massive explosion with which *Le prophète* ended almost literally brought down the house.

The transformation of the singing came with Rossini. His contract with the Département des Beaux-Arts and the Maison du Roi was twofold: mainly, he was to write new works for the Opéra as *premier compositeur du roi,* but he was also given a wider brief as *inspecteur général du chant en France.* The latter title was honorary, but it had a basis in reality because Rossini was who he was—the apostle of bel canto. Yelling and barking were not acceptable in Rossini's operas. His brief directorship of the Théâtre Italien was over and above his other responsibilities, but it acted as a significant impetus to French singers: if they were going to sing what was widely expected to be a prolific stream of new Rossini works for the Opéra, then they were going to have to mend their ways. And they did. But the language of the Opéra was French, not Italian, and Rossini first had to improve his own grasp of the language. The coronation of Charles X came too early for a suitable work in French; instead, he wrote the colorful pageant *Il viaggio a Reims* in Italian for the Bouffes. Then he adapted two of his Neapolitan operas for the Opéra (*Le siège de Corinthe,* derived from *Maometto II,* and *Moïse et Pharaon,* from *Mosè in Egitto*). Finally, he wrote two very different pieces for the Opéra—*Le comte Ory,* which was a return to his comedic vein, and the hugely ambitious grand opéra *Guillaume Tell.* And *Tell,* it turned out, was his last opera. He was thirty-seven.

The remaining thirty-nine years of Rossini's life were spent mostly in Paris, and there was a sense in which the honorific "inspector general of singing" now became his most important role. He was of great assistance to other composers—Bellini, Donizetti, and Meyerbeer most of all—but he was also an avuncular critic, and sometimes coach, to all manner of singers. Pasta, Malibran, Grisi, Rubini, Mario, Lablache, Tamburini, and all the great Italian singers clustered around him. Later, they were joined by a new generation—Adelina Patti, Enrico Tamberlik, Christine Nilsson from Sweden, and the great French bass Jean-Baptiste Faure. Occasionally, Rossini adopted protégées of his own, generally those whose voices and abilities reminded him of the singers of his earlier life. The contralto Marietta Alboni was one of them; the Marchisio sisters from Italy, Carlotta and Barbara, for whom he wrote the soprano and contralto parts in the *Petite messe solennelle,* were others.

But it was French singers who had most to gain from his presence in Paris, and one in particular, Laure Cinti-Damoreau. Rossini chose her to create principal female roles in all five of his Paris operas—and with good reason, because her studies at the Conservatoire, where piano was her major, singing only her minor, had enabled her to circumvent the barking disease. She was that rarity among French singers—a talented youngster who made her debut not at the Opéra or the Opéra-Comique or one of the other French theaters, but at the Théâtre Italien. She was only fifteen when she sang in Martín y Soler's *Una cosa rara,* and it was at the Bouffes that she learned from her Italian colleagues the art of florid, melodic singing that set her apart from the Caroline Branchus and other more senior French sopranos. By the time Rossini arrived in France, she had established herself (in London and

Brussels as well as in Paris) as a clear-toned Italianate singer whose first language was French, and who was therefore perfectly suited to Rossini's needs when he came to compose for the Opéra. He celebrated the purity of her voice in the great role of Mathilde, which is central to *Guillaume Tell*. It can be heard best of all in Mathilde's moving farewell to Arnold, "Sur la rive étrangère."

The year before she sang Mathilde, Cinti-Damoreau had created Elvire in Auber's *La muette de Portici*. It was this work, and not *Tell*, that had the honor of being the first grand opéra in what was to become a category peculiar to Paris. Beginning with *Robert le diable*, written two years after *Tell*, Meyerbeer would quickly become the greatest exponent of the new genre—at least until Verdi finally mastered it with *Don Carlos* in 1867—and its very grandness was perhaps one element in Rossini's decision to write no more operas after *Tell*. It demanded huge ballets, armies of choristers and extras, special effects, a very large orchestra—and singers with power that was alien to the Rossinian method. It was equally alien to a fine Rossinian singer like Cinti-Damoreau. As became the first lady of the Opéra, she dutifully created Isabelle in *Robert le diable*, but she was intelligent enough to know that she was being over-parted. She wisely left to sing at the Opéra-Comique, spurred on, no doubt, by the tragic example of the only French soprano who might have supplanted her in the affections of Rossini. Joséphine Fodor-Maineville, whose career had run parallel to Cinti-Damoreau's for several years, including some successful seasons at the Théâtre Italien, had won for herself, in competition with Pasta, the title role in *Semiramide* for its Paris premiere in 1825. On opening night, singing while indisposed, she did irreversible damage to her voice. For all intents and purposes, her career ended on that awful night.

Fodor-Maineville's story, and several very similar ones, were reminders that the human voice, however well trained, could not stand a great deal of abuse. Most of Paris's opera houses were fairly large—the Opéra's Salle Le Peletier and the Opéra-Comique's Salle Favart, rebuilt in 1840, had capacities close to two thousand—but it was not so much the size of the house that bothered the singers: it was the size of the orchestra, the density of the scoring, and very often the length of the evening. Grands opéras were almost always in five acts; they were melodramas with very large casts and massive sets: they were exhausting. Cornélie Falcon's short career was an example of the toll they could take.

The term *falcon* is used to describe a type of voice—a dramatic soprano —that has much in common with the lirico spinto voice of Verdi's middle and later periods. *Spinto* means "pushed" (which, in itself, is very different from "forced"). The "pushed lyric" voice is one that probably will not possess the florid agility of the bel canto soprano, but it will have fullness and richness over a very wide range, it will be capable of power and incisiveness at moments of dramatic tension, and it will be equally capable of high piano notes at moments of pathos. Puccini's Mimi is a typical spinto role. In the vocabulary of French singing, *falcon* describes such a voice, and it was introduced to the language of singing on an extraordinary night in July 1832.

The Paris Opéra was full to overflowing that night. Rossini was there, so were Berlioz, Cherubini, and Auber. María Malibran was there, so were Caroline Branchu and most of the leading singers not otherwise engaged. France's two greatest actresses were there—Mlle Mars and Mlle George of the Comédie-Française. And the critics were out in force, led by Théophile Gautier and Alfred de Musset. Yet this was not a premiere, nor even a gala evening. It was, in fact, the forty-first performance of Meyerbeer's *Robert le diable,* which had been given its premiere eight months before—a routine performance, in every way but one.

For weeks, it had been touted in the press as *the* night to be at the Salle Le Peletier. Dr. Louis Véron, the energetic director of the Opéra, had used all the might of his redoubtable publicity machine to get the movers and shakers to attend. What they were promised was what they got—a sensational debut by a twenty-year-old singer just graduated from the Conservatoire. Her name was Cornélie Falcon. She was tall of stature; she had long black hair and dark good looks; she was a wonderful actress; and she had this sumptuous and very unusual voice that gave her performance of Alice a vibrancy and an edge that was entirely unexpected. From low B to high D, she seemed to have absolute command of her instrument and a tessitura (texture) that was uniquely her own. Alice had been created by Julie Dorus-Gras, fine soprano that she was, but this was different, and the audience knew it.

Cornélie Falcon (1812–1897). In his *Histoire de l'opéra* (1875), Alphonse Royer wrote: "Before Cornélie Falcon there had not been seen on the stage of the Académie Royale an artist uniting in the one person so many natural means, so much distinction and beauty." (Bibliothèque Nationale de France.)

From that day on, Falcon was the star of the Opéra. She was the protégée of Adolphe Nourrit, the leading tenor of the Opéra and the creator of the title role in *Robert le diable*. He was a great figure in Paris—a hero of the barricades, an outstanding Rossinian singer, and an influential teacher at the Conservatoire, where he was *professeur de déclamation* and had done more than most to rid French singing of the *urlo francese*. Falcon revered him and adored him, and their careers from this time on had a fateful affinity.

Together, they sang the great roles of grand opéra—in Rossini's *Guillaume Tell,* Halévy's *La juive,* Auber's *Gustave III,* Meyerbeer's *Les Huguenots*—until their voices could no longer cope with the incessant demands. In 1837, a yet more brilliant tenor arrived on the scene—Gilbert-Louis Duprez, who had already created Edgardo in Donizetti's *Lucia di Lammermoor.* Duprez's voice was big enough and strong enough to take over the grand opéra roles that had been Nourrit's domain; he was able to sing Arnold in *Guillaume Tell* without any apparent strain, which had never been the case with Nourrit, and he did something that no tenor before him had been able to do on a regular basis—he sang his high Cs from the chest rather than falsetto, which was the usual practice of the time. In a profound depression, Nourrit left Paris and went to Naples.

Less than a year later, Falcon joined him. She was suffering from constant hoarseness, her voice was in tatters. She had started too young and put too much pressure on what was basically a lovely mezzo-soprano instrument, forcing it to take on a tessitura that was too high and too demanding. The Rachel of *La juive* probably sat quite naturally for it, but the Valentine of *Les Huguenots,* which she also created, frequently went up to sustained high Cs, and it was written in concerted music so that it could not easily be transposed. Today, it would be rare to find the same singer cast as both Rachel and Valentine—the parts are so different in their demands. Falcon paid the price for trying to be all things to all composers.

Nourrit, in one of the saddest chapters of opera history, committed suicide in Naples by jumping from a window in 1839. As Berlioz described the funeral: "A young woman in mourning hid in a corner of the nave, sobbing painfully. It was Mlle Falcon, an artist who could not die."[4] Nor did she die just yet: she lived to be eighty-five, but she never again sang in public—except for one fearful evening at the Opéra in 1840 when she attempted to give a farewell performance. "None of the audience will ever forget that pitiful evening," wrote Gautier.[5] It ended, not soon enough, when Cornélie Falcon, twenty-eight years old, fainted in front of the curtain.

Victoire Noël was made of sterner stuff, though even she, calculating lady that she was, could only eke out a career of a dozen years. She was the daughter of a family of caretakers on the Boulevard du Montparnasse in Paris, and she came to the Opéra the hard way, after several years of chorus duty and small parts in Brussels, Antwerp, and the Netherlands. Her path can be mapped by a dizzying succession of stage names — Rosine Niva, Mlle Ternaux, Mlle Héloïse Stoltz, and finally Rosine Stoltz. It was as Rosine Stoltz that she sang Rachel in Halévy's *La juive* in Brussels in 1836, with Nourrit as her Eléazar, and it was Nourrit who recommended her to the Paris Opéra for the same role the following year. It was not the magical triumph of Falcon's debut five years earlier, but it was a triumph nonetheless, and Rosine Stoltz never looked back. She quickly became Falcon's successor, and she made her mark in other ways as well, most notably by becoming the all-powerful mistress of the Opéra's director, Léon Pillet. From 1840 until her fall from grace in 1847, she more or less ran the Opéra, and everyone knew it.

It is hard to know to what extent Rosine Stoltz warped the development of French opera, or whether she did so at all. The 1840s were a time when the emphasis in Italian opera was moving away from the low soprano voices of Pasta and Malibran to the high sopranos of Sontag, Lind, and Persiani. Whether French opera would have followed suit is arguable: there are good reasons to suppose that the Opéra's principal composers were more wedded to the mezzo voice — higher than Pasta's and Malibran's, certainly, with more emphasis on medium and head registers and the powerful, brilliant high notes of the dramatic soprano, yet still containing enough of the chest registers to command a very wide range overall. But composers had to make use of the resources they were given, and the one resource that was a given at the Opéra for most of the 1840s was the mezzo voice of Rosine Stoltz. Any female singer she saw as a potential competitor simply did not sing there (Jenny Lind never did), and new operas were neither commissioned nor allowed to become part of the repertory unless they contained a starring role for the director's mistress.

Stoltz was a good singer, hard working and very capable, but she was paranoid. She saw Julie Dorus-Gras as her principal rival and she set out to destroy her. There were stories of Stoltz crossing the stage eating a plate of macaroni, in full view of the audience, while Dorus-Gras was in mid-aria.[6] Dorus-Gras, great singer that she was, who had served the Opéra faithfully since 1826, who had created the roles of Alice in *Robert le diable* and Marguerite de Valois in *Les Huguenots,* finally threw in the towel in 1845 and left the Opéra for good. In the meantime, composers anxious to have their works performed were ensuring that Stoltz was kept happy. Donizetti wrote the Léonor of *La favorite* for her, as well as the Zayda of *Dom Sébastien;* she was Berlioz's Ascanio in *Benvenuto Cellini,* and she created roles for Halévy, Auber, and several others. But she overplayed both her hand and her voice. By the end of 1846 her singing was ragged and erratic. She was booed by audiences, and the board of the Opéra called Pillet to account—not just for his reliance on her as a singer but for the chaotic state of the house's finances that had resulted from her dominance. In April 1847 she gave her farewell performance, and the audience cheered her, perhaps from relief at her going, or because the claque had been well paid, or, maybe, out of nostalgia for her better years.

Rosine Stoltz was finished in Paris, but there was the rest of the world to conquer, and not just as an opera singer. She came close to earning herself an entry in the *Guinness Book of Records* by a series of marriages almost as giddying as her former stage names. She became successively a baroness, a countess, and a princess.[7] When she established herself as mistress to the Emperor Dom Pedro of Brazil there were hopes of her achieving a unique grand slam, but that was not to be.

One man who would have nothing to do with her was Meyerbeer. After his success with *Robert le diable* (1831) and *Les Huguenots* (1836), his next work was eagerly awaited. It was to be *Le prophète,* but there was no way he was going to allow the great role of Fidès to be performed by Stoltz. It was put aside until the coast was clear. In the meantime he wrote *Ein Feldlager in Schlesien* for Jenny Lind in Berlin. Finally, with the Opéra suitably purged, *Le prophète* was staged in 1849 with Pauline Viardot as his chosen Fidès.

Viardot, of course, was Malibran's sister, but her claim to fame is much greater than that. She was thirteen years younger than Malibran and she was much less influenced by their father, Manuel García, who died when she was eleven, but her young voice (a natural mezzo-soprano) was given the same sort of training as her sister's, including an artificial extension into the upper register, and later, a similar but less forced extension into the contralto registers below. It was not naturally an Italianate voice like Malibran's (in fact, Viardot never sang in Italy). She nevertheless made her stage debut in London as Rossini's Desdemona when she was only seventeen, and quickly became a popular member of the Théâtre Italien's company in Paris. Two years later, she married the writer and impresario Louis Viardot, and from that time on she was at the center of a circle of intellectuals—musicians, writers, artists—who gravitated to her wherever she was. She had a particular empathy with Russian music and literature (she later became Turgenev's companion and collaborator in several operettas), and she was the first major European singer to perform regularly *in Russian* in Moscow and St. Petersburg, at a time when Glinka and Dargomïzhsky were establishing Russian as a language of opera for the first time.

Malibran had been an enthusiastic actress, often over the top. Viardot was more natural onstage, less theatrical, much more effective. And her voice, with its beautiful texture and great range, was a dramatic composer's dream. Certainly Meyerbeer dreamed about it. He had started to sketch *Le prophète* in 1836, immediately following the great success of *Les Huguenots,* and he had Cornélie Falcon in mind as Fidès. But Falcon's voice was already in trouble and the project was first shelved, then put as far out of sight as possible when Rosine Stoltz appeared on the scene—not least because Meyerbeer had already heard the young Viardot sing in Paris and he knew instinctively that she should be his Fidès. He also knew that she was never going to sing at the Opéra while Stoltz held the reins. Eventually, with Stoltz dethroned, *Le prophète* could go forward.

Fidès is not, in fact, the "first lady" of *Le prophète:* that title should properly belong to Berthe, the fiancée of John of Leyden, who is the prophet of the title. Fidès is actually the prophet's mother—a role rather similar to Azucena in Verdi's *Il trovatore,* which had its triumphant premiere in Rome only three years later. But Meyerbeer was not greatly enamored of the voice or capabilities of Jeanne Castellan, who was cast as Berthe: she had a reputation for poor intonation and overelaborate ornamentations. Meyerbeer grudgingly wrote a *cavatine* for her and then expunged it from the printed score. Instead, he put the weight of the distaff side (indeed, of the entire opera) on the person of Fidès, as portrayed by Viardot. It is one of

Pauline Viardot (1821–1910). Although as a singer she never quite equaled the fame of her elder sister María (Malibran), Viardot had a much greater influence on the development of opera. She promoted, in particular, the careers of Berlioz, Gounod, Massenet, Saint-Saëns, and Fauré.
(Royal College of Music, London.)

the great roles of grand opéra, and one can only imagine the effect this story of the Anabaptist uprising in sixteenth-century Germany must have had on an audience that had so recently witnessed the Paris uprising of 1848. By all accounts, Viardot's performance was astounding—"she reached unprecedented tragic heights both as a singer and as an actress," Meyerbeer himself wrote,[8] and Berlioz called her "one of the greatest artists in the history of music."[9]

But Fidès was not Viardot's most famous role. In 1859, ten years after the premiere of *Le prophète*, Berlioz prepared a new edition of Gluck's *Orphée et Euridyce*, and Viardot sang 138 performances of Orpheus during the next three years. This was not at the Opéra, nor even at the Opéra-Comique, but at the Théâtre Lyrique on the Place du Châtelet, the theater established in 1851 for performance of opera in the vernacular—in many ways the forerunner of London's Sadler's Wells Theatre eighty years later. The Lyrique had a distinguished run during the Second Empire, until it was demolished by fire during the Commune in 1871.

Orphée was both the summit and the end of Viardot's stage career, but she still had almost fifty years to live (she died in 1910), and her opinion continued to be valued by composers and singers alike. She had created the title role in Gounod's *Sapho* in 1851, and she remained a great champion of Gounod's music, as she was of Massenet's and Fauré's at the beginning of their careers. Saint-Saëns wrote Dalila in *Samson et Dalila* with her in mind, and Berlioz did the same with Didon in *Les troyens*. For all these composers, Viardot was a friend, a trusted adviser, and very often a sounding board as well. Berlioz had particular reason to be grateful to her because she was one of the first to recognize *Les troyens* for what it was—the towering achievement of nineteenth-century French opera—and she was the first to perform Didon, though only at a private performance of excerpts. Poor Berlioz never saw a complete performance of the work; he had to content himself with having the last three acts performed at the Théâtre Lyrique, though with a different Didon. At about the same time, it looked as though Wagner would suffer a similar fate with *Tristan und Isolde,* and had not young King Ludwig of Bavaria intervened in 1864 he probably would have. In the meantime, like Berlioz, Wagner had had the compensation of a private performance of act two of the great work, with Viardot as Isolde (Wagner himself sang Tristan, and Berlioz was one of only two privileged spectators).

For all the disaster of its collapse in 1870 in one of the most unnecessary wars ever staged, the Second Empire was a period of glittering splendor in France's history, a period whose legacy of art, literature, and style prevails to this day. Neither Napoleon III nor his wife, the Empress Eugénie, were very interested in musical theater, but they were well aware of its importance. The Opéra continued to be the focal point of Parisian society; the Théâtre Italien remained the headquarters of Italian singing (though the singing was less spectacular than in the great years of Rubini, Pasta, Lablache, and Malibran); the Opéra-Comique, run by the resourceful Émile Perrin, enjoyed its proudest years as a literary-musical institution, spurred on, no doubt, by competition with the brave new Théâtre Lyrique; and the Parisian scene was immeasurably added to by the wit and gaiety of Offenbach's Bouffes-Parisiens, founded in 1855.

Dance, spectacle, and grand opéra continued to be the principal obsessions of the Opéra, but its reputation for innovation was beginning to lag. After *Le prophète* in 1849, Meyerbeer wrote only one more work for it— his enormous and visually stunning *L'Africaine,* performed posthumously in 1865. In the meantime, he had staged both *Dinorah* and *L'étoile du nord* for the Comique. Another foreigner, Giuseppe Verdi, sought to conquer Paris. His original connection had been through the Théâtre Italien, but Paris was a city in which he spent much of his time during the 1840s and 1850s and grand opéra was a genre in which he longed to succeed. *Les vêpres siciliennes* in 1855 was, at best, a marginal success. Sophie Cruvelli, the German soprano who created the role of Hélène, had a huge voice with a range to match (almost three octaves), and she performed the part with the sort of ferocity that early Verdian heroines might seem to demand (Abigaille in *Nabucco* and Odabella in *Attila* were similar sounding ladies), but it was a style that was alien to French sensibilities. It was to be another twelve years before Verdi returned to Paris with *Don Carlos,* arguably the finest of all grands opéras, and the singers cast in the leading female roles on that occasion were French speakers rather than Italian or German (they were actually Belgian).

By that time, the emphasis was beginning to shift away from grand opéra. Meyerbeer's *L'Africaine* was a spectacular success in 1865, and his earlier works remained popular, as did those of Halévy, Auber, and others, but the Opéra was well aware that pioneering work in French opera had been taking place elsewhere—at the Lyrique and the Opéra-Comique—and it needed to get on the bandwagon. As early as 1851 it had given the premiere of Gounod's *Sapho,* a lyrical piece, classical in theme, and (most revolutionary of all) three acts instead of five. But Gounod had quickly departed for the Lyrique, where he enjoyed his period of greatest productivity. At the same time, the Opéra-Comique was catering to the literary taste of Parisian audiences, and the Bouffes-Parisiens to the demand for broad comedy and farce. It was at the Comique that most of France's leading composers gathered— Adolphe Adam, Ambroise Thomas, Victor Massé, Georges Bizet, and many others. The Opéra needed to attract them, too, and it began to do so in 1868 when Thomas crossed the road. He had been writing successfully for the Opéra-Comique for more than quarter of a century and had recently had a triumph there with *Mignon*. Now the Opéra commissioned *Hamlet* from him and enjoyed a considerable artistic success, despite its ridiculous happy ending.

But neither *Faust* nor *Carmen*—probably the most popular works ever composed for the opera stage—originated at the Opéra. They came, respectively, from the Lyrique and the Comique.

The resources of the Lyrique were limited, but they included Caroline Carvalho, a fine soprano with a light lyric voice and enviable coloratura, who also happened to be the wife of the Lyrique's manager, Léon Carvalho. Caroline Miolan, as she was then known, had had a major career underway long before she met and married Carvalho: she had been singing at the Opéra since 1849—a well-regarded Isabelle in *Robert le diable* and a favorite Rachel in *La juive*. The transfer to the Lyrique gave her the opportunity to create four roles for Gounod—Marguerite in *Faust* (1859), Baucis in *Philémon et Baucis* (1860), the title role in *Mireille* (1864), and Juliette in *Roméo et Juliette* (1867). Not all these works were successful. For Parisians in love with Offenbach's *Orphée aux enfers* (Orpheus in the Underworld), *Philémon* was a pretty tame setting of mythology, and rehearsals for *Mireille* were bedeviled by Gounod's temporary falling out with the Carvalhos; but *Faust* and *Roméo et Juliette* quickly became part of the repertory, and Caroline Carvalho found herself in demand to sing them in cities as far apart as London, Berlin, and St. Petersburg. Her range was unusually large: Mozart's Cherubino seemed to be as natural to her as Rossini's Mathilde in *Guillaume Tell* or Verdi's Gilda in *Rigoletto*—added to which she was a very good actress. Unfairly, she is not much celebrated in histories of opera, perhaps because she did her most innovative work in one of opera's lesser-known theaters. But innovative it was: Berlioz pointed out that some of the best-loved sections of *Faust* were so strange to the original audiences in 1859 that they were incomprehensible.[10]

When *Faust* finally made it to the Opéra ten years later, with sung recitatives and a grand new ballet, Carvalho was available, but not selected. The role of Marguerite went, as of right, to the Swedish soprano who was newly enthroned as the first lady of the Opéra, Christine Nilsson. She was twenty-six years old, "tall and handsome, with fair hair and light blue eyes, elegant and engaging in manner, and possessing a voice eminently pure, flexible, and true in the upper range."[11] She was hailed, of course, as "the second Swedish Nightingale," yet it was hard to take comparisons with Jenny Lind much further than their common nationality and precocity. Like Lind, Nilsson had been a childhood prodigy in Sweden, but unlike her, she did not begin singing professionally until she was twenty-one, and then it was as a member of Léon Carvalho's company at the Théâtre Lyrique in Paris. She made her debut as Violetta in a French version of *La traviata* and quickly followed it with Mozart's Queen of the Night and Flotow's *Martha* (supervised by the composer). It was in the last of these operas, as Lady Henriette, that she made the greatest impression, singing it more than a hundred times in three seasons. Not surprisingly, the Opéra called, and she crossed the road to the Salle Le Peletier with Thomas to create Ophélie for him in 1868. She was also the Marguerite of the Opéra's magnificent new production of *Faust* the following year. The move to the Opéra meant that she missed out on creating the role of Catherine in Bizet's *La jolie fille de Perth:* it was written for her, but she was busy with Ophélie when it came to be performed.

Marguerite could certainly have been Nilsson's calling card for the remainder of her career—whether in French or Italian, she never ceased to sing the role, and that included the opening night of New York's Metropolitan Opera House in 1883 (a theater that one critic later remarked might more accurately be known as the "Faustspielhaus")—but, in fact, she had a very large repertory, ranging from her famously accurate Queen of the Night to the Elisabeth of Wagner's *Tannhäuser,* and taking in the Leonore of Verdi's *Il trovatore* along the way. She was not a great "creator"—very few new roles were written for her after Thomas's Ophélie, and none that were important. Rather, she was one of the first representatives of a new breed of soprano: a fine technician, able to select her roles from what was now a very large, and fast growing, repertory, and able to travel much more efficiently and quickly than her immediate predecessors. Nilsson crossed the Atlantic regularly; she undertook major, and highly remunerative, concert tours of the United States, traveling across the country by train, and she sang all over Europe. She was never afraid to learn new roles—she introduced Boito's

Célestine Galli-Marié (1840–1905). Forever associated with the roles of
Carmen and Mignon, both of which she created, Galli-Marié was actually
a repertory singer at the Opéra-Comique for almost three decades.
(Bibliothèque Nationale de France.)

Mefistofele to London and Ponchielli's *La gioconda* to New York—and she
managed always to keep her voice in good repair (though that's rather more
than could be said for her figure by the end). It was not a large voice, but it
was pure and flexible and perfectly even over two and a half octaves.

Célestine Galli-Marié was not a great international figure like Nilsson.
She had been brought up in and around the Opéra, where her father was a
singer, but her parents and teachers had the good sense, early on, to real-
ize that her voice and her dramatic talents were better suited to the Opéra-
Comique. So that was where she sang for almost thirty years, with a few side
trips, later on, to Italy, Spain, and England. Those foreign engagements, such
as they were, were inspired by the fact that she was Carmen—the first Carmen, and, by all accounts, one of the greatest. She created the role for Bizet
in 1875, and she became so closely identified with it, in its birth pangs as
well as its ultimate fame, that that was how she was generally thought of—as
Carmen. Yet she was always a member of a repertory company, the Opéra-

Comique, that performed almost every night of the year, so she actually sang a very large number of roles. As early as 1866, four years after joining the company, she had created Mignon for Ambroise Thomas, and she would go on to originate more than a dozen other roles for composers ranging from Offenbach to Massenet. She was the leading mezzo-soprano of the Comique, and every composer who worked there wanted to make use of her. The voice was neither large nor particularly beautiful—it was often harsh at the top—but there was a warmth to it and a texture that tended to remain in the listener's memory. As an actress, she had few equals on the operatic stage.

Carmen was a time bomb. Ever since its inception at the end of the sixteenth century, opera had avoided reality. It had tackled mythology and history with great confidence (even quite recent history), but it was important that its performers were always presented in period costume. It did not generally concern itself with the contemporary world, and if it did, it avoided the more squalid aspects of it. Opera buffa had frequently transgressed into the recognizable modern world, though it generally portrayed a fairly sanitized version of it. That was what Pergolesi had done as early as 1733 in *La serva padrona;* it was what Mozart and Da Ponte had done rather more shamelessly when they brought *Le nozze di Figaro* to the stage in 1786; and it was what Verdi had done when he wrote *La traviata* to be performed in "modern dress" (circa 1853), though it was never actually performed that way until the early twentieth century. Bizet's "crime" was much more blatant: he actually presented some of the most horrific aspects of "reality" right there on the stage—Carmen's undisguised sexuality, an unseemly chorus of girls who smoked and fought with one another, and a brutal murder. Verismo opera would do all this and more ten years later, but in 1875 it was new and disconcerting. As a result, *Carmen*'s reception was cautious, even tepid, and Bizet died three months after the premiere without knowing that he had created one of the masterworks of opera.

In fact, he owed a great deal to Galli-Marié, not just for her stunning performance as Carmen, but also for the considerable part she played in bringing it to the stage uncut and unadulterated. The directors of the Opéra-Comique, nervous of audience reaction, wanted it toned down, even abandoned—one of them called the score "Cochin-Chinese" music.[12] The orchestra was unhappy—players found the scoring difficult and unusual. Chorus members were downright hostile—they were not used to being asked to act as individuals, expecting instead to be moved around as a group in unison. But Galli-Marié, together with Paul Lhérie, the tenor who created Don José, backed Bizet all the way, and *Carmen* came to the stage almost exactly as Bizet had conceived it.

No one was more impressed than Tchaikovsky. Now in his mid-thirties and traveling restlessly in Europe (*Onegin* was still more than a year away), he visited the Opéra-Comique in March of 1876 and was beguiled and fascinated by Galli-Marié's performance. His brother Modest, who was with him, wrote of her "unbridled passion and an element of mystical fatalism," which aroused in Tchaikovsky "an almost unwholesome passion for this opera."[13] Like Carmen, Tchaikovsky believed himself to be fated (it is the dominant motif of his music), and in the years ahead, right up to his own death in 1893, he would play over and over in his mind the eerie remembrance of Galli-Marié's dark voice in the Card Trio: "Spades—a grave! What matters it? If you are to die, try the cards a hundred times, they will fall the same—spades, a grave."

Paris was still a city in which great singers needed to be heard—but not quite as often, maybe. The Théâtre Italien had been steadily declining for several years, and it finally ended its honorable existence in 1881. Milan was now the undisputed headquarters of Italian opera—it had even survived a boycott by Giuseppe Verdi between 1845 and 1869. London was almost as popular with Italian singers, and certainly with non-Italian singers who specialized in the Italian repertory: it was the place where Therese Tietjens, and later Adelina Patti, most often strutted their stuff. But the French repertory had been so greatly enlarged in the nineteenth century that Paris no longer needed to rely on the Italian tradition: it had its own, and it was widely respected and widely performed.

Christine Nilsson might have been the greatest star of the Opéra in the 1860s, but she was frequently absent, performing elsewhere, and Tietjens and Patti made their homes in London. This meant that many of the best opportunities in Paris fell to two Belgian singers, Marie Sasse and Pauline Guéymard-Lauters. Sasse had started out in Italy, but without much success. She moved to Paris and made her living as one of the café-concert singers who were then a popular feature of the Parisian scene. That was how Léon Carvalho came to hear her, and he quickly recruited her to the Théâtre Lyrique, where she became famous as the Eurydice in Berlioz's setting of Gluck's *Orphée et Euridyce*, singing opposite Pauline Viardot in more than a hundred performances. From then on, she became an important part of operatic history as it was played out in Paris. Crossing to the Opéra, she was the Elisabeth of the tumultuous (and very short) run of Wagner's *Tannhäuser* in 1861; she created Sélika in Meyerbeer's *L'Africaine* in 1865; and two years later she was Verdi's Elisabeth de Valois in *Don Carlos*. In that opera, and in many others, one of her principal colleagues was Guéymard-Lauters, who created the role of Eboli. She was the same age as Sasse and she had come to the Opéra by the same route, via the Lyrique, but slightly earlier. Both ladies sang Valentine in *Les Huguenots* (a role that has never seen much distinction between sopranos and mezzo-sopranos), and they shared several other roles, including Leonore in *Il trovatore*, for although she had the lower tessitura of the mezzo range, Guéymard-Lauters also had a brilliant top to her voice. She created Balkis in Gounod's *La reine de Saba* and the Queen in Thomas's *Hamlet* opposite Nilsson's Ophélie; she followed Viardot as Fidès in *Le prophète*, and she was one of Rosine Stoltz's successors as Léonor in Donizetti's popular *La favorite*.

But neither Marie Sasse nor Pauline Guéymard-Lauters, nor even Christine Nilsson, was the real prima donna of Paris in the 1860s. Without a shadow of a doubt, that title belonged to Hortense Schneider. Yet you could not hear Mme Schneider at the Opéra or the Comique or the Lyrique. Instead, if you were lucky enough to get a ticket, you might hear her at the Bouffes-Parisiens or the Variétés or the Palais-Royal.

In the summer of 1867, at the glittering pinnacle of the Second Empire, when all the world came to Paris to visit the Great Universal Exposition, Hortense Schneider was Offenbach's Grande-Duchesse de Gérolstein, the toast of Paris. Everyone, it seemed, came to see her. The czar of Russia was sitting in a box at the Variétés barely three hours after he arrived in the city; the Prince of Wales came without a ticket and had to beg one from the great lady herself; even Count Otto von Bismarck paid her a visit, just three years before he was to conquer Paris with his Prussian armies.

Hortense Schneider had arrived in Offenbach's life in 1855, just as he

Hortense Schneider (1833–1920) as the Grande-Duchesse de Gérolstein, the role she created for Offenbach in 1867. The opera appeared to make everyone happy—except the censor, who saw the libretto (by Meilhac and Halévy, who would later supply Bizet with the libretto for *Carmen*) as a satire on German militarism and the scandals at the court of Napoleon III. Schneider was ordered to remove the ribbon of an imaginary order she was planning to wear across her bosom, causing her to throw a tantrum and walk out of rehearsals—temporarily. (Lebrecht Collection.)

was launching his tiny new theater off the Champs-Élysées. She was twenty-two at the time, a young singer from Bordeaux scratching a living as a café-concert performer on the Boulevard des Italiens. She turned up at his home one day and demanded an audition. Offenbach, it was said, heard her sing only a few bars before he booked her for the Bouffes-Parisiens, where she was an instant success. Her voice was not large, but it was pure and clear and beautifully projected, and she had a natural gift for comedy. She sang the great tunes of *La belle Hélène* and *Barbe-bleue,* and many another Offenbach score, and at the same time she used her speaking voice and her talents as an actress to underline the innuendo and satire that were always part of the librettos. She was a terrible handful for those who worked with her, especially librettists: her version of the text was often markedly different from theirs, and she generally got her way. She was litigious, temperamental, and very expensive—but everyone knew she was the drawing card, so they put up with her tantrums and did everything they could to keep her happy. If she insisted on being treated like royalty—well, who was going to gainsay her? One afternoon in the summer of 1867 she arrived at the gates of the Exposition and announced her intention of driving around the grounds in her carriage. When it was explained to her that only royalty had such a privilege she informed the gatekeeper "I am the Grand Duchess of Gérolstein." She was promptly admitted, carriage and all.[14]

Hortense Schneider might have behaved like royalty, and Jenny Lind might have felt she was able to call on royalty (which she did, dropping in unannounced on Queen Victoria), but prime donne were *not* royalty. Nor were they aristocrats, even though some might have married into the aristocracy (Sontag permanently; Rosine Stoltz whenever the fancy took her). Europe was still hidebound in its social setup, and those who had titles and positions *as of right* were keen to keep the entertainers in their place, however rich and famous they might become. Great singers were often invited to perform at aristocratic salons, and they were generally given extravagant presents for doing so, but that in itself defined their position: they were "guns for hire." It was true that they had come a long way from the near-courtesan status of a singer as recent in memory as Isabella Colbran (certainly in her pre-Mme

Rossini days), and it was equally true that some of them had become exceedingly rich (was not Patti encamped in the castle of Craig-y-Nos in all her glory?), but there was nothing particularly new about that: the great castrati, like Caffarelli and Farinelli, had purchased dukedoms and expensive villas a hundred years before.

Singers had been powerful ever since they had discovered their importance to the box office in seventeenth-century Venice, but they had also been held in check (female singers, in particular) by the extent to which they were socially and economically dependent. That was no longer true of the nineteenth-century prima donna. Her celebrity and her earning power made her a free woman, much less willing to be patronized by the social elite, much more determined to get her own way in things artistic as well as in matters of business. She might not be accepted as the social equal of a duchess or a countess, but why should she care? She did not need to be *prima inter pares* when, in her own world, she was already *prima assoluta*.

By and large, nineteenth-century prime donne did not exercise this power indiscriminately. Many of them were loved and admired by their colleagues as well as their audiences. In artistic matters, they had a lot of license: it was generally accepted they could rearrange, transpose, or even cut sections of music that did not sit well for them, and opera house managements were generally their willing allies in this. In other matters, particularly contract negotiations, they fought the managements with every weapon at their disposal, and with considerable success. But that was business, and opera singers had every right to play the laws of supply and demand in the same way everyone else did.

What the world of opera was not prepared for, however, was a figure so powerful—at once so angelic and so monstrous—that she could impose a tyranny. The tyrant duly arrived, and her name was Nellie Melba. For the most part, her story lies outside the bounds of this book, but it is well to remember that her extraordinary and ruthless career was made possible by the advances made by her immediate predecessors. The angels of nineteenth-century opera had created for themselves a nascent power that would only be equaled and exceeded when the Hollywood film star came of age in the twentieth century.

CHAPTER EIGHT

Dramatic Singing

The Verdian Soprano

Other than Mozart, no opera composer has ever written more singable music than Giuseppe Verdi. That does not mean his music is always easy—no Abigaille or Aida or Violetta would ever say that—but most female singers would agree that it generally lies well for the voice and that it can be performed without having to resort to unnatural forcing. Male singers have often been more critical, particularly the early baritones for whom Verdi was one of the first composers to write major roles. Some of them, like Felice Varesi and Giorgio Ronconi, found his writing fearsomely high and accused him of being obsessed with the "upper fifth" of the voice.

Verdi took it for granted that his music was within the compass of professional singers who were normally equipped and properly trained. What he did *not* take for granted, because he had too much evidence to the contrary, was that these people could do anything other than sing. To his way of thinking, an opera singer who had a wonderful voice but was unwilling to study and absorb the dramatic aspects of the work, and then to act them out on the stage in concert with his or her colleagues, was no opera singer at all. As his career developed, and as his reputation and stature grew to unprecedented heights, he was increasingly able to impose his views on the managements of opera houses and to make sure that those who sang his operas were intelligent and credible actors as well as very good singers.

In a letter to Varesi, the first Macbeth and the first Rigoletto, Verdi explained what he wanted: "I will never stop urging you to study the dramatic situation and the words; the music will come by itself."[1]

That was not an easy concept to explain to nineteenth-century Italian singers who were not familiar with the idea of a stage director. It was true that composers like Weber and Meyerbeer had begun to take much more active roles in the staging and directing of their operas, and it was true that some French and German opera houses had begun to hire permanent *régisseurs*, or *metteurs-en-scène*, like Edmond Duponchel at the Paris Opéra, but most Italian houses still operated under the eighteenth-century system whereby a *regolatore di scena* (hardly more than a stage manager armed with a prompt book) was broadly responsible for getting singers and choruses on-stage on cue, and for positioning them once they were there. A few houses (the San Carlo in Naples and La Fenice in Venice were examples) employed resident poets. Their principal duties were literary, but some of them, like Francesco Maria Piave in Venice, who was Verdi's most prolific librettist, also took on some of the duties of stage director: they supervised rehearsals, liaised between scenery, costume, and machine departments, and generally attempted to explain to singers and choruses the dramatic context of each scene and character. As far back as Monteverdi's time there had been examples of production manuals being assembled to provide future producers with a record of how the original production had been staged, but they were difficult to put together in the hurly-burly of rehearsals and deadlines, and they were done only rarely.

Verdi was not the first Italian composer to be concerned about dramatic and production values, but he was the first to make a fetish of them. The more successful he became, the more control he exerted. His contracts increasingly specified the sort of terms composers like Rossini could not have dreamed of—that his scores, once published, could not be truncated or bastardized, for instance—and he eventually adopted the Paris method of publishing a *livret de mise en scène* (production book) for each of his operas after *Les vêpres siciliennes* in 1855. Known as *disposizioni sceniche,* they were records of the original production, supervised by Verdi himself, complete with diagrams and detailed descriptions of the blocking of every scene. They were clearly intended to be templates for all future productions.

The contracts of Rossini, Bellini, and Donizetti were very clear: they were required to compose operas for *particular* singers with *particular* vocal abilities for *particular* occasions. Thus, for a large part of his active career, Rossini was under contract to the San Carlo in Naples, where he was required to deliver two new operas a year for a roster of singers that included Isabella Colbran, a bunch of distinguished tenors (David, Nozzari, García, and Rubini), and the bass Michele Benedetti. That explained the format and vocal mixture of most of his Neapolitan operas (three major tenor roles in *Otello,* for instance). As a guest composer in other cities, he was generally bound by very similar conditions, though he was occasionally able to suggest that a theater employ a certain singer who would suit his purposes, which is how Geltrude Righetti-Giorgi, his childhood friend, came to create Rosina and Angelina. Because these works were modeled on particular singers, it did not mean they could not be sung by anyone else: it was a time when both singers and composers expected parts to be freely transposed in order to suit voices that were often very different from the creators'. We can assume that Pasta's Semiramide varied quite considerably from Colbran's (not just in interpretation but in the actual notes they sang), and that Malibran's varied from them yet again. It was a singer's world. Composers were hired hands; they generally owned no copyright in their works, they were paid a fraction of the amount singers were paid, and they were expected to write at great speed against deadlines that would be unthinkable today.

Verdi could not change this system overnight, but in the course of his fifty-five-year career as an active opera composer he eventually changed almost every part of it—methods of payment, copyright ownership, control of residual rights, and much more. (He even decided which theaters could produce his works and on what terms: for several years, while he was boycotting La Scala because of the theater's business practices, his contracts actually stipulated "not La Scala.") Most of all, however, Verdi changed the relationship between drama and music. He did not see them as separate departments, and he was not prepared to let singers do so either. He believed passionately in the earliest definition of opera—dramma per musica (drama expressed through music)—so he required his singers to "study the dramatic situation." He wrote for specific singers, or certainly for types of singers—he was only prepared to go ahead with *Macbeth,* for instance, when he knew Varesi was available—but his chief concern was always to write music that placed his characters within their dramatic situations. Provided the singers understood what those situations were, then, as he told Varesi, "the music will come by itself."

But singers did not always study the dramatic situations closely enough, and the music did not always come by itself—not in time for first nights, anyway. Verdi sometimes felt his singers had not served him well, and he vented his spleen in morning-after letters to his friends: "If I had had singers—I will not say sublime singers, but just singers who could sing— *Ernani* would have come off as well as *Nabucco* and *Lombardi* in Milan,"[2] he wrote to one; to another: "*La Traviata,* last night, fiasco. Is it my fault or the singers? Time will tell."[3]

Verdi began his career at La Scala in 1839, at a time when Milan, still under Austrian occupation, was fast becoming the most important commercial and industrial center in Italy. It was a wealthy, go-ahead city, and La Scala provided it with opera to match. In the 1830s alone, the theater gave forty world premieres. Its roster of singers was certainly the best in Italy, though it might not yet have been as good as that of the Théâtre Italien in Paris. It was no surprise, therefore, to find that *Oberto,* Verdi's very first commission, was destined for the most prestigious trio of singers available in Italy—Giuseppina Strepponi, Giorgio Ronconi, and Napoleone Moriani, the tenor who was known as "the Swan of the Arno." No composer could have asked for more. As it happened, none of those singers eventually appeared in *Oberto* because the premiere was postponed until the autumn, partly as a result of Strepponi's health problems. Earlier in the year she had given birth to her second child in thirteen months, and she had done so just six hours after completing a performance of Bianca in Mercadante's *Il giuramento* in Florence. Less than two weeks later she was beginning rehearsals for yet another opera in Venice. No one, except Strepponi, was surprised that she had problems. When *Oberto* was finally staged in November, the role of Leonora was sung not by Strepponi but by Antonietta Raineri-Marini, a very good soprano though not as well-known as her husband, Ignazio Marini, the bass who created the title role for Verdi.

The year 1839 was Strepponi's first season at La Scala. She was twenty-four years old, a fairly recent winner of the prestigious bel canto award at the Milan Conservatory, and already acclaimed in cities as important as Vienna, Bologna, and Venice. But 1839 was also the peak of her career. The voice, which many people thought was as good as Grisi's, maybe even Pasta's, was seriously overworked. There were good reasons and bad. Her father had died while she was still at the Conservatory, and she had immediately become the breadwinner for her mother and four siblings. As a result, she sang at every opportunity—she even sang Norma on five consecutive nights![4] Worse, she was driven by a group of greedy agents and managers who saw her as a potential gold mine. And worse again, this time entirely of her own making, she formed unwise liaisons that resulted in unwanted pregnancies. Between 1839 and 1842, she was able to capitalize on her initial fame, but it soon became clear that the voice was a ruin. She created Abigaille in *Nabucco* for Verdi in 1842, and went on singing sporadically for four years after that, but it was no secret that Giuseppina Strepponi's career was a might-have-been. Had she not gone on to be Verdi's partner of more than fifty years, she would be remembered only as a singer who did something less than justice to the role of Abigaille.

Abigaille requires power and a very wide range. It is written for a coloratura soprano who also has the strong, deep chest notes of a mezzo-soprano. It is intensely dramatic, yet somewhat static. Abigaille's mood swings and emotions give the story its impetus: they must be projected almost entirely in the voice since the tableau-like structure of the work gives few opportunities for physical acting. It is an exhausting role, notoriously difficult to cast.

Strepponi was a highly intelligent woman. When she looked back later in life she must have known she had blown an incredible opportunity. La Scala (in fact, Italian opera in general) was desperately in need of a new prima donna at the beginning of the 1840s. Pasta had retired in 1835, Malibran had died the following year, Henriette Sontag was the Countess Rossi and would not return to the stage until 1849, and Giulia Grisi, while she was undoubtedly the greatest Italian prima donna of the day, refused to sing in Italy. One of the more interesting speculations of the story of opera is what effect it would have had on Verdi's work if Grisi had been available to him as a creator.

In her absence, and with Strepponi in terminal decline, the most talented sopranos in Italy were Erminia Frezzolini, Eugenia Tadolini, and Marianna Barbieri-Nini. To them should be added a German soprano, Sophie

Löwe, who sang in Italy between 1841 and her retirement from the stage in 1848, when she became the Princess von Liechtenstein. What these ladies had in common, aside from the fact that they all created roles for Verdi, was that they were very dramatic singers with powerful, flexible voices; they had chest registers deep enough for Norma and head notes high enough for the *Sonnambula* Amina. This meant that they would normally be categorized as low sopranos like Pasta and Malibran, rather than high sopranos like Sontag and Lind, but under the influence of Verdi's music they developed, almost surreptitiously, into the first generation of a new type of singer—one who would later be called a *lirico spinto* (or "pushed" lyric soprano), but would more immediately be recognized as a much more dramatic soprano than had previously been heard. These women had been brought up to sing roles like Lucrezia Borgia and Anna Bolena, so it was not a huge step to Joan of Arc and Lady Macbeth, but it was an important step.

Frezzolini was the darling of La Scala in the 1840s. She created Giselda in *I Lombardi,* as well as the title role in *Giovanna d'Arco,* both of them with great success. She was still in her mid-twenties, famously beautiful, with a powerful, brilliant voice that was especially capable of the sort of long legato line that Verdi called for in Giselda's prayer. She and her husband were friends of Verdi's, and Strepponi's letters to Verdi, with their shy requests for news of Frezzolini's progress, betray an acute awareness that Frezzolini was where she was because Strepponi had failed to live up to her promise.[5] But that was not the only reason she was there. She was a very capable singer who made the most of her opportunities. By 1848–49 she was embarking on profitable concert tours in North America and making even more richly remunerated appearances in St. Petersburg. In 1857, with her voice still in good condition, she was Gilda in *Rigoletto* and Leonora in *Il trovatore* at the French premieres of those operas at the Théâtre Italien in Paris.

Eugenia Tadolini was nine years older than Frezzolini. She had conquered the Théâtre Italien much earlier—in the 1830 season, when she was a twenty-one-year-old debutante singing Zoraide in Rossini's *Ricciardo e Zoraide* in the presence of the composer. Her success led her on to a fine career as a bel canto soprano in Milan, Venice, Florence, and Vienna. It was in Vienna that she created the title roles of *Linda di Chamounix* (1842) and

Maria di Rohan (1843) for Donizetti, and it was in Naples that she created Alzira for Verdi. Only once before—with his second opera for La Scala, the comedy *Un giorno di regno*—had Verdi tasted failure. *Alzira* was not as bad as that, but it was, at best, an inauspicious beginning to Verdi's attempt to conquer the south (many years later, when a friend asked him about it, he replied, "That one is really ugly"). But he did not blame Tadolini.[6] He had, in fact, had difficulty getting the San Carlo to cast her at all. He had originally been threatened with an English soprano named Anna Bishop who was then under contract to the theater: Bishop orchestrated a frenetic press campaign to get the part for herself, and nearly succeeded. Tadolini had already won her spurs as a Verdi singer in Venice, and she did her best with Alzira in front of a wary Neapolitan audience, who thought of Verdi (at this stage, but not for much longer) as a northern composer—that is, a foreigner. Two years later, Tadolini missed out on the part she most craved—Lady Macbeth. Verdi rejected her on the devastating grounds that her voice was too beautiful for the role. It went instead to Marianna Barbieri-Nini.

Verdi had had a great deal of success by 1847, but *Macbeth* was the first of his operas to be perceived as out of the ordinary. A few critics recognized it as such, and a good many people in Florence's Teatro della Pergola did so as well (Verdi took thirty curtain calls at the premiere), but it was the singers who most truly understood its originality, which lay in the synchronicity of its music and drama. For the first time, Verdi devoted almost as much labor to the staging, the lighting, and the sets as he did to the music. He had adapted plays before—Victor Hugo's *Hernani* was a recent and very successful example—but he had never before encountered a play in whose "drama as theater" he had so much confidence. He knew Shakespeare better than most English people did—"He is one of my very special poets; I have had him in my hands from my very earliest youth and I read and re-read him continually"[7]—but he was also aware that Shakespeare's plays did not necessarily work for Italian audiences. As recently as 1842, *Othello* had been the first of the plays to be staged in a public theater in Italy. Despite a fine cast led by Gustavo Modena, one of the most celebrated actors of the time, it was more or less booed off the stage and closed after only one performance.[8] So Verdi knew that the adaptation of *Macbeth* was both a risk and an experiment, but at least he would arm himself with the very best singers for the task.

He would not have composed *Macbeth* at all, he said, unless Felice Varesi had been available to sing the title role.[9] As for Lady Macbeth, he originally wanted Sophie Löwe, but she was in the early stages of pregnancy and unwilling to take any risks; instead, he was glad to know that Barbieri-Nini would do it. She had already created Lucrezia for him in *I due Foscari* (and would later create Gulnara in *Il corsaro*), so he knew her to have a big voice and (very importantly) to be a better than average actress.

For all the time and attention he lavished on this opera, both in the writing and the rehearsing, Verdi always maintained that the most important moment was the sleepwalking scene and the duet that follows it. "For three months, morning and evening," Barbieri-Nini later recalled, Verdi kept her at it, "attempting to impersonate someone who speaks in her sleep, who (as the maestro put it) utters words . . . almost without moving her lips, the rest of the face motionless, the eyes shut."[10] Even at the public dress rehearsal, while the audience waited impatiently in the auditorium for the opera to begin, Verdi ordered the two principals to rehearse the scene yet again in the foyer of the theater. When Varesi accused him of having rehearsed it 150 times already, Verdi replied "You won't be saying that in half an hour's time: it will be 151 by then." As Barbieri-Nini recalled, "We were forced to obey the tyrant."[11] Yet she and Varesi also understood that it was this obsessive regard for dramatic detail that made the opera work so well, and that made it the most important success of each of their distinguished careers. It was an opera Verdi would later tamper with for its French premiere in 1865, adding some beautiful music, but the 1847 version bears all the marks of the real Verdi that was now emerging—Verdi the music-dramatist. This side of him was writ large in a letter he sent to the director of an opera house the following year, begging him (once again) *not* to cast Eugenia Tadolini as Lady Macbeth: "You know how much I admire Tadolini, and she knows it herself; but in our common interest we should stop and consider. Tadolini has too great qualities for this role. Perhaps you think this is a contradiction! Tadolini's appearance is good and beautiful, and I would like Lady Macbeth twisted and ugly. Tadolini sings to perfection, and I don't wish Lady Macbeth to sing at all. Tadolini has a marvelous, brilliant, clear, powerful voice, and for Lady Macbeth I should like a raw, choked, hollow voice. Tadolini's voice has something angelic. Lady Macbeth's voice should have something devilish."[12]

The year after *Macbeth*, the same emphasis on music-drama was applied to *Il corsaro*. Neither the libretto nor the music of this opera won much praise, then or later, and Verdi, who was in Paris, made no effort to get to Trieste for the premiere (the revolutionary year of 1848 was not a good time to be traveling in Europe). Instead, he wrote Barbieri-Nini, who was to create Gulnara, a long and detailed letter about her role—not so much about the music as about the ways (sometimes unmusical ways) in which she was to deliver it: "You know better than I that anger is not always expressed in shouting, but sometimes in a suffocated voice; and that is the case here. Sing the whole movement *sotto voce*, then, except for the last four notes; wait until [the] bass has almost left the stage before exploding with a shout, accompanied by a terrifying gesture, almost a premonition of the crime you are about to commit."[13]

Verdi clearly got on well with Barbieri-Nini and admired her as a singer and an actress. He admired Sophie Löwe as well, but he did not always get on with her. She was a German singer who had studied first in Vienna, then in Milan, and had sung mainly in Germany and Austria during the 1830s. She became a personality at La Scala when she created the title role in *Maria Padilla* for Donizetti in 1841, and Verdi was pleased enough to find that she would be the Elvira for the premiere of *Ernani* in Venice in 1844. He was coming off the La Scala successes of *Nabucco* and *I Lombardi,* and his new opera was greatly anticipated. But it was not a good time for Verdi: he was not well, *I Lombardi* failed in its Venice production, and he had difficulty finding an adequate tenor for *Ernani*. Then Sophie Löwe decided she did not like the trio that ended the opera: she would prefer a brilliant solo for herself and she actually asked Francesco Maria Piave, the librettist, to supply the words. For the first time in his career (but not the last) Verdi went ballistic with a singer and forbade the slightest change. Whether as a result of all these problems, or more probably because of last-minute production problems at La Fenice, the premiere was not a success. Löwe sang flat for much of the

Sophie Löwe (1812–1866). The volatile German soprano had a great career between 1832 and 1848, creating the title role in *Maria Padilla* for Donizetti (1841) and, for Verdi, Elvira in *Ernani* (1844) and Odabella in *Attila* (1846). (Private Collection/Lebrecht Collection.)

evening and the tenor Guasco was hoarse from a shouting match he'd had with the theater staff before the performance began. But the opera was generally deemed a success, and subsequent performances were very well received. Verdi did not wait to see them: he left Venice without even the courtesy of calling on his leading lady—he left her a visiting card instead.[14]

If Löwe had met her match, then it was also true that Verdi knew he would need her again. There were few enough singers in Italy who could do justice to his operas, musically and dramatically, and Löwe was one of them. Relations were repaired in time for *Attila* in 1846, when Löwe created the huge role of Odabella. "I never would have believed that a German could display such patriotic fire," Verdi wrote chauvinistically of her performance,[15] and it certainly did not pass notice that the lady portraying the flower of

Italian womanhood had more in common with the Hun than she did with most of the audience at La Fenice. Despite the usual wobbly Verdian first night, *Attila* was an enormous success, and it was undoubtedly Löwe's performance as Odabella that made Verdi ask for her the next year for Lady Macbeth. That was not to be: first her pregnancy, then her marriage to the Prince of Liechtenstein led to her retirement from the stage in 1848, and the loss of what was probably the most exciting and powerful female voice of early Verdi.

Finding such voices was a very real problem in the 1840s, just as it is for opera houses at the beginning of the twenty-first century. As early as 1842, when it became clear that Strepponi's voice was too far gone to tackle the second run of *Nabucco* performances scheduled for La Scala's autumn season, Verdi had sought out a young woman named Teresa De Giuli Borsi, whose voice, he had heard, might be strong enough. It was, and Verdi followed her ensuing career with interest, doubtless looking for an opportunity to express his gratitude in the form of a role created especially for her. The opportunity came in the explosive political circumstances of Rome in 1849. For a few brief months, with the pope in exile, Rome was an independent republic—and Verdi was there. He had missed the historic *cinque giornate* (Five Days) that had rocked the Austrian hold on Milan the previous year— instead, he had been in Paris, where he had witnessed equally remarkable events, culminating in free elections. Reviewing all that was happening in Europe at this most revolutionary of times, he had no doubt that it was the right moment for him to embark on a more overtly patriotic opera than anything he had dared attempt before. His chosen vehicle was *La battaglia di Legnano,* which celebrated the defeat of the Emperor Frederick Barbarossa at the hands of the Lombard League in 1176. Its martial tunes and nationalistic sentiments were clearly intended as a contribution to what would soon become the *Risorgimento*. That it was produced in Rome in the immediate aftermath of free elections and at the height of revolutionary excitement was a happy coincidence for Verdi, and it gave him the single greatest success of the first half of his career. At the public dress rehearsal alone, he took twenty curtain calls. At the official premiere, the entire last act was encored. And it was the tenor Gaetano Fraschini as the dying hero Arrigo, and Teresa De

Giuli Borsi as the pure-as-milk heroine Lida, who had the honor of floating the final, soaring phrase out into the auditorium: *Chi muore per la patria alma sì rea non ha!* (He who dies for the homeland cannot have such an evil soul).

Inevitably, *La battaglia* had a checkered career with censors thereafter, but Italian memories were long and anyone who had taken part in those first performances in the early weeks of 1849 was honored as a patriot. Verdi was glad to have given De Giuli Borsi her own role at last, and was full of admiration for the way she handled it. Four years later, when *Il trovatore* was given its premiere in Rome, she was his first choice for Leonora, though she did not, in the end, sing the role.

Verdi sometimes found himself with the wrong singer, but once (and maybe only once) he found himself with the wrong *kind* of singer. When he accepted the commission to write *I masnadieri* for London in 1847, he knew it would be for Jenny Lind. Emanuele Muzio, who was then studying with Verdi and acting as his secretary and amanuensis, went ahead to London and reported on Lind's vocal abilities: "Her voice is a bit sharp at the top, weak at the bottom, but through study she has reached the point where she is able to make it flexible at the top, so that she can perform the most difficult passages. No one can match her trill; she has an agility like no other singer, and generally, to let people hear her *bravura* in singing, she sins in performing too many *fioriture, gruppetti,* [and] trills, things that were pleasing to audiences in the last century, but are not in 1847."[16]

Verdi could write the long, smooth melodies of *cantilene* in the style of Bellini—he had done so for Frezzolini in *Giovanna d'Arco*—but it was not in his nature to write highly ornamented music, nor did he think it appropriate dramatically. He did his best for Lind: he gave her a couple of ornamented arias so that she could demonstrate her well-known agility, but the role of Amalia was not ideally suited to her talents, and she never sang it again. The opera, as a whole, was well received in the theater, but it was not successful in the long term, largely because its musical raison d'être was at odds with its dramatic values (a most un-Verdian situation). Moreover, the production featured one of those dramatic anomalies that drove Verdi to distraction. The role of Massimiliano, the elderly count who is released from prison, starving and emaciated, was played by the most famous of basses, Luigi Lablache—

a giant of a man with a massive girth, renowned for his healthy demeanor. It was the sort of situation Verdi would confront even more brutally in the first staging of *La traviata,* and he hated it.

While he was rehearsing *I masnadieri* at Her Majesty's Theatre, Verdi was very much aware of what was going on down the road at Covent Garden. There, the team of Grisi, Mario, and Ronconi was in the middle of a hugely successful run of *I due Foscari,* having just come off an equally successful run of *I Lombardi.* It was, in a way, Verdi's "dream team," and it must have been frustrating to know that they were not going to be singing in Italy any time soon—never again, in the cases of Grisi and Mario.

Because he was at odds with La Scala, Verdi had no "home base" for his operas after 1845, but he was rarely short of commissions. The last of his great predecessors, Donizetti, had written his final opera in 1843 and died in 1848; Rossini would live another twenty years in Paris, but not as an active opera composer. Verdi stood head and shoulders above everyone else, and his preeminence was buttressed by the fact that he had come to embody the idea of Italian nationhood. So by the time he moved back to his childhood home of Busseto in the summer of 1849, he was generally in a position to delay signing a contract for a new opera until he knew who the singers would be. Even then, it didn't always work out well. He accepted Marietta Gazzaniga for the title role of *Luisa Miller* in Naples because there seemed to be no alternative (he was much more concerned about the tenor, who had to be replaced in the middle of rehearsals), and he accepted her again for the crucial role of Lina in *Stiffelio* the following year, but neither opera was a great success and Verdi blamed the singers almost as much as the censors. Gazzaniga was, in fact, a very dedicated Verdian—she eventually had eleven Verdi roles in her repertory[17]—but she never aroused much enthusiasm in the composer. He disliked her Gilda, which he saw in Bergamo, and he dismissed her from the list of candidates to create Violetta on the grounds that he had been "unhappy" with her work in the past.[18]

In the 1840s, Verdi had been fortunate in his female singers, but thereafter, until Teresa Stolz's arrival in Italy in 1863, though he may have had more to choose from, they were not generally of the quality of Sophie Löwe,

Erminia Frezzolini, Eugenia Tadolini, and Marianna Barbieri-Nini—some of whom were still available in the 1850s (Barbieri-Nini was on the short list for Violetta). At the same time, Verdi himself was developing as a composer: the drama and the music were becoming ever more intertwined in the way he conceived his operas and wished to see them realized. That did not necessarily require new singers, but it did require singers who were prepared to "study the dramatic situation," as he had explained to Varesi at the time of *Macbeth*.

The three great operas of the early 1850s—*Rigoletto*, *Il trovatore*, and *La traviata* (the last two with premieres only six weeks apart)—are generally regarded as the first works of Verdi's maturity. *Il trovatore* is really a throwback to his earlier style—a very superior version of *Ernani*, perhaps— but *Rigoletto* and *La traviata* are distinguished from previous works by the way both the characters and the storytelling are developed in the music. The portraits of Rigoletto and Gilda, and of Violetta and Alfredo, are fully developed characterizations—believable people confronting recognizable moral dilemmas. Verdi had been there before—very recently, in fact, with *Stiffelio*, in which a Protestant minister had confronted the infidelity of his wife and been unable to summon up enough Christian charity to forgive her—but he had never quite succeeded in combining music and drama into a seamless whole. Now he did so—and, in doing so, he placed himself, for all time, in the hands of the singers: if they failed to unite the music and the drama in their own performances, if they were not prepared to "study the dramatic situation" and work within it, the results would be laughable. Verdi found that out to his cost, and it is still true today.

Il trovatore, the second of the three operas, was not the problem. It was a *singfest*, a miracle of big tunes and dramatic music, and its success in Rome in 1853 was assured by a red-blooded Italian cast that contained no great stars, just a group of fine repertory singers—though it would have been rash to point that out to Rosina Penco, who sang Leonora. Salvadore Cammarano's libretto was a battle against mortality (he died before it was quite complete), and even the astonishing score could not transform the opera into dramma per musica of the sort Verdi had so recently achieved in *Rigoletto*. Astute observers did, however, notice one very unusual thing about *Il trova-*

tore (which, luckily, was lost on Penco): the soprano was not the leading female protagonist. Clearly, the central figure in the drama was Azucena, the troubadour's gypsy mother, and that was a mezzo-soprano role sung by Emilia Goggi at the premiere. Penco was not so oblivious to this situation that she did not pick a number of fights with Goggi during rehearsals (Verdi had been warned by his friend Cesare De Sanctis that she would probably do so),[19] but at least she did not appear to have discovered that the enlargement of her own role into one comparable with those of the other three principals was an afterthought that took place very late in the day (and one that, unfortunately, served to obscure the real drama of the work). Azucena, on the other hand, became the first of a wonderful succession of mezzo and contralto roles with which Verdi would stud his operas from now on—Ulrica, Eboli, Amneris, Mistress Quickly.

The real test for singers was not *Il trovatore* but the two operas given their premieres in Venice. *Rigoletto* in 1851 was a triumph, *La traviata* in 1853 was a fiasco. What made the difference then (and it is just as often the difference between success and failure today) was that one set of singers was dramatically believable, the other was not. "Ten years ago I would not have dared to tackle *Rigoletto*," Verdi wrote to a friend in 1853. "Today I would refuse subjects of the kind of *Nabucco, Foscari,* etc. . . . They harp on one chord, elevated, if you like, but monotonous . . . I think the best, the most effective, subject I have so far set to music . . . is *Rigoletto*. It has very powerful situations, variety, brio, pathos. All the sudden changes of fortune are brought about by the lighthearted, libertine character of the Duke, who arouses Rigoletto's fears, Gilda's passion, etc., which form many excellent dramatic points, among them the quartet."[20]

Verdi thought Victor Hugo's play *Le roi s'amuse* was "one of the greatest creations of the modern theater,"[21] but its immediate attraction to him in 1850–51 was that he was due to write an opera for Venice and he knew Felice Varesi was on the roster at La Fenice. Just as he had written Macbeth for Varesi four years before, so he now wrote Rigoletto for him. It followed that the Gilda would be Teresa Brambilla, since she too was under contract to La Fenice that season. She was a happy choice, not just because she scored a personal success in what turned out to be a great collective triumph on the first night, but also because she happened to have gone to school with Giuseppina Strepponi, who was now living openly with Verdi at Busseto.[22] The Brambilla family was a musical dynasty from Milan: Uncle Paolo, recently deceased, had been quite a well-known opera composer; cousin Amalia was one of Italy's leading bel canto sopranos; and Teresa's four sisters were all reputable singers—Marietta, a true contralto, had created Orsini in Donizetti's *Lucrezia Borgia,* and the much younger Giuseppina, also a contralto, was Verdi's choice for the Fool in *Re Lear,* had that opera ever come into being. Teresa's voice had an unusually wide compass (she was best known as Abigaille in *Nabucco*), and Verdi entrusted her with the very high tessitura of Gilda. In addition, she was a fine actress and a striking-looking woman, and Verdi also trusted her, in her thirty-eighth year, to be dramatically credible as Rigoletto's young daughter. On both counts, his trust was justified. The real success of *Rigoletto,* though, was that its cast formed a genuine ensemble—Varesi as the Jester, Raffaele Mirate as the duke, Teresa Brambilla as Gilda—three fine singers who were prepared to "study the dramatic situation and the words" and then to allow the music, as Verdi promised it would, "to come by itself."

That is not what happened in *La traviata* two years later, and it was no great surprise to the composer, though he was nevertheless furious about it. From the beginning, he had been concerned about the casting of Violetta. At various times, he had suggested a number of singers to the management of La Fenice and had finally agreed upon Carolina Alajmo, a very capable artiste who was not a frontline singer but was an excellent actress. Alajmo fell ill and Verdi was forced, against his better judgment, to accept Fanny Salvini-Donatelli. What he wanted, he told his librettist, Piave, was "an elegant figure, young, who can sing passionately."[23] What he got was a very fine singer, aged thirty-eight, and large. Varesi, who was to sing Germont *père,* wrote a friend at La Fenice that he had read an Italian translation of Dumas's *La dame aux camélias,* and thought the role of Violetta "very unsuited to Salvini-Donatelli's figure": how could she possibly play a consumptive?[24]

That turned out to be the conclusion of the first-night audience, too. Ironically, while Varesi sang badly and the tenor, Carlo Graziani, was hoarse, Salvini-Donatelli sang wonderfully and took all the vocal honors in the first

Fanny Salvini-Donatelli (c.1815–1891). Aside from the role of Violetta in *La traviata*, which won her fame (and infamy), Salvini-Donatelli was greatly esteemed as Lady Macbeth, Lucrezia (in *I due Foscari*), and Elvira (in *Ernani*). (Private Collection/Lebrecht Collection.)

two acts. But when the audience was asked to accept that this vision of healthy eating was dying of consumption it simply refused to suspend its disbelief. People laughed, and with the laughter went all the dramatic credibility Verdi had labored so hard to create. "Is it my fault or the singers'?" he wrote. "Time will tell."[25]

Time did tell. A year later, again in Venice but this time at a different theater, Verdi relaunched *La traviata* with a new cast and scored a great triumph. "Then it was a *fiasco;* now it is creating a *furore,*" he wrote to a friend.[26] The new Violetta was Maria Spezia—not so great a singer as Salvini-Donatelli, perhaps, but in every other way a better choice. She had already sung Gilda with success, and two or three other Verdi heroines as well.

Piave, who directed the rehearsals at the Teatro San Benedetto, wrote with a librettist's pride to the publisher Ricordi: "In this opera, she is a woman different from those in all the other [works], and her very pallor, her exhaustion, and her entire person, everything in her comes together to make her the true incarnation of the ideas of Dumas, of Verdi, and also of myself."[27]

The lesson of La traviata was that Verdi was approaching that point at which music and drama were joined in a near-perfect union: to emphasize one element at the expense of the other was to undermine the whole. Wagner was struggling with the same dilemma during his long exile from Germany, and other composers were beginning to think the same way—Bizet's Carmen was only a dozen years away. But Verdi had already got there, and his position in the world of opera was now so commanding that he could afford to dictate his terms. The first term was that he would never again allow his operas to be produced with inadequate singers—by which he meant singers who could not, or would not, accept that "the dramatic situation" was a vital part of their responsibility.

Nothing illustrates Verdi's determination better than the events surrounding the opera that never was. Re Lear (Shakespeare's King Lear) had been a recurring item on Verdi's list of possible subjects since 1843, when he considered it for Venice instead of Ernani. By 1850 he had a draft libretto in hand (by Cammarano, from whose deathbed he was quick to reclaim it), and in 1857 he was almost ready to compose it for the San Carlo in Naples. What held him back was the knowledge that the San Carlo did not have the necessary singers—but surely it could import them if it really wanted the opera? For Lear himself, "a baritone artist, in every sense of the word" would be needed, and Verdi clearly thought that was soluble.[28] The sticking points were the soprano to sing Cordelia and, to a lesser extent, the contralto to sing the Fool. Verdi knew who he wanted for these roles—Marietta Piccolomini for Cordelia and Giuseppina Brambilla (Teresa's younger sister) for the Fool—but it was not what the San Carlo management had in mind. Instead, Rosina Penco was suggested as the soprano. She might have done well enough as the original Leonora in Il trovatore four years before, but Verdi knew she was wrong for Cordelia: "It is my habit not to let any artist be forced upon me, not even if Malibran were to come back from the dead. All the gold on earth would not make me give up this principle. I have all possible respect for Penco's talent, but I don't want her to be able to say to me: 'Signor Maestro, give me the part in your opera, I want it, I have the right to it.'"[29]

Verdi himself had already entered into negotiations with Piccolomini. She was still in her early twenties, aristocratic and very attractive, and she had established herself as *the* Violetta in *La traviata*. The voice was acceptable, but no one ever accused it of being exceptional: it was her acting and her stage presence that made her so remarkable. Verdi knew what a fine singer could do with Violetta (Fanny Salvini-Donatelli had always sung it wonderfully), but he also knew that she could be laughed off the stage if she did not look the part and could not act it. Piccolomini's Violetta was entirely credible; audiences in London and Paris had acclaimed it. Verdi saw her in the Paris production, and he must have heard about, and enjoyed, the disapproving notice written of her performance in London by the straitlaced critic Henry Chorley: "Never did any young lady, whose private claims to modest respect were so great as hers are known to be, with such self-denial fling off her protection in her resolution to lay hold of the public at all costs. Her performances at times approached offence against maidenly reticence and delicacy."[30]

Verdi had no doubt that this was his Cordelia. But it was not to be. The San Carlo management stood firm, and so did Verdi: "Believe me, it is a great mistake to risk *Re Lear* with a company of singers who, good as they are, are not—one might say—made to order for those roles. I would perhaps ruin an opera, and you, to some extent, would ruin your management. Let me scrounge around among other plays, and it will be fine when I finally find a subject."[31]

What he found, after some delay, was Scribe's libretto *Gustave III, ou Le bal masqué,* originally written for Auber in 1833. It became *Un ballo in maschera.*

The intense activity of the years up to *La traviata* (nineteen operas in fifteen years) was succeeded by a more measured pace (nine operas in forty years, plus some major rewrites and revisions). Verdi traveled a good deal—*Les vêpres siciliennes* and *Don Carlos* were composed for Paris, *La forza del destino* for St. Petersburg—and he took a close interest in performances of his works all over Europe and the Americas. These were now becoming prolific. With the advent of *Rigoletto, Il trovatore,* and *La traviata,* he finally outpaced his great predecessors and became the most performed opera composer in the world. There was one day in London—May 25, 1858—when all three musical theaters were performing *La traviata* at the same time: Violetta was performed by Piccolomini at Her Majesty's, Salvini-Donatelli at Drury Lane, and Angiolina Bosio at Covent Garden.[32] Verdi watched all this activity with satisfaction, but his particular interest, as his letters to Ricordi attest, was most often in the singers and the production standards. He wanted to know who could be relied on and who could not.

Sophie Cruvelli could not—even though in Paris she was hailed as "the second Malibran." She had been born Johanne Sophie Crüwell in Germany and had followed her countrywoman Sophie Löwe to Italy, where she made her professional debut in 1847 as Odabella. Like Löwe again, her career was cut short by an advantageous marriage—to Baron De Vigier in 1856—but not before she had become one of the most admired, and certainly one of the most highly paid, singers in Paris, first at the Théâtre Italien, then at the Opéra. It was at the Opéra that she was chosen to create the role of Hélène in *Les vêpres siciliennes,* Verdi's first really concentrated attempt to write a grand opéra in the French style. Unfortunately, Cruvelli was famously eccentric, and she was also in love. In the middle of rehearsals she simply disappeared—for a whole month. It later transpired that she had spent the time on the Côte d'Azur with her fiancé, Baron De Vigier, but it had not occurred to her to notify anyone that she was going away or when she would be returning. When she did get back, she gave a fine performance as Hélène, and seemed quite unable to understand the composer's bafflement that a professional singer might suddenly decide to take a holiday in the midst of rehearsals for a world premiere.

Verdi did not find Eugènie Julienne-Déjean much more reliable. She was the Frenchwoman who created Amelia in *Un ballo in maschera* in Rome in 1859. This was the opera that should have been *Re Lear* in Naples. When the San Carlo failed to come up with the sopranos Verdi wanted, it became

Un ballo—and promptly fell afoul of the Neapolitan censor. That was why it was given its premiere in Rome (and even then, in a colonial Boston setting rather than the Swedish setting of Gustavus's actual assassination). Like Cruvelli, Julienne-Déjean eventually turned in a very good performance, but not before she had greatly displeased Verdi by asking him to give her special coaching in her role. He inferred (rightly or wrongly is not known) that she had not yet memorized her music, and he sent her away with a flea in her ear. Luckily for her, she was protected by Strepponi, whose pupil she probably was.[33]

Emma La Grua, on the other hand, was a nonevent. She was a Sicilian singer who, in 1861, was at the height of what was to be her short-lived fame. Like many of the singers Verdi favored, her voice was adequate but not spectacular. It was her acting that made her special. In Vienna she had been hailed as "the greatest actress to be found on the stage in Europe."[34] It was for her that Verdi wrote the Leonora of *La forza del destino,* and journeyed all the way to St. Petersburg to direct it. When he got there, she was ill. After several weeks of rehearsing with the rest of the cast, she was still ill. There was no possibility of finding a replacement in Russia, so eventually Verdi left for home, promising to return the following season—which he did. La Grua was no longer in Russia and the role fell instead to Caroline Douvry Barbot, the young Frenchwoman who was married to Joseph Barbot, creator of Gounod's Faust. Caroline Barbot got the role because Verdi insisted on her: if he could not have La Grua, then it must be Barbot. When the director of the theater in St. Petersburg advised him that another singer, Constance Nantier-Didiée, who was to sing the small but eye-catching role of Preziosilla, was campaigning to have Barbot taken out of consideration, Verdi wrote from Paris: "I know that if I were director, I would set fire to the four corners of the theater rather than put up with such demands!"[35] Arson was avoided: Barbot and Nantier-Didiée both performed, and Verdi scored a modest success, though *La forza* did not come into its own until 1869, when he rewrote parts of it and staged it at La Scala with Teresa Stolz as Leonora.

These were all singers who could reasonably claim that Verdi had written roles for them. He had—and yet he hadn't. Only a decade or two earlier it had undoubtedly been true that Rossini and his contemporaries were composing for very specific singers—for Colbran, say, or Pasta—but that was never quite true of Verdi.

First, working with a librettist, he conceived a dramatic character—Hélène, maybe, or Amelia, or Leonora—and he probably made some sketches of the music, but by this time he already knew the sort of singer he was looking for (the voice type, the overall range, but, most of all, the appearance and dramatic capabilities of the singer), and he generally sent the opera house, via Ricordi, a list of "possibles." Occasionally he was stymied by deadlines or badly written contracts (that was the problem with *La traviata:* even though he knew Salvini-Donatelli was wrong for Violetta, his contract did not allow him to stop the production), but he generally avoided signing contracts until the necessary singers were in place. He might then adjust what he had written to suit the individual singers—Cruvelli, or Julienne-Déjean, or Barbot—but it was never true to say that he had written the roles *for* them. It would be more accurate to use the parlance of the dance world: he had created the roles *on* them. As early as *Nabucco* in 1842, it was evident that Verdi was writing for posterity: he expected his operas to be restaged again and again, with many different singers assuming the parts. He knew these parts were eminently singable, but just singing them was not enough: they also had to be dramatized and acted, and that took a different kind of singer, one that was intelligent, physically presentable, interested in the dramatic context, and willing to become part of an ensemble. Such singers were rare in the nineteenth century.

Verdi heard two of them in London in the spring of 1862. He was there for the first performance of his cantata *L'inno delle nazioni* (The Hymn of the Nations) at the International Exhibition. He had written it for a tenor soloist, Enrico Tamberlik, but, since Tamberlik was under contract to Covent Garden and the cantata was to be given its first performance at Her Majesty's Theatre, he had to "adjust" it so that the undisputed star of Her Majesty's could sing it. That was Therese Tietjens, the German soprano who now made her home in London and was well on her way to becoming one of the best-loved singers the English ever laid claim to. She had been the first London Hélène in *Les vêpres siciliennes*, and, at the time of Verdi's visit, she was about to become the first London Amelia in *Un ballo in maschera*. Like everyone else, Verdi was impressed with her both as a singer and a human being. She was intensely musical; she sang happily in Italian, French and German (an unusual accomplishment for a singer at that time), and she had a voice of great power and flexibility. By the time of her tragically early death from cancer in 1877 (she was still in her early forties, probably at the peak of her powers) she had six of Verdi's heroines in her repertory, from the *Ernani* Elvira to the *Forza* Leonora, and for most Londoners she had provided the introduction to these operas.

The other lady Verdi first heard in London in that spring of 1862 made an even greater impression. She was nineteen years old, trained and educated in America, and her name was Adelina Patti. What so impressed Verdi about her (and he took pains to see her in several different operas) was that she was "a perfect balance between singer and actress"—she was, in fact, as close to being his ideal singer as anyone was ever to become:

> A *born* artist in every sense of the word. When I heard her for the first time in London . . . I was stunned, not only by the marvelous technique, but by several moments in the drama in which she showed that she was a great actress. I remember her chaste, modest behavior when she sits on the soldier's bed in *La sonnambula* and when she, defiled, rushes out of the Libertine's room in *Don Giovanni*. I remember a certain action in the background during Don Bartolo's aria in *Barbiere;* and more than anything else the rec[itative] before the quartet in *Rigoletto,* when her father shows her her lover in the Tavern, saying "And you still love him" and she answers "I love him." No words can express the sublime effect she achieved when she said these words . . . I judged her to be a marvelous actress and singer the first time I heard her in London. An exceptional artist.[36]

Fifteen years later, when she made her triumphant tour of Italy, Verdi heard her again. He was alarmed to hear she was planning to make a cut in the third act of *Aida* at La Scala, but when he heard her in Genoa he knew immediately that she was still the same wonderful singer-actress: "The talent, the instinct for the theater, the singing are the same, the same, the same," he wrote. "[Her] artistic nature [is] so complete that perhaps there has never been anyone to equal her! Oh! Oh! And Malibran? Very, very great, but not always even! Sometimes sublime and sometimes exaggerated! Her singing style was not very pure, her acting was not always right, her voice shrill in the top notes! In spite of everything, a very great artist, marvelous! But Patti is more complete. A marvelous voice, an extremely pure singing style; stupendous actress with a charm and a naturalness that no one else has." [37]

Amid the fanfare surrounding her conquest of Milan there were, inevitably, one or two naysayers. One of them wrote Verdi a less than glowing account of Patti's Aida: her high notes were forced, there were whole stretches of the opera she apparently did not like or could not interpret. Verdi doubtless took the letter with a grain of salt, because the writer was Teresa Stolz. [38]

Of all the female singers Verdi knew and worked with in his long career (not excepting Strepponi), Stolz was probably the one he trusted the most in artistic matters. From the moment he first heard her—as Elisabetta in the 1869 Milan production of *Don Carlo* that marked Verdi's return to La Scala after an absence of twenty-five years—he knew she would be his first-choice soprano. He immediately agreed that she should "re-create" Leonora in the revised version of *La forza* that La Scala staged the same year, and he undoubtedly thought of her as the first Aida (though she did not, in fact, originate the role—like Verdi himself, she was not in Cairo for the world premiere on Christmas Eve 1871, though she was already learning the role for the La Scala production two months later).

In that Carnival season of 1872, when *Aida* was seen in Milan for the first time, Verdi had reason to believe he had found not just one soprano, but two—and that was just as well since most of his operas now involved a major mezzo-soprano role as well as the soprano lead. The mezzo side of the partnership was Maria Waldmann: she sang Amneris to Stolz's Aida at La Scala, and later at the Théâtre Italien in Paris as well, and together they sang in the first performances of the *Requiem* in Milan in 1874, followed by the triumphant tour of London and Paris.

Although they quickly became the most important female singers in Italy, neither of these ladies was Italian. Stolz was a Bohemian who made her early career in Odessa, Constantinople, and Tiblisi. She did not sing professionally in Italy until 1864, when she was thirty, though she already had a number of Verdian roles in her repertory and it soon became clear that she was ideally equipped for them. She possessed the lirico spinto voice for which Verdi was writing—a voice that could "push" to the great dramatic moments, had a wide compass (two and a half octaves, in her case), and had the control necessary to float a piano note that would hold an audience spellbound. "Vigorous, flexible, dramatic, limpid, brilliant," was how one reviewer described her voice.[39] She was a passionate but dignified actress, an extremely intelligent woman, and a dedicated Verdian. During the last five years of her career, between 1872 and 1877, she sang only two roles that were not Verdi's, and it was no coincidence that those two were Alice in *Robert le diable* and Rachel in *La juive*—the most famous roles of Cornélie Falcon, the first real spinto singer at the Paris Opéra forty years before.[40]

Waldmann was Austrian, eight years younger than Stolz. She made her debut in Germany in 1865 and spent six years singing around Europe, from Amsterdam to Moscow and as far south as Trieste. Verdi heard good reports of her, so when he was planning his La Scala production of *Aida* he asked Ricordi to have her contracted to La Scala for the 1871–72 season: he would then be able to hear her in other parts before offering Amneris (La Scala, he said, was the only place to judge a singer).[41] That Verdi could add singers to La Scala's roster says much about his power in the world of opera at this time, but what really impressed Stolz and Waldmann when they turned up for rehearsals was another condition Verdi had placed on the management. The orchestra, he said, had to be in a pit, out of sight of the audience: "The idea is not mine. It is Wagner's. It is excellent. How can we bear the sight of those wretched frock coats and white ties in the midst of Egyptian, Assyrian and Druid costumes?"[42]

It was one of several innovations in the 1870s and 1880s that improved the presentation of opera and had major consequences for the singers. The other important one was the lowering of house lights during a performance. Up to about 1820, theaters had relied on candlelight or oil lamps, which were smelly and smoky. Then had come coal gas, which was safer and allowed innovative theaters like the Paris Opéra to create all sorts of startling effects on the stage (the spectacles d'optique and, later, limelight). But the real breakthrough came around 1875, when theaters were able to lower (but not extinguish) the gas lamps in the auditorium when the performance began. A few years later, with the advent of electricity, house lights could be completely extinguished. The Paris Opéra converted its foyer and auditorium to electricity in 1881, the same year that Richard D'Oyly Carte's new Savoy Theatre in London, home of the Gilbert and Sullivan operettas, converted its stage lighting to electricity. Covent Garden and Bayreuth followed suit in the early 1890s and New York's Metropolitan Opera in 1893. This was the real revolution for the singers: their performances became focused on the stage, and they were able to sing and act without the distraction of being able to see the audience all the time. For audiences, it was not all gain. For hundreds of years they had been able to follow the action by reading from librettos or translations as the opera progressed; now they were consigned to darkness, and very often, unless they had done their homework in advance, to incomprehension—until the invention of projected supertitles in the 1970s, greatly reviled by critics and even more greatly appreciated by audiences.

For Verdi, so deeply committed to drama, hiding the orchestra and lowering the house lights were important advances, but he still relied, first and foremost, on the passing parade of singers. Just as their marriages to aristocrats had robbed him of the two Sophies, Löwe and Cruvelli, so it was with Maria Waldmann. In 1876, soon after the great success of *Aida* at the Théâtre Italien in Paris, she retired from the stage in order to marry Count (late Duke) Galeazzo Massari. The next year, Teresa Stolz, now in her mid-forties, also decided to retire. In their different ways, both these ladies remained important friends of Verdi's right up to his death a quarter of a century later— Waldmann as a faithful correspondent and occasional visitor, Stolz as a very close friend and, eventually, companion to Verdi and Strepponi in their old age. The ménage à trois suffered some strains and tensions along the way, but there is no reason to suppose (as scurrilous gossips inevitably did) that Verdi's relationship with Stolz was ever more than a close friendship.

Meanwhile, Verdi, by virtue of his longevity and the miracle that he continued to compose, was once again in need of singers. *Simon Boccanegra* had been a failure at La Fenice in 1857, mainly on account of its libretto, which even the principal author, Piave, had difficulty understanding. When Arrigo Boito began his great collaboration with Verdi in 1879, the rewriting of *Boccanegra* was the test piece he was given to see if he would be up to *Otello*. He passed with flying colors, and so did the singers, though that was more than Verdi had expected. When he was offered La Scala's "A-team" of Anna D'Angeri, Francesco Tamagno, Victor Maurel, and Edouard De Reske, he wrote disparagingly to Ricordi: "'Either the operas for the singers or the singers for the operas'—an old proverb that no impresario ever knew how to follow, and without which no success is possible in the theater. You have a good company for La Scala, but it is not suited to *Boccanegra*."[43]

Some of the singers shared Verdi's skepticism. The tenor Tamagno and the soprano D'Angeri waited for him to arrive in Milan for rehearsals before they announced that their roles (Adorno and Amelia, respectively) were too high and not important enough. Verdi kept his temper and rehearsals went ahead, but he did not anticipate a success. When it turned out that the revisions, the production, and the singers combined for a considerable success he was sufficiently pleased to allow thoughts of *Otello* to begin to percolate. It was a long process (seven years to completion), and when it came to finding a cast his first choices were all members of the *Boccanegra* team—Tamagno, for whose trumpetlike tenor the role of Otello was clearly written, Maurel as Iago, and D'Angeri as Desdemona—but the soprano (yet another Austrian) had in the meantime married Vittorio Dalem, director of the Teatro Rossetti in Trieste, and was unwilling to come out of retirement, even though she was still in her early thirties.

So Verdi was in search of a Desdemona. There appeared to be two candidates—Gemma Bellincioni, a twenty-two-year-old sensation whose claim was championed by Giulio Ricordi, and Romilda Pantaleoni, forty years old and renowned as a singing actress (indeed, she was often compared to the greatest Italian actress of the time, Eleonora Duse). Pantaleoni also had powerful backers—Teresa Stolz, who promised she would work on Verdi, and Franco Faccio, who had been chief conductor at La Scala since 1872 and would be the conductor of *Otello,* as he had been of *Aida* fifteen years earlier. But Faccio was Pantaleoni's lover . . . In the end, it was up to Verdi. He made a special trip to Milan to hear Bellincioni, and he also met with

Stolz to hear the case for Pantaleoni. As usual, he came down on the side of the better and more experienced actress, Pantaleoni, and he was probably right. He had liked Bellincioni's Violetta, but he may also have detected what soon became apparent, that she had little sympathy with the "old-fashioned" operatic style that Verdi now represented. Just three years after the premiere of *Otello,* she would create the role of Santuzza in Mascagni's *Cavalleria rusticana* and thus become the undisputed champion of the verismo (realistic) school of opera. Carmen and Tosca were two of her greatest portrayals, but the crowning achievement of her long career (she was still performing in 1924, her sixtieth year) was Salome, a role she first sang under Richard Strauss at the Italian premiere in 1906 and would sing more than a hundred times. At the peak of her career, which was probably in the ten years that spanned the nineteenth and twentieth centuries, she was the most explosive and exciting singer in Europe, and a very fine actress besides.

So Romilda Pantaleoni was Verdi's Desdemona, and a very creditable one, though Verdi gave her few signs of approval. In the months before the premiere she was coached intensively, first by the composer at Sant'Agata, his home in the Po Valley, and then by Faccio in Milan. Verdi supervised the final month of rehearsals at La Scala, giving all the principals individual coaching and very precise instructions about their acting, and the opening night, on February 5, 1887, was a historic triumph. Fifteen years after his last Italian premiere *(Aida),* Verdi gave La Scala an opera that was recognizably by the same composer as *Nabucco* and *Ernani,* but was light-years removed from them. It was virtually a "through-composed" work with no stand-alone arias (Desdemona's Willow Song, which was encored on the opening night, was really the only such piece). Pantaleoni's performance was much praised at the time, but afterwards, in the extended process of casting myriad new productions in Italy and throughout Europe, Verdi was very lukewarm about her, and hurtfully so. But the fact was that he probably never heard a better Desdemona, and he was lucky to find one at the outset who was such an accomplished actress.

Though she had several Verdi heroines in her repertory, Pantaleoni was certainly not the dedicated Verdian that Stolz was. She was always adventurous and supportive of new composers—Ponchielli, Mascagni, even Wagner (she was much acclaimed as Elsa in *Lohengrin*). Three years before *Otello* she had sung the role of Anna in the first Milan performance of an opera called *Le villi*, the earliest stage work of a young man called Giacomo Puccini; in 1889 she would create the role of Tigrana in his next opera, *Edgar*, and she would follow the much younger Bellincioni into the world of verismo in the role of Santuzza. But personal problems were closing in on her: Franco Faccio was clearly ill, and it was affecting his mind. One awful night at La Scala he insisted that *Die Meistersinger* had no third act and they could all go home.[44] He had to be confined in an institution at Monza, and he died there in 1891. Pantaleoni never sang again.

For the better part of forty years Verdi had so dominated the opera scene in Italy that few other living composers had achieved popular name recognition. Boito had emerged with *Mefistofele* (the revised version of 1875, at any rate: the original in 1868 was a fiasco), but after that he concentrated on writing librettos for Verdi and others—his only other opera, *Nerone*, was a work-in-progress for the last thirty years of his life and had to be completed by others after his death. Ponchielli had also emerged with *La gioconda* in 1876, to a libretto by Boito, and he at least contributed a major new role to the soprano repertory. The "joyful girl," or ballad singer, of the title quickly became a favorite part for dramatic sopranos, none more so than the composer's wife, Teresa Brambilla-Ponchielli (not to be confused with her aunt, the Teresa Brambilla who had created Gilda in 1851). But as the 1880s wore on, with Verdi generally assumed to be in retirement at Sant'Agata, more young composers emerged. Puccini, Mascagni, Leoncavallo, Giordano, Catalani, and Franchetti all made promising beginnings, and some of them (Mascagni and Leoncavallo, in particular) branched out into verismo opera, which made even greater demands on the dramatic credibility of singers than did Verdi's operas.

So by the time Verdi surprised the world of opera with *Falstaff* in 1893, his eightieth year, female singers were measuring their voices by their ability to stand up to the very large orchestrations these new composers favored. Gemma Bellincioni's Santuzza in *Cavalleria rusticana* was matched two years later by Adelina Stehle's Nedda in *I pagliacci;* Cesira Ferrani created two crucially important roles for Puccini—Manon Lescaut in 1893 and Mimì in 1896; and the Romanian soprano Hariclea Darclée created the title roles in *La Wally, Iris,* and *Tosca* for Catalani, Mascagni, and Puccini, respectively.

All these ladies had generous, powerful voices that were variously described as *drammatico* (Darclée), *lirico* (Ferrani), or *lirico spinto* (Stehle).

Adelina Stehle was yet another of those Austrians who made their livings in Italy. She had started out as what was called a *soprano leggiero* (light soprano—the sort of voice needed for Norina in Donizetti's *Don Pasquale*, or perhaps Despina in *Così fan tutte*), and it was as such that she must have been engaged to sing Nannetta in *Falstaff*. But her voice was already developing into the drammatico or even lirico spinto category that was to make her most famous in the great verismo roles—she had actually created Nedda for Leoncavallo nine months before she did *Falstaff*. Perhaps the most enduring result of her appearance in *Falstaff*, however, was that she formed a relationship with her Fenton, Edoardo Garbin, and they subsequently married. Verdi did not like Garbin and found him the least effective member of the cast, but he and Stehle, separately and together, went on to become extremely successful. Three years later, in 1896, Puccini came to owe them a particular debt for the way they rescued *La bohème* after its not very successful premiere in Turin: their performances as Mimì and Rodolfo in Palermo proved to be the turning point for that opera, from which it never looked back.

At one stage, less than three months before *Falstaff* was due to go into rehearsal, it looked as though the opera would be called off altogether. Victor Maurel, the French baritone who had created Iago, had always assumed he would be the Fat Knight (to be fair, he was never given any indication he would not be). As a result, when it came time for contract negotiations he had put together a remarkable list of "requirements." According to Verdi, they included fees of four thousand lire a night, ten thousand lire for attendance at rehearsals (no one had ever been paid for rehearsals before), and the exclusive right to perform *Falstaff* in Florence, Rome, Madrid, and the United States. Faced with a very angry composer, Maurel retreated, but not before Verdi, as he later put it, "unsheathed my claws and said, 'The opera is mine and I do not permit anyone to have rights over my property.'"[45]

Meanwhile, Verdi struck up real friendships with the two principal female members of the cast. Emma Zilli was Alice Ford and Giuseppina Pasqua was Mistress Quickly. Pasqua was in her late thirties and probably as famous in Europe as Maurel. She had started out as a soprano pupil of Marietta Piccolomini, the Violetta Verdi had so much admired in the 1850s (and the woman who would probably have created Cordelia in *Re Lear,* had that project ever come to the stage), but Pasqua's voice had changed to the mezzo range at about the time she turned thirty and she had quickly turned to roles like Amneris and Azucena. Her Quickly proved that she was also a very accomplished comic actress. Zilli was another fine actress: she was nine years younger than Pasqua and only six years into what was to be a short but interesting career in which Alice Ford and Manon Lescaut were her specialties. Unluckily, she died of yellow fever in Cuba in the same month that Verdi also died in 1901.

Any man of eighty has intimations of mortality, and Verdi certainly knew that *Falstaff* would be his last opera. The opening night in February 1893 was another tremendous triumph. All the world, it seemed, was there. Adelina Patti (now in her sixth or seventh year of "farewell performances") was in Milan during rehearsals. So was Nellie Melba, who was making her La Scala debut as Lucia that season. On opening night, Teresa Stolz and Maria Waldmann had their accustomed places in the audience, and Mascagni and Puccini were both present as well (Puccini had come straight from Turin, where *Manon Lescaut* had had its brilliant premiere ten days before). As always, Verdi stayed on in Milan for the second and third performances, and then took leave of the singers. A few months later, he wrote to Emma Zilli: "Do you remember the third *Falstaff?!!* . . . I took my leave of you all; and you were all somewhat moved, especially you and Pasqua. Imagine what my greeting implied, since it meant: '*We will never meet again as artists!!*'"[46]

Meeting with singers, writing for singers, directing singers onstage— these were among the most important and enjoyable activities of Verdi's career. Better than all his predecessors and most of his successors, he understood that composers had to be in partnership with singers, and that the partnership extended beyond purely musical considerations to characterization, acting, and all aspects of the dramatic presentation of an opera. If the composer was not prepared to do this, then who else would—and who else could?

Though they were born in the same year and became the dominant personalities in nineteenth-century opera, Verdi and Wagner never met. Verdi liked some of Wagner's ideas (the sunken orchestra pit, for instance), but he admired neither his music nor his idea of *musik drama*. When he saw *Lohengrin* in Bologna in 1871 (it was the first performance of a Wagner opera in Italy), he made notes on his score during the performance and, at the end, summarized his reactions: "Mediocre impression. Beautiful music; when it is clear, it is throughout. The action runs slowly, as do the words. From that, boredom. Beautiful effects in the instruments. Abuse of notes held too long, and that makes it heavy."[47]

"Slowly," "boredom," "heavy"—all descriptions that conspired against drama in Verdi's opinion. Wagner, for his part, found Verdi's music beneath contempt. He worshiped Gluck; he admired Bellini; he thought Bizet's *Carmen* was not without merit, though repellent overall; but when he discussed Verdi, he referred his listeners to Spontini's scorching description of Italian musicians—*cochons* (swine).[48]

To the extent that they had anything in common, it was their commitment to the idea of music drama, which each of them proclaimed as his objective. What constituted music drama for Wagner was the amalgamation of the composer and librettist in a single person (himself), the writing of a "through-composed" score with recurring leitmotifs that identified individual characters, moods, and events within the opera, and the achievement of a narrative in words and music, but one that did not necessarily have to represent the dramatic action on the stage—often, it was good enough just to refer to it in the music.

Verdi's concept included some of these aspects, but rejected others. As time went on, he moved closer to "through composition," though it was not until *Otello* that he properly achieved it. Leitmotifs were part of his vocabulary almost as early as they surfaced in Wagner's (in *Ernani*, for instance, in 1843, which was about the time *Der fliegende Holländer* was being performed for the first time in Dresden), but Verdi always used them much more sparingly than Wagner. The major difference was over what constituted dramma per musica. Verdi believed there were three essential elements—words, music, *and stage action*—and they should be seamlessly intertwined throughout an opera.

Then and now, most people have seen Wagner as the true revolutionary, while Verdi is thought of as a conservative figure (of tremendous talent, admittedly) who simply continued the three-hundred-year-old tradition of

Italian opera. There was some truth in that—and a great deal of untruth, for Verdi's revolution, though it was subtle, was every bit as profound as Wagner's, and probably more influential in the long run.

Opera had long been recognized as a legitimate branch of theater, but it was also accepted that its very artificiality (the substitution of singing for speaking) excused it from the standards of dramatic credibility that were generally imposed on the straight theater. The development of Verdi's canon—twenty-eight operas over fifty-four years—could be seen as a rejection of any such special pleading. He believed that all theater was artificial to some degree, and acknowledged that on the surface opera was more artificial than most others because of its musical format, but he felt that this was not necessarily a dramatic weakness. On the contrary, he believed it ought to be a great strength. So, instead of excusing opera from the need to be staged and acted as dramatically as any straight play would be, Verdi insisted on standards at least as high, if not higher.

The people most affected by this, of course, were the singers. They were required to interpret their characters in light of the overall dramatic context; they were required to be credible representatives of those characters, both in looks and in their acting; and they were allowed (actually, they were required) to sacrifice beautiful singing in favor of ugly or more expressive singing when it was appropriate. It was not that Verdi wanted them to be completely realistic—the closest he came to verismo was *La traviata,* and that was not very close—but he did want them to be believable, and, as we have seen, that was frequently as important a criterion in his choice of singers as their vocal and musical ability.

The twentieth century found it hard to live up to Verdi's standards. It supplied a lot of Fanny Salvini-Donatellis—fine singers who lacked dramatic credibility in the roles they assumed. So often was this the case that audiences got used to it and were prepared, as a matter of course, to suspend belief. That was opera's loss, and it was a loss of which Verdi would have been contemptuous.

Performing Wagner was, of course, a different matter—because it really did need a different kind of singer, and one that had not really existed before Wagner's own time.

CHAPTER NINE

Heroic Singing

The Wagnerian Soprano

"Dear child, you have a voice like a house," said Joseph Haydn.[1] The compliment (for such it was intended to be) was addressed to Anna Milder, a pupil of Salieri's who had become a sensation at the Theater an der Wien in 1803, when she was only seventeen. Already the voice was powerful and very dramatic, and young Anna, though she was never to be a particularly good actress, was a striking and handsome woman. Two years later, when it was suggested she should create the title role in *Fidelio*, Salieri would have had no difficulty reassuring Beethoven that she was ideal for the part—that rare singer who could look like the boy Fidelio while being equally convincing as the wife Leonore, and whose voice was big enough, and exciting enough, to partner with Beethoven's large orchestra in the great set pieces of the opera.

In fact, Milder "created" Fidelio three times—first, in the three-act version of 1805, which was given three performances in front of an audience divided almost equally between frightened Viennese patrons and French soldiers who had swept triumphantly into Vienna the previous week; then in a new two-act version the following year, again performed only three times before Beethoven fell out with the impresario and withdrew his score; and finally, in 1814, in another revised version, staged to celebrate the Congress of Vienna. The Congress, whose modest agenda was to plan the post-Napoleonic world, brought all the leaders of Europe to Vienna. Most of them visited the Kärntnertortheater at least once, and Milder quickly became the toast of Vienna.

Fidelio so clearly mirrored the aspirations of the moment—liberation, freedom from tyranny, a new age of hope and optimism—that no one, not even Napoleon himself, had ever personified a historical moment as clearly as Fidelio, in the person of Anna Milder, did in Vienna in the summer of 1814. For her part, she was twenty-nine years old, now appearing under her married name of Pauline Anna Milder-Hauptmann, and secure in the esteem of the world's greatest living composer (Beethoven ungallantly observed of her marriage to the jeweler Hauptmann, which was not a success and did not last long, that it mattered little since he, Beethoven, would remain her *hauptmann*, or "head man").[2] She had started out as a lyric soprano in the eighteenth-century tradition—a fine interpreter of Gluck's Alceste, Iphigénie, and Armide—but her transition to dramatic soprano can be traced by the roles she increasingly took on. Cherubini, the most popular composer in Europe, invited her to sing Médée at the Viennese premiere, and later composed the title role in *Faniska* for her. Faniska was a very dramatic part and very similar to Fidelio. Both were the heroines of what were called "rescue operas"—stories about men and women who were saved from death in the nick of time; the template had been provided by Henri-Montan Berton's hugely popular *Les rigueurs du cloître* in 1790, in which a young nun was saved from entombment at the hands of a corrupt mother superior. Beethoven was one of Cherubini's many admirers in Vienna (Weber was another), and it was partly under his influence that the vocal line of Leonore evolved from lyric soprano to dramatic soprano in the nine years between the first and last versions of *Fidelio*.

Evolving with the role, Milder thus became the model for a new type of singer—a German soprano who might best be described as lyric-dramatic, and who was well on the way to becoming the heroic soprano for whom Richard Wagner would call in the not too distant future.

There had been great German singers before, but not many of them, and even fewer who got to sing regularly in German opera (as opposed to Italian opera translated into German). The German-speaking states had always accepted that opera was basically an Italian art form: the greatest German composers—Handel, Hasse, Gluck, Mozart—wrote mainly in Italian, and the princely courts rarely performed in any language other than Italian. It was true that German opera did exist, but it was comparatively rare in Germany itself and had almost no currency outside the German-speaking world.

If one leaves aside the almost accidental incidence of German opera represented by Heinrich Schütz in the 1620s and Agostino Steffani in the 1680s and 1690s, then there had been two really notable developments. The first was the sixty-year existence of the Theater auf dem Gänsemarkt in Hamburg between 1678 and 1738. The Goose Market had much in common with the public theaters that had flourished in Venice a few years earlier: it was commercial, dependent on box office, and it performed always in the vernacular—German. For almost forty years, Reinhard Keiser presided over it, writing more than a hundred operas in German. It was where Handel got his start (as a violinist), and it was where he wrote his first four operas, all in German. It was where, in the 1720s, Handel's friend Georg Philipp Telemann pioneered a form of opera buffa (even before the Italians had gotten around to inventing it) that became the peculiarly German institution of Singspiel. That was the second notable development.

The "song-play," with musical numbers separated by spoken dialogue, was clearly related to French opéra comique and English ballad opera, and yet it was uniquely German and ideally suited to the bands of traveling players that proliferated in northern Europe in the eighteenth century. On the few occasions that Mozart wrote German opera at the end of the century, as he did with *Die Entführung aus dem Serail* and *Die Zauberflöte,* it was in the style of Singspiel, and the same was true of Beethoven's *Fidelio,* though Mozart and Beethoven wrote music so elevated that it is hard to compare their works with the run-of-the-mill *Singspiele* that were routinely performed in every town and village of the German principalities.

The traveling troupes that performed most of these Singspiele invariably consisted of actors who could sing rather than exceptional singers. At the other end of the scale, the princely courts, performing a strict diet of Italian opera, preferred to hire singers from Italy. Not surprisingly then, there were few German singers of the first rank. What is even more surprising, perhaps, is that the few who did manage to break through the language and culture barriers to establish themselves as international celebrities generally managed to do so without studying in Italy. Regina Mingotti, who was at least half German, received most of her training in Silesia before becoming a pupil of Porpora's in Dresden; Madame Mara, perhaps the greatest German singer of the eighteenth century, did not visit Italy at all until she was twenty years into her career and at the height of her fame, yet she almost always sang in Italian; Antonia Bernasconi, one of Gluck's favorite singers, for whom Mozart wrote Aspasia in *Mitridate,* was born Antonia Wagele in Stuttgart and owed her training to an Italian stepfather (whose name she took); and Caterina Cavalieri, the most illustrious of Mozart's singers, seems never to have left Austria in her entire life.

Anna Milder was different. As the daughter of an Austrian diplomat, she was born in Constantinople and was well traveled. It was Schikaneder, once Mozart's partner in *Die Zauberflöte,* who first noticed her and sent her to Salieri, and it was Salieri who introduced her first to opera and then to Beethoven. If she was fortunate to be in the right place at the right time, then it was also true that she developed into a very fine vocalist—fine enough for Schubert to compose one of his loveliest songs for her, *Der Hirt auf dem Felsen.*

After the Congress of Vienna, Milder sang for another two decades, into her fifties, alternating the lyric roles of the previous century with the much more dramatic roles that were being written around her, and some-times for her. The itinerant composer Luigi Spontini (now based in Berlin and writing in German) cast her as Statira in the Berlin premiere of *Olimpie,* and he subsequently wrote the role of Irmengard for her in *Agnes von Hohenstaufen* (1829). *Agnes,* coming after Weber's *Euryanthe* (1823) and be-fore Wagner's *Rienzi* (1842)—all stories of medieval pageantry set to grand and dramatic music—confirmed the Romantic course of German opera.

There was another development taking place alongside this Romanti-cism, and it could be heard and seen at the Schauspielhaus in Berlin just a few weeks after the premiere of *Olimpie*—in fact, it very quickly wiped all mem-ory of *Olimpie* from the minds of German operagoers. *Der Freischütz* was undoubtedly Romantic, but it was also the most articulate statement Weber would ever make of his ideal of opera—a combination of music, drama, and the visual aspects of theater in a unified work of art (what Wagner would later call a *Gesamtkunstwerk*). Weber was not the only composer pursuing this ideal. In various degrees, E. T. A. Hoffmann, Ludwig Spohr, and Heinrich Marschner were also involved, but it was *Der Freischütz* that made the deepest and most lasting impression on the German consciousness. It also began to define the types of singers that would be needed for this new German enterprise.

Of all the sopranos who sang Agathe in *Der Freischütz* in the years following its premiere in 1821, none was more greatly admired than Wilhelmine Schröder-Devrient. Weber thought the world of her, Wagner virtually worshiped her, and Beethoven would certainly have joined her band of admirers had his deafness not prevented him from hearing her properly when she stepped into Anna Milder's shoes in Vienna to sing Fidelio in 1822. She was still only eighteen, but already two years into a professional career that had begun with Pamina in *Die Zauberflöte,* quickly followed by Agathe in performances conducted by Weber himself. By the time Wagner got to hear her in 1829 she was a mature twenty-five-year-old (while he was an extraordinarily confident, not to say arrogant, sixteen-year-old). Years later, writing in his autobiography, *Mein Leben* (My Life), Wagner recalled the impression she had made on him: "When I review my entire life I can discover hardly another occurrence which affected me so profoundly. Whoever remembers that remarkable woman at that stage of her career will testify to the almost demoniacal warmth radiated by the human-ecstatic achievement of this incomparable artist. After the performance, I dashed to the home of a friend of mine to write her a letter in which I solemnly stated that, as of that day, my life had acquired its meaning, and that if she was ever to hear my name mentioned as of consequence in the world of art, she should remember that on this evening she had made me what I herewith vowed to become. I dropped the letter at her hotel and dashed off into the night."[3]

Schröder-Devrient not only kept the letter, but was able to repeat it verbatim to Wagner when they worked together in Dresden in 1842.[4] By that time she had conquered Paris and London as well as the German states. Because she was so famous as Fidelio and Agathe, and because she later created three roles for Wagner, it was easy to dismiss her as just a German singer, but she was much more than that. Her great contemporaries were

Wilhelmine Schröder-Devrient (1804–1860) as Leonore in *Fidelio,* a role in which she was rehearsed by Beethoven. Wagner, for whom she created three roles in Dresden near the end of her career, thought she was the most important singer-actress of her generation. In *Über Schauspieler und Sänger,* written thirteen years after her death, he included a detailed critique of her artistry. (Lebrecht Collection.)

Pasta, Malibran, and Sontag, and she sang many of the French and Italian roles that they performed. Schröder-Devrient's Desdemona and Romeo (in the operas of Rossini and Bellini, respectively) were as highly esteemed as anyone's: she performed them at Covent Garden and the Théâtre Italien in Paris to great acclaim. Her range can be guessed at from the variety of roles she took on—Donna Anna, Amina in *La sonnambula,* Norma, even Valentine in *Les Huguenots.* Nevertheless, she clearly did not possess the facility that Sontag (another native German speaker) had in the Italian and French repertoires, nor did she command the extraordinary agility and coloratura technique of Pasta, but she was a more dramatic singer than either of them. Chopin heard her perform with Malibran at the Théâtre Italien in 1830, in what must have been a most unusual evening's entertainment: "I also heard la Schröder-Devrient, who doesn't arouse the same furore here as in Germany. She played the role of Desdemona and Madame Malibran that of Otello. La Malibran petite and the German enormous! It seemed as though the German was going to smother Otello. It was expensive to attend this performance. Twenty-four francs for all seats to see la Malibran completely black and in a role for which she is not renowned."[5]

Three years later, at Covent Garden, the roles were reversed: Malibran was in her more familiar guise as Desdemona and Schröder-Devrient was blacked up as the Moor.[6] Stealing male roles like Otello was a party game for these singers, but one that was appreciated by the audience and paid for accordingly. Malibran and Schröder-Devrient were not bosom friends, but they were clearly admiring and respectful colleagues.

The same might be said of Schröder-Devrient and Wagner when they finally worked together in 1835. It was in Magdeburg, where Wagner was music director of the opera house, and he conducted Schröder-Devrient in performances of both *I Capuleti e I Montecchi* and *Otello*. It was in the Bellini work that, as Wagner later put it, she "kindled a fresh flame in my breast."[7] Seven years later, however, when she came to Dresden to create the travesti role of Adriano Colonna in *Rienzi,* she was past her best. In his memoirs, Wagner wrote that her "maternal" stoutness was inappropriate to the portrayal of a young man, and he admitted that it "made too great a demand upon the imagination . . . Her voice, which in point of quality had never been an exceptionally good medium for song, often landed her in difficulties, and in particular she was forced, when singing, to drag the time a little all through . . . A fact which caused me even greater trouble, however, was that she did not grasp music easily, and the study of a new part involved difficulties which meant many a painful hour for the composer who had to make her master his work. Her difficulty in learning new parts, and particularly that of Adriano in *Rienzi,* entailed disappointments for her which caused me a good deal of trouble."[8]

As usual, Wagner was more concerned about the trouble to which he had been put than the trouble others might have had in grasping his requirements. Nevertheless, Schröder-Devrient's performance as Adriano was one of the principal reasons for *Rienzi*'s stunning success, despite its hugely long running time. Three months later, when *Der fliegende Holländer* was given its premiere, her performance as Senta was the only reason the opera survived its first night at all—despite the fact that she was ill, that her love life was in disarray (a not unusual circumstance for her), and that she had once again had terrible difficulties learning the music. She was back again for *Tannhäuser* two years later, this time in the somewhat smaller role of Venus. It was a role that Wagner later admitted was sketchy and underwritten (he fleshed it out considerably for the Paris performances in 1861), and Schröder-Devrient, "who could hide her age and matronly appearance no longer,"[9] was able to do very little with it. In any case, the failure of *Tannhäuser* in 1845 had much more to do with the inadequacies of Joseph Tichatschek, the vain and pompous popinjay who had been so successful in the silver armor of Rienzi but never seemed to have any idea what *Tannhäuser* was about.

Most critics agreed that there were deficiencies in Schröder-Devrient's voice, and some put them down to a lack of proper training. Certainly, she started very early (a professional debut at sixteen), yet her father, Friedrich Schröder, was a good singer—the first German Don Giovanni—and her early mentors, of whom Weber was one, do not appear to have detected problems. A much more likely cause of the alleged deficiencies was Schröder-Devrient's own lack of interest in the bel canto ideals of her contemporaries. Hearing her in London, Chorley noted "a strong soprano . . . with an inherent expressiveness of tone," but he also remarked that "her tones were delivered without any care, save to give them due force."[10] She was, above all, a dramatic singer. Many people, including Berlioz, thought her acting was exaggerated, her declamation too emphatic, her dramatic style generally inclined to go over the top—not in the undisciplined way of Malibran, but in a carefully rehearsed way that was calculated to affect the audience.[11] And that was clearly what it did, Berlioz notwithstanding. Young Wagner was quite bowled over by it, as was almost anyone who ever saw her as Fidelio or Agathe.

In 1875, fifteen years after her death, Wagner acknowledged his debt to her in the construction of a frieze that was attached to the facade of Haus Wahnfried, the home he built for himself in Bayreuth. It depicted the figures of Tragedy, Ancient Myth, and Music, and the features of the figures were clearly modeled on those of the most important people in his life—Music on his second wife, Cosima; Ancient Myth on the great tenor who created Tristan, Ludwig Schnorr von Carolsfeld; and Tragedy on Wilhelmine Schröder-Devrient, still remembered with gratitude and affection.

One of the people who would have passed beneath that frieze soon after its construction, and who would instantly have recognized the features of Schröder-Devrient, was Johanna Wagner, the composer's niece. Johanna made her first visit to Bayreuth in 1872, on the day Wagner laid the corner-stone of his new Festspielhaus. That afternoon, in the old baroque opera house that had stood in Bayreuth since 1748, she sang the solo alto part in Beethoven's Ninth Symphony, conducted by Wagner. She no longer pos-sessed a fine voice, but Wagner, for once in his life, was looking backward as well as forward on that day, and Johanna represented an important part of the past. Ironically, it had been jealousy of her that eventually caused Schröder-Devrient to fall out with Wagner, but Johanna was there in 1872 (and would be there again in 1876 to sing small parts in the first complete production of *The Ring*) for a much more positive reason—because she, more than any of the commonly cited mistresses and muses in Wagner's life, had been the inspiration for three of his greatest creations—Elisabeth in *Tannhäuser*, Elsa in *Lohengrin*, and Brünnhilde in *Die Walküre*.[12] Elisabeth was the only one she created, but Wagner never forgot the eighteen-year-old girl she then was, and she seems to have remained an ideal for him long thereafter. "The youthful appearance of my niece [in *Tannhäuser*]," he wrote, "her tall and slender form, the decidedly German cast of her features, as well as the incomparable beauty of her voice, with its expression of almost child-like innocence, helped her to gain the hearts of the audience, even though her talent was more theatrical than dramatic."[13]

Not surprisingly, this image of Johanna was still in Wagner's mind in the months immediately following the premiere of *Tannhäuser* when he was writing *Lohengrin*—we can clearly see it in the character and music of Elsa. What is much more surprising is that it should still have been there twelve years later, when he completed *Die Walküre* in Zurich and tried to lure her away from Berlin to create Brünnhilde.

Johanna was described as Wagner's niece, but she was actually the adopted daughter of his elder brother Albert, and not therefore a blood re-

Johanna Wagner (1826–1894) created Elisabeth in *Tannhäuser* as a nineteen-year-old, sang in the first complete production of *The Ring* as a fifty-year-old, and was, in between, Wagner's model for Brünnhilde, though she never sang the role. (Lebrecht Collection.)

lation. Wagner first heard her sing in 1842, when she was fifteen, on a visit to his brother in Halle. He was struck by Johanna's personality and "child-like nature," and the "extraordinarily beautiful quality" of her voice.[14] Two years later, Wagner persuaded Albert to let her become a member of his Dresden company, alongside Schröder-Devrient. She made her debut as Agathe in 1844 and created Elisabeth the following year. She was still not twenty. She had the good sense to know that she had a lot of learning still to do, and that Paris was the best place to do it. She spent three years there as a pupil of Manuel García the younger and his sister, Pauline Viardot. By the time she returned to Germany—first to Hamburg and then to Berlin, where she was prima donna at the Hofoper right through the 1850s—she commanded a very powerful voice with a notably wide range. She seems to have retained the brightness and clarity of her top notes, but most of her roles were in the lower-lying territories of what might be called the Malibran/Viardot repertory—Rossini's Tancredi, Donizetti's Lucrezia Borgia, and Bellini's Romeo (the three roles with which she scored a huge success in London in 1856), together with Meyerbeer's Fidès. She continued to sing Elisabeth, and eventually the *Lohengrin* Ortrud as well, but Wagner's confidence in her was somewhat undermined by family politics and by her determination to go her own way without regard to his wishes and interests. In 1854, she annoyed him considerably by taking part in the premiere of Heinrich Dorn's *Die Nibelungen*—for by that time Wagner had completed the texts of the four operas that would comprise his own cycle, *Der Ring des Nibelungen*, and was beginning to write the music: "When I attempted to turn Brunhilda's first address to Siegfried into song my courage failed me completely, for I could not help asking myself if the singer had yet been born who was capable of vitalizing this heroic female figure. The idea of my niece Johanna occurred to me, whom, as a matter of fact, I had already destined for this role when I was still in Dresden on account of her personal charms. She had now entered upon the career of prima donna in Hamburg but, judging from all the reports I had received, and especially from the attitude towards me she openly adopted in her letters to her family, I could only conclude that my modest hopes of enlisting her talents on my behalf were doomed to disappointment."[15]

Nevertheless, the idealized image of Johanna remained obstinately in his memory, and he continued to hope she might come to Switzerland to create the Brünnhilde of *Die Walküre* (Wagner had been banned from setting foot in the German states as a result of his participation in the 1849 Dresden uprising: he was not allowed to visit any of them until 1860, and he could not return to Saxony until the amnesty of 1862). In the end, however, the problem solved itself. In 1861, Johanna lost her voice—certainly, it was no longer in a condition that enabled her to continue as prima donna in Berlin. Instead, she became a "straight" actress, and a very successful one, and hardly sang at all until her fiftieth year, 1876, when her uncle, remembering what she had once meant to him as a muse and inspiration, asked her to sing two quite small but important roles in the first complete production of *The Ring* at Bayreuth—the Valkyrie Schwertleite and the First Norn.

There were, perhaps, two Johanna Wagners. One was the virginal teen-age singer Wagner first met in Halle and brought to Dresden to be his Elisabeth. She was beautiful, gifted, a natural actress, though seriously lacking in vocal training—but at least she was *real*. The other was an idealized version of this young woman that Wagner carried around with him ever after and came to equate with Brünnhilde. This Johanna was certainly beautiful and gifted, and innocent and virginal too, but she was also an immensely powerful singer with rock-solid technique, unbelievable stamina, and a gift for sustained melodic utterance. Unfortunately, this Johanna did not actually exist.

So he wrote for a mythical singer who would have to be invented if the great operas of his maturity—in particular *Tristan und Isolde* and *The Ring*—were ever to be performed in the way he intended them to be.

It is unlikely Wagner ever heard any of the great roles of those operas performed as he intended, but there is good reason to believe that the singers of his own time may have come closer to his ideal than any singers since. He was certainly very pleased with Ludwig Schnorr von Carolsfeld's Tristan at the premiere of that work in 1865, and he once said that an 1881 performance of *Tannhäuser* (in Italian) in Rome had included a rendering of Wolfram by the baritone Mattia Battistini that was "sung as he had only dreamed it could be."[16] So far as the women were concerned, the nearest he got to his ideal was the young Lilli Lehmann, who was one of Johanna Wagner's partners among the Valkyries in the Bayreuth *Ring* of 1876, as well as a Rhinemaiden and the Woodbird: Wagner knew instinctively that she would later become a great Brünnhilde and Isolde, and he was right, though he did not live to see it.

The twentieth century so brutalized Wagnerian singing that it is hard for us to comprehend what Wagner really had in mind. In any comparison of the two giants of nineteenth-century European opera, Verdi and Wagner, Verdi is generally assumed to be the one who inherited the bel canto tradition, while Wagner is accused of having reacted against it to the extent of writing a species of ugly *Sprechstimme* (spoken song). In fact, Wagner was obsessed with bel canto; he believed that legato was an essential element in the performance of all his vocal music (which is why he so loved Battistini's performance of Wolfram), and he would have been horrified by the "Bayreuth bark" that developed in the years after his death, and for which his widow must bear the responsibility. Verdi was certainly appreciative of bel canto too, but he thought Italian opera had taken it much too far and sacrificed the dramatic and theatrical side of the art form in the process: he spent much of his time searching for singers who were prepared to violate the rules of bel canto in order to achieve dramatic effect.

Bel canto and legato were legitimate ambitions for Wagner, but many people thought they were often rendered impossible by the music he wrote and the demands he placed on his singers. On the one hand, there was the orchestra, which was always Wagner's principal narrator. It was as large as any known symphonic force and it frequently became a protagonist in the drama, sometimes in direct opposition to the singers. It was hard to think of it as an accompanist. On the other hand, there was the declamatory nature of the singers' roles—a continuous dialogue, normally one on one, which sometimes involved individual singers for thirty or forty minutes at a time. There were virtually no pauses for arias or set pieces: the dialectic never ceased.

But Wagner did not expect the singers simply to declaim their lines in competition with the orchestra. On the contrary, he claimed to have set the words in continuous melody—not to big tunes you could hum along with, but according to the strictest definition of melody (that is, successions of notes that had organized and recognizable shapes). Tunes are scarce in Wagner, but melody is almost always present. As early as 1850, he explained his system in a letter to Liszt: "I have been so intent upon weighing and indicating the verbal emphases of speech, that the singers need only sing the notes, exactly according to their value in the given tempo, in order to get precisely by that means the declamatory expression." [17]

In his heart of hearts, Wagner knew it was not that simple. As a composer, he could "hear" what he put down on paper, but as an impresario (which is what he increasingly became as he searched for ways to get his operas performed) he knew that there were very few singers capable of re-producing it. The problem came into the open with *Tristan und Isolde,* and it became manifest with *The Ring.*

There were times when Wagner himself wondered if the roles he had written for Tristan and Isolde were capable of being sung. It was not so much the tenor role that he worried about, since he had known for some time that there was a German tenor, Ludwig Schnorr von Carolsfeld, who would be capable of singing it—and to make sure, he traveled to Karlsruhe in 1862 to hear him sing Lohengrin. The only doubt about Schnorr was his health, which, for so large a man, was uncharacteristically delicate. About his voice there could be no possible doubt, and Wagner knew immediately that he would be able to sing Tristan exactly as he had written it. The fact that he turned out also to be a hugely intelligent man, and a disciple of Wagner's to boot, added to the certainty. But who could be his Isolde? Up to that time, Pauline Viardot was the only professional singer who had sung any part of the role, and that had been in a private performance of act two in 1860: Viardot, who was sight-reading, and Wagner had divided the roles between them, with Karl Klindworth, the great German pianist, as accom-panist. There was an audience of two, one of whom was Berlioz, who ap-parently was so taken aback by Wagner's singing that at the end he was only able to compliment him on the *chaleur* (heat, passion) of his delivery. Wagner never knew whether the compliment was real or backhanded.[18]

The soprano Wagner heard in the Karlsruhe *Lohengrin* was Schnorr's newly wedded wife, Malvina. She was eleven years older than Schnorr, and she would ultimately outlive him by almost forty years. As Malvina Garri-gues, she had moved from her home in Denmark to become a pupil of Man-uel García the younger in Paris (five years before Johanna Wagner had gone to García, and about the time Jenny Lind was consulting him). For thir-teen years, she sang in German theaters as a well-respected soprano with a powerful voice and ringing tone—until, in 1854, she and the eighteen-year-old Schnorr arrived in Karlsruhe at more or less the same time. It was Mal-vina's partnership with the young Schnorr that raised her above the ordinary and that led to the two of them being lured to Dresden in 1860 (the Karlsruhe

Lohengrin that Wagner saw in 1862 was a long-promised guest appearance in the city that had made them famous).

Wagner's attention in Karlsruhe had been directed principally toward Schnorr, with whom he had a long nocturnal conversation about the role of Tristan. As for Malvina, he had recognized in her "a great and well-developed theatrical talent," though he made no comment on her voice.[19] Nevertheless, it seems likely that Wagner persuaded the Schnorrs, there and then, that they should create Tristan and Isolde. Shortly afterward, when they visited him in Biebrich, they apparently sang through the opera in the presence of Wagner, Hans von Bülow (who would eventually conduct the premiere), and Bülow's young wife, Cosima (Liszt's illegitimate daughter and Wagner's future mistress and wife). Wagner's only written comment on the Schnorrs' performance was that he found "both were a good deal lacking in clearness of enunciation."[20]

But Karlsruhe was not willing to stage *Tristan,* even if Dresden could once again be persuaded to lend the Schnorrs, and Dresden, from which Wagner had been expelled in 1849, was clearly not an option. So Wagner had to contemplate the possibility of *Tristan* taking place without the Schnorrs. Vienna was the only city that appeared to be interested.

The Vienna Hofoper had no male singer to compare with Schnorr. The best it could offer was Aloys Ander, a lyric tenor from Bohemia who specialized in the operas Vienna was importing from Paris almost as fast as they were written. He sang John of Leyden in *Le prophète,* Raul in *Les Huguenots,* and even the newly minted title role of *Faust.* Wagner had heard him sing Lohengrin in Vienna in 1861 (it was, in fact, the first time Wagner had ever heard his opera in performance: when it had been given its premiere in Weimar in 1850 he had already been placed on the wanted lists of all the German states, and no other opportunity had ever presented itself). He had found Ander's performance quite pleasing—but that was before he heard Schnorr.

Even more pleasing was Vienna's Elsa in that same production. She was Louise Dustmann-Meyer, a fine dramatic soprano with the usual wide-ranging repertory expected of a leading prima donna—she sang Norma,

Marguerite, the Queen of the Night, and Amelia in Verdi's *Un ballo in maschera*; she sang Gluck, Donizetti, Meyerbeer, and Weber; and she had quickly become Vienna's leading female Wagnerian as Senta and Elisabeth in addition to Elsa (she would later add Ortrud and Eva). Wagner clearly saw her as a viable candidate for Isolde, and when negotiations with Karlsruhe broke down he began to teach the title roles to her and Ander.

For a time, it seemed that the premiere of *Tristan* really might take place in Vienna in 1863. Wagner's life at this stage was more frenetic than usual—he was dashing around Europe arranging concerts of his works in increasingly desperate attempts to pay off his debtors—but when he called in at Vienna he found that rehearsals were going well: "I was astonished at the really passable performance of the tenor, while from Frau Dustmann I could not withhold my sincerest congratulations on her admirable execution of her difficult part."[21] Beneath the surface, however, things were going wrong, and it was largely because of Wagner's own arrogance and tactlessness. First, Frau Dustmann was disturbed by what appeared to be an inappropriate relationship between Wagner and her sister, the actress Friederike Meyer (for once in his life, Wagner was innocent). Then Dr. Eduard Hanslick, the powerful critic of *Die Presse,* whose opinions were of great importance to the Hofoper and who appeared to have been reconciled to Wagner in a meeting carefully choreographed by Frau Dustmann, was gratuitously insulted when he was invited to a reading of the recently completed poem of *Die Meistersinger.* In front of some of Vienna's most influential citizens, he heard himself caricatured as the curmudgeonly Beckmesser—and just in case there could be any doubt, the character, at that stage, was called Veit Hanslich (only later did he become Beckmesser).

The final straw, however, was not of Wagner's making. Ander had reported severe vocal problems the previous year, but now he completely lost his voice. Both rehearsals and production plans were aborted. The rumor mill quickly confirmed what the anti-Wagner camp had forecast all along—that the role of Tristan simply could not be undertaken without risking severe damage to the voice. By implication, the same applied to Isolde. In fact, it turned out that Ander's problems were not just vocal: the following year, shortly after a performance of Arnold in Rossini's *Guillaume Tell,* he collapsed and died. As for Louise Dustmann-Meyer, although she was the first to learn the role, she never did sing Isolde on the stage.

In the meantime, Ludwig, the teenage King of Bavaria, had come to Wagner's rescue, and *Tristan* was performed in Munich in the early summer of 1865. Throughout the dreamlike year since Ludwig's cabinet secretary, Franz Seraph von Pfistermeister, had sought Wagner out in Stuttgart and given him the news that Ludwig wished to relieve him of all "material cares," Wagner had known that *Tristan* was finally to be performed and he had been able to plan accordingly. It was always understood that Schnorr would sing Tristan, and his name was entered beside the opera in the *Program for the King* that Wagner presented less than a month after arriving in Munich. The program set out an eight-year schedule during which all Wagner's new works, including *Tristan, Die Meistersinger, The Ring,* and *Parsifal* (and a revised version of *Tannhäuser*) would be performed. There would also be a staging of the one that eventually got away — *Die Sieger* (The Victors), a Buddhist drama based, like *Tristan,* on themes of renunciation and redemption.[22] What was not stated was who would sing Isolde.

But Wagner had made up his mind. Only three weeks after his arrival in Munich, on May 24, 1864, he wrote to Therese Tietjens offering her the role and promising that cuts could be made in it if she so desired.[23] Frau Dustmann and Frau Schnorr were suddenly thrown overboard, and only the woman who was generally thought to be the greatest living German soprano would do. Tietjens was then at the height of her powers and settled in London. Her voice, extending over three octaves, was equaled only by Patti's, and she was still, in her early thirties, a very elegant figure on stage (she later became extremely stout). But Tietjens was not interested in Isolde. Ortrud was the only Wagner role she would ever attempt, and that was shortly before the end of her abbreviated life in 1877. In 1864 she had no intention of risking her voice on such an enterprise.

So Wagner had to fall back on Plan A — Malvina Schnorr von Carolsfeld — and he was delighted with the results. She had the advantage of having been acquainted with the music for three years already, and the even greater advantage of being coached by Wagner, Bülow, and her husband throughout the long rehearsal schedule. When the day of the premiere found her hoarse and unable to sing, a three-week postponement was immediately arranged. The four performances that finally resulted were hugely gratifying to Wagner and Ludwig, and a revelation to everyone else (if not always a welcome revelation). Everyone agreed that the Schnorrs, husband and wife, were the heroes of the hour. If nothing else, they had proved that the two great roles could be sung without ill effects.

Then, three weeks later, back in Dresden, Ludwig Schnorr von Carolsfeld died — of typhus according to some reports, of rheumatic fever according to others. Inevitably, there were some who said he died of "Tristan," and they may have been more right than wrong. Schnorr was obese; he had always had delicate health; he had been worried from the beginning about the physical demands of the role. He was also highly emotional, and nothing excited him more than the music and the presence of Richard Wagner. Whatever disease it was that snared him on his return to Dresden, it seems probable that he had been drained, physically and emotionally, by the experience of *Tristan* in Munich, and had no reserves with which to fight the malady. One description called it *"Springende Gicht* [leaping gout] . . . that traveled from his knee joint to his brain."[24]

As for Malvina, Wagner had outdone himself with superlatives in Munich ("Frau Schnorr is perfect; no living artist of her sex may in any way be placed beside her," and "From her, one will be able to learn what a tragedienne is!"), and he fully intended to remain close to her. He understood her determination not to sing in public after her husband's death, but he persuaded Ludwig to give her a pension and he encouraged her to move to Munich to begin teaching a new generation of Wagnerian singers. Unfortunately, Malvina wanted more than that. She wanted to be Cosima—not as mistress of the bed, but as mistress of all other parts of Wagner's life. She descended on Triebschen, the house on Lake Lucerne to which Wagner and Cosima had escaped when things got too hot for them in Munich, and brought with her a singing pupil named Isidore von Reutter. Reutter, it transpired, was more than a singing pupil: she was also a medium. She convinced Malvina (without much difficulty) that her late husband's spirit urgently recommended that Malvina immediately assume the roles of principal adviser and chief of staff to the great composer—and, by the way, the spirit also recommended that Wagner should be required to introduce his new adviser's medium to King Ludwig with a view to those two soul mates being wed. Wagner's failure to adhere to this program, or any part of it, resulted in Malvina telling the king what everyone else already knew, that Wagner was having it away with Bülow's wife.[25]

Bülow, however, continued to worship at the shrine. He not only publicly and legally accepted paternity of the two daughters Cosima bore to Wagner, he continued to conduct the composer's music in Munich with great faithfulness. The breaking point came in June 1869, when he learned that Cosima had given birth to a son, Siegfried, after months of denying to Bülow that she was pregnant at all. The discovery coincided with the staging of the first revival of *Tristan und Isolde,* once again under Bülow's direction but this time without any involvement from Wagner, who had opposed the revival. Musically and artistically, the performances were a triumph, but for Bülow they were, as he wrote in a bitter letter to Cosima, "le coup de grâce."[26] As soon as they were over, he resigned and left Munich.

The question mark over the new *Tristan* had been who would take the place of the Schnorrs. It turned out to be another husband and wife team, Heinrich and Therese Vogl. They were both twenty-four when they first assumed the roles in 1869, and for the best part of a decade they would have a virtual lock on the opera—in fact, Therese Vogl was the only person who sang Isolde in Germany during that time. Partly because they were in the right place at the right time (the Munich Hofoper at the time when Wagner's mature operas were first being performed) and partly because they were blessed with magnificent and powerful voices, they, along with the bass Franz Betz, became the leading creators and interpreters of Wagner's music. Heinrich Vogl created Loge and Siegmund; he later sang both Tristan and Parsifal at Bayreuth; and he was a famous Siegfried in New York, London, and many European cities. Therese's record was almost as impressive: she created Sieglinde in Munich in 1870 (and would have sung it again at Bayreuth in 1876 had she not become pregnant), and she quickly became one of the leading Brünnhildes in Europe. Unlike most of her colleagues, she was an accomplished horsewoman and was able to mount Grane, Brünnhilde's horse, and ride him into the flames at the end of *Götterdämmerung* ("circus tricks," Cosima disparagingly called it in a conversation with Lilli Lehmann).[27] Both Vogls were renowned for their stamina—Heinrich was willing to sing Loge, Siegmund, and the two Siegfrieds on successive days in *Ring* cycles—and it was their example, probably more than anyone else's, that convinced the opera profession that Wagner's music could be sung without risking immediate death. When Heinrich died in 1900, aged only fifty-five, it was, luckily, four days after singing Leoncavallo's Canio, not a Wagner role. Therese lived to be a very respectable seventy-three.

The Schnorrs undoubtedly had voices of the type Wagner was writing for, but *Tristan* was the only one of Wagner's mature operas they ever performed, and that only four times. So it is from the Vogls that we first get an understanding of what Wagner's new music was doing to the singing profession in Germany.

It was forcing the abandonment of a tradition that had, rather remarkably, remained supreme throughout the first two-thirds of the nineteenth century—the vocal tradition of the Italian school. There may have been variations of style and form, but the way opera singers sang, regardless of what country they came from, was Italianate. That had been the rule ever since French opera had gotten over its differences and joined up with the rest of Europe at the beginning of the century. Certainly, it was the style of all the greatest singers of the 1860s—of the American Patti, the German Tietjens, the Swede Nilsson, and the Belgian Marie Sasse—just as it had been the style of their great predecessors, Colbran, Pasta, Malibran, Sontag, Falcon, and Viardot. Even a singer as undeniably German as Wilhelmine Schröder-Devrient had been trained in the Italian style and unfailingly performed in it.

What this style consisted of, first and foremost, was "beautiful singing," bel canto. The principal components of bel canto were purity of tone, legato phrasing (in which the notes were "bound together" in smooth portamento delivery, in one breath), and the ability to embellish and ornament the music. The end result was lyrical rather than declamatory, with the emphasis on vowel sounds rather than consonants. It required consummate technique and disciplined breath control; it also required an intimate knowledge of *music*.

There is absolutely no doubt that Wagner intended his music to be performed in this way, and it very often was in his lifetime, but he nevertheless put up barriers that many singers found insuperable. The most obvious was the size of the orchestra, though it was not until after Wagner's death in 1883 that conductors (with the honorable exception of those, like Richter, Seidl, and Fischer, who had been trained at Bayreuth under Wagner) allowed orchestras to get out of control. The test of this was simple: Wagner wrote vocal parts in the same way, and for the same purpose, that he wrote instrumental parts—the voices were intended to be part of an overall musical tapestry that narrated the story and commented on the action. If the voices could not be heard—just as if individual instruments could not be heard—then the conductor was not doing his job.

The other substantial problem for singers was the sheer weight of words, and the importance of them. A Wagnerian opera was a Gesamstkunstwerk, an "integrated work of art," symphonic in structure, in which set pieces were rare and lines and phrases were almost never repeated, as they so often were in the Italian architecture of arias, duets, and choruses. Moreover, Wagner wrote in German, with its guttural sound patterns: it was frankly easier for singers to get across the words by emphasizing consonants rather than vowel sounds. What this added up to was a declamatory style rather than the traditional lyric Italian style. And in time, though not until after Wagner's death, it led to one of the most dreadful developments in the history of opera, "the Bayreuth bark." This was the substitution of *Sprechgesang,* or Sprechstimme, for Wagner's beloved legato, and the guilty ones were Cosima Wagner (because she should have known better) and Julius Kniese, the chorus master at Bayreuth, who had far more influence than was good for the institution. Early recordings made by singers trained by Wagner himself (Lilli Lehmann, of course, but also Marianne Brandt, the first Kundry, and Hermann Winkelmann, the first Parsifal) show that they knew better: they retained the legato style and the essentially musical approach to his operas. Even while the "bark" was being encouraged at Bayreuth, most of the really outstanding performances of Wagner's operas were being given outside Germany (and sometimes not in the German language at all) by great Italian stylists like Jean de Reszke, Olive Fremstad, and Clarence Whitehill.[28]

The Bayreuth bark and the overzealous orchestra were still thirty years in the future when Heinrich and Therese Vogl began to confront the problems of *Tristan* and *The Ring,* but they still had to deal with a very large orchestral sound and the absolute requirement that the words be heard. On the one hand, they were expected to sing in the Italian legato style, which was what they had been taught; on the other hand, there was a premium on declamation. The via media between these often conflicting requirements was a clarion delivery that was musical, yet came clearly through the orchestra, with tone as pure as any instrument, and that had sufficient reserves of strength and brilliance to rise to thrilling climaxes. It was often lyrical, almost always dramatic, and the word that was coined for it was *helden* (heroic). Such a voice was rarely necessary in the French or Italian repertories, but for Wagnerian singers, both male and female, it was essential. It was the form and sound that the Schnorrs had pioneered and that the Vogls, still in their mid-twenties, adopted—an automatic response, maybe, to vocal requirements that had no precedent in the story of opera. The style obviously boasted ancestry within the Italian tradition, but it was recognizably different—the first of what would, very soon, become a number of distinctively national vocal styles.

It was Wagner's great good fortune that the singers and musicians of what was formally known as the *Hof- und Nationaltheater* in Munich were so outstanding in the 1860s and 1870s. The man responsible was Karl von Perfall, intendant of the royal theaters, who was greatly abused by Wagner yet remained a fervent champion of his operas and later persuaded King Ludwig to bail out Bayreuth when it looked as though Wagner had finally committed financial suicide. It was Perfall who saw to it that the extraordinary resources needed to stage the operas in Munich were made available—from carpenters and scene builders to singers and orchestral players (players like Franz

Strauss, the first horn player, who abominated Wagner and derided his writing for the horn, yet played his music like a god—and whose son Richard was born the year before the *Tristan* premiere).

In addition to the Vogls, the company included August Kindermann, who was over fifty when he created Wotan in *Das Rheingold* and *Die Walküre* in Munich (and would be sixty-five when he created Titurel at Bayreuth in 1882), and two very fine sopranos, Mathilde Mallinger and Sophie Stehle. Perfall was also able to obtain the services of other singers when necessary, including Franz Betz, who was recruited from Berlin to create the huge role of Hans Sachs.

Notwithstanding all that was to happen at Bayreuth, Wagner and Cosima had little doubt that the greatest triumph of Wagner's career was the premiere of *Die Meistersinger* at Munich in 1868. The undisguised nationalism of the opera, with its glorification of *die heil'ge deutsche Kunst* (holy German art), coincided with the crescendo of chauvinism that was to culminate less than two years later in the Prussian invasion of France and the proclamation of the German Reich at Versailles. Not even Bismarck could have written a better propaganda document for the unification of the German states than *Die Meistersinger*. This was the atmosphere in which the nervous citizens of the Wittelsbach kingdom of Bavaria (nervous of being gobbled up by Bismarck's Prussia in the process of unification) hailed Wagner as the poet laureate of die heil'ge deutsche Kunst—the Hans Sachs of their own time. Along with Perfall's theater and its staff, the heroes were Betz as Sachs and Mathilde Mallinger as Eva. She was a twenty-one-year-old Croatian singer who had come to Munich from Zagreb, via Prague and Vienna. Her debut role in Munich, at nineteen, had been Norma! She had already sung Elsa, and now she created the most sympathetic and appealing of all Wagner's womenfolk. Her voice was neither large nor heroic—essentially, she was a lyric soprano—but her technique was such that she regularly sang heavy roles such as Fidelio and Valentine without any appearance of strain. In 1868, moreover, she was exceptionally slender and very pretty. King Ludwig ordered a bust of her.

The year after *Meistersinger*, Mallinger left Munich and moved to Berlin, where she sang alongside her Sachs, Franz Betz, for a dozen years. However unfairly, she was best remembered in Berlin as the woman who saw off Pauline Lucca. Lucca, an Austrian soprano, was six years older than Mallinger and had been singing in Berlin since 1861. She was very well established there, not only as an outstanding singer, which she undoubtedly was, but as a somewhat controversial ornament of the social scene: she was said to be "romantically linked" to the kaiser. She had been a protégée of Meyerbeer's and had quickly become an international star—she was particularly popular in London and St. Petersburg—and having a rival appear on her home turf was the last thing she would have expected in 1869. Inevitably, Berliners took sides, and the rivalry culminated in a very nasty display of booing during a performance of Mozart's *Figaro* in 1872. Mallinger and Lucca were both onstage, as the Countess and Cherubino respectively, but it was Lucca who was booed. She promptly broke her contract in Berlin and went to New York, where she sang at the Academy of Music for two years before resuming her European career, but this time from a base in Vienna.

The distinction of being the first woman to sing Brünnhilde fell to Sophie Stehle in the premiere of *Die Walküre* in Munich in 1870. The previous year she had sung Fricka in the first performance of *Das Rheingold*, and once it was established that Therese Vogl would sing Sieglinde (with her husband Heinrich as Siegmund), Stehle became the logical choice for Brünnhilde. These performances of *Rheingold* and *Walküre* were ordered by King Ludwig (and he had every right to do so since he had paid Wagner, handsomely, for the copyrights at the very beginning of their relationship), but they took place without Bülow, who had retired to lick his wounds, and without Wagner himself, who did everything in his power to have them stopped. Wagner had written *The Ring* for a theater of his own imagination, yet to be built, and he was loath to see the enterprise go off at half-cock in the confined spaces of the National Theater—or that was the reason he and Cosima later made official. In fact, Wagner had always intended that the *Ring* operas should first be showcased in Munich, if only to accustom singers and musicians to their demands, but when it was time to begin—with *Rheingold* in 1869—Wagner's relations with the city, the court, and the press were such that he could not spend more than a day or two in Munich at a time—certainly not the several weeks that would be needed to direct the production. Without Bülow, whom he himself had driven away, there was no one in whom the king, Baron Perfall, and Wagner could all have confidence. The twenty-six-year-old Hans Richter, whom Wagner sent to represent him and to conduct the performance, never had the trust of the other two parties, and proved them right when he treacherously withdrew from the production after the dress rehearsal in an effort to sabotage it.

Bayreuth historians have generally concluded that the Munich productions of *Rheingold* and *Walküre* were embarrassing failures.[29] In fact, they seem to have been quite successful. Scenically, there is much evidence to suggest that they were better, and certainly more efficient, than the Bayreuth premieres. So far as the singing was concerned, Franz Betz, motivated by Wagner, withdrew, like Richter, after the dress rehearsal, but August Kindermann, the local singer, was ready to replace him within a month. As for Brünnhilde, it was not a role that Stehle ever sang again (she retired four years later when she was only thirty-six), but she certainly sang it very creditably, no doubt aided by the efforts of Franz Wüllner, the conductor hurriedly recruited to replace Richter, who kept down the orchestral volume in the relatively small theater. Stehle was a sterling singer, already well grounded in Wagner (she had sung Senta, Elisabeth, and Elsa), and she evidently succeeded in alternating Fricka and Brünnhilde when *Rheingold* and *Walküre* were offered on successive evenings in the fall of 1870.

Thus, by the time Wagner announced that the first full cycles of *The Ring* would take place at Bayreuth in the summer of 1876, there was already a small pool of Wagnerian singers he could call upon. He quickly learned, however, that it was not going to be easy to cast *The Ring*. To begin with, he was not proposing to pay the singers or musicians—he would cover their expenses, but there would be no fees—yet he was demanding an enormous amount of their time: six weeks in the summer of 1875 for rehearsals and eight weeks more for rehearsals the next summer, followed by the three complete cycles in three consecutive weeks. In a time before summer festivals, it was customary for singers to take vacations in July and August, but they still needed the permission of their parent houses to sing elsewhere. Managements were not generally keen to release their leading singers for

Bayreuth, some of them out of antipathy for Wagner, some of them because they genuinely feared that the singers would damage their voices—or worse: Schnorr's death was too recent to have been forgotten, and things were made worse when Julius Campe died prematurely shortly after singing Beckmesser in Vienna.[30] It says much for Wagner's personal magnetism, and the singers' awareness that history was in the making, that they accepted his terms and gave up their summer holidays two years in succession. "Please note," Wagner wrote to them, "that all participants will have to give up any thought of financial gain, and indeed the will to make sacrifices should be taken for granted."[31]

Amid all the problems of designing, funding, and building the new Festspielhaus, Wagner and Cosima, who was now his wife, raced around Germany looking for singers with voices and techniques capable of meeting the demands of the many roles. They found alarmingly few, and several mistakes were made. Siegfried might have had a fine creator in Albert Niemann, the unfortunate tenor of the interrupted performances of *Tannhäuser* in Paris in 1861, but Wagner wanted him for Siegmund (he felt he was too old for Siegfried). Niemann would gladly have sung *both* roles, but Wagner decided that Siegmund and Siegfried should not be portrayed by the same singer within a single cycle. So, after two other "possibles" had fallen by the wayside, Georg Unger was "discovered" by Richter and eventually proved a great disappointment as Siegfried.

Sieglinde, on the other hand, had never seemed likely to be a problem because Therese Vogl was available, with her husband, Heinrich, repeating his Loge. But Therese got pregnant and Wagner, uncharacteristically bowing to expediency, gave the role to a young woman he believed to be a favorite of King Ludwig's. Josefine Scheffsky, it was true, had once tried to charm the king, but her efforts had only gotten her into trouble: she overcharged the royal chancery for a present and was denounced in front of the entire company of the Royal Court Opera, on Ludwig's orders. Writing of her performance at Bayreuth, Lilli Lehmann later characterized Scheffsky as "a big, strong woman with a powerful voice, but possessed of neither poetry nor the intelligence to express in the very least what, as a matter of fact, she did not even feel, not to mention the inadequacy of her technique."[32]

Of all the female roles in *The Ring*, Brünnhilde is clearly the biggest and the most important. Sophie Stehle, the Munich Brünnhilde, was now retired, and it seemed logical that Therese Vogl, the reigning Isolde, would be promoted to that role. Wagner thought otherwise—and he may have been right, because, when Therese Vogl did get to sing Brünnhilde for Angelo Neumann's touring company, she was never very highly esteemed in the role. Instead, Brünnhilde went to an Austrian soprano who was virtually unknown outside Vienna. Amalie Materna was thirty-two years old, a matronly looking woman with a very powerful voice. She had sung in a concert of excerpts from *Götterdämmerung*, conducted by Wagner, and had ridden the huge sound of the orchestra with apparent ease. Wagner had no hesitation in giving her the role, and never regretted it, though he had to pay a high price: the management of the Hofoper made it a condition of her release that he would spend several weeks in Vienna in the fall of 1875, when he could least spare the time, supervising productions of *Lohengrin* and *Tannhäuser*.

Materna's performance in *The Ring* was greatly admired by critics as dismissive of the enterprise as a whole as Tchaikovsky and Hanslick. She even survived what appears to have been formidable competition from Cocotte, the magnificent black stallion presented by King Ludwig for the role of Grane, who was characterized by Ernest Newman in his *Life of Richard Wagner* as the "one model member of the company with whom Wagner had no trouble from first to last."[33] Materna returned to Bayreuth in 1882 to create Kundry in *Parsifal* (a role she sang there in six more festivals after Wagner's death), and continued her career in Vienna until 1894, interrupting it for visits to New York, where she sang with the Metropolitan Opera in 1885 and the Damrosch company in the 1890s. With its heavy concentration on German opera, New York arguably possessed a better roster of German singers and players than any city in Europe, and under Anton Seidl, who had been one of Wagner's music assistants at Bayreuth, staged some of the finest performances of Wagner's operas that were heard anywhere in the nineteenth century.

Many of those great New York performances, including the Metropolitan Opera's first complete *Ring* cycle in 1889, featured another veteran of the 1876 Bayreuth festival. Then, she had been a Rhinemaiden, a Valkyrie, and the Woodbird, but in the 1880s and 1890s she was the incomparable Brünn-hilde of two continents. Wagner had been a part of her life since she was a teenager (he almost always addressed her as "dear Child"), but she was a great deal more than just a Wagnerian singer. She had begun her career in Prague in 1869 as the First Boy in *Die Zauberflöte* (she would eventually add every other soprano role in that opera!); she was famous as Lucia, Gilda, Vio-letta, and Vielka (the role Meyerbeer wrote for Jenny Lind); she made her Metropolitan debut as Carmen; she was superb as Valentine, Fidelio, Donna Anna, and Constanze; and if there were four roles for which she would even-tually be best remembered they were Sieglinde, Isolde, Brünnhilde . . . and Norma. She was a coloratura soprano with a range and technique to com-pare with Malibran's, a dramatic soprano as powerful and exciting as Teresa Stolz in Italy, and she was the heroic soprano of Wagner's dreams. By the end of her stage career in 1910 (though she continued to sing on the concert plat-form until 1920, when she was seventy-two), she was reputed to have sung 170 roles in 119 different operas. Her name was Lilli Lehmann.

When Wagner was in Magdeburg in 1835, one of the singers he engaged was a young Jewish woman named Marie Löwe, whom he had known and courted during his student days in Leipzig.[34] Almost thirty years later, visit-ing Prague to give a concert, he came across her again. She was now a harp-ist in the orchestra and was known by her married name, Marie Löwe-Lehmann. Wagner was charmed by her fifteen-year-old daughter, Lilli. Lilli, it has to be said, was not so taken with Wagner. According to one of Wagner's later biographers, Robert Gutman, he frightened her. "He had appeared in a yellow damask dressing gown, pink tie, and voluminous black velvet cape lined with rose satin. Thoroughly frightened by this apparition and its im-petuous hugs and kisses, [Lilli] had to be quieted by Mamma Marie, who later joked with her old friend about his bantering proposal to adopt the talented young charmer."[35]

To begin with, there was little doubt that Lilli would be a lyric and col-oratura soprano. She joined the Berlin company in 1870, at the age of twenty-one, and was soon singing Lucia, Constanze, Lucrezia Borgia, and other formidable bel canto roles. The invitation to Bayreuth in 1876 was not unexpected (as a friend of the family, if nothing else), and her parts were carefully chosen. She was as natural for the Woodbird as Joan Sutherland would be in a later generation, and Wagner was keen to have Lilli and her talented younger sister Marie as two of the three Rhinemaidens, whose scenes at the beginning and end of the cycle are of such importance. It was thus that Lilli learned the dangerous art of singing complicated music over a large and loud orchestra (albeit a hooded one at Bayreuth) while being trundled around the stage lying on machines that had been specially designed by Wagner to make it appear that she and her colleagues were swimming. The machines were very successful, but Lilli did not enjoy singing on them, any more than she appreciated being "squeezed into tight corsets" for the role.[36] She was happier as Helmwige, the Valkyrie girl, which she sang alongside Johanna Wagner, who was returning to the opera stage at the age of fifty.

It was not until 1882 that Lilli's career began to change course. In that year, she went back to Bayreuth at Wagner's request to sing one of the Flower Maidens in *Parsifal* and to take responsibility for rehearsing all the Flower Maidens collectively. In the event, she withdrew from the production just before the dress rehearsal—not because she had any quarrel with Bayreuth or Wagner, but because she was uncomfortable having to work so closely with her former fiancé, who was Bayreuth's technical director. In any case, she had already made the decision to move into more dramatic roles than she had been singing in Berlin. Within a few months she was tackling Marguerite de Valois in Meyerbeer's *Les Huguenots* in Vienna and beginning what would be a long association with that city, including many memorable performances under Mahler. Two years later, in London, she sang Isolde for the first time under Richter, and in November 1885 she made her Metropolitan debut as Carmen, breaking her lifetime contract in Berlin in order to extend her stay in New York. Her punishment was to be heavily fined and banned by the kaiser from singing in any German opera house for six years—an inconsiderable penalty in light of the huge advantages that fell to her as darling of the Met during the seven seasons she sang there.

A few years later, when she started taking pupils of her own, Lehmann was generally described as a martinet (or worse) by those she taught, but she was teaching them no more than she had taught herself. By her own ac-

Above: Wagner designed special "swimming machines" for the three Rhinemaidens in the first complete production of *The Ring,* at Bayreuth in 1876. *Below:* Minna Lammert, Lilli Lehmann, and her sister Marie Lehmann, as seen from the audience. (Lebrecht Collection; Richard Wagner Museum.)

count, she worked incredibly hard to make the transition from coloratura soprano to dramatic soprano to heroic soprano.[37] She practiced every phrase hundreds of times, "gradually increasing my physical and vocal endurance," but the greatest wonder was that she accomplished it without surrendering the vocal qualities that enabled her to sing the great coloratura roles as well as anyone had ever sung them. Her explanation, with which Wagner would surely have agreed, was that legato was the indispensable art of song, and that applied whether one was singing Isolde or Norma, Brünnhilde or Lucia. Lehmann was decidedly a first generation Wagnerian: she had learned it from the Master and she unreservedly abhorred the Sprechgesang style imposed by Cosima and Kniese after Wagner's death. In fact, she fell out with Cosima very early. Affronted by an invitation to sing Brangäne rather than Isolde in the first Bayreuth *Tristan* in 1886 (Rosa Sucher was preferred as Isolde), she refused to take part at all. She did return in 1896, however, to sing Brünnhilde in the first revival of *The Ring,* though even then she had to share the role with the Swedish singer Ellen Gulbranson, who would remain Bayreuth's preferred Brünnhilde right up to 1914. In 1896, Lehmann was so much the most famous Brünnhilde in the world that it would have been hard *not* to ask her, but neither Cosima nor Lehmann enjoyed working together. Lehmann was slapped down every time she made a suggestion based on the 1876 experience, and Cosima made it clear that she alone was The Authority. Lehmann remembered the experience with bitterness: "All roads may lead to Rome but to the Bayreuth of today there is but one—the road of slavish subjection. There is no true conception of how valuable individual artistry can be."[38]

Fach is the German word for "fold" (as in *zweifach*, "twofold"), and in opera it is used to describe the place where a particular role sits in the voice. Singers can, and often do, move from one category of opera to another—from lyric to dramatic, and back again, for instance—but they need to work at each individual part to get it into the right fach of the voice. For Lilli Lehmann this never seems to have been a problem. Like Therese Tietjens, she would sometimes sing five different roles in a week; she frequently went from Isolde to Norma in a matter of days, and she sang that broad spectrum of roles not just for a year or two as she transitioned from one fach to another, but for more than twenty years at the center of her career. Her strengths were at the top and bottom of the voice: her singing was characterized by immensely powerful chest notes and pure and accurate head tones with very little vibrato, and they were still resplendent in 1907, when she made her few recordings at the age of fifty-nine, though the middle of the voice was decidedly worn by then.

Today, we are awed by the very idea of a voice that could encompass such a range of roles, and could be used so often and so exuberantly over so long a period. Maybe it was the constant inclusion of coloratura roles that kept the voice so well oiled and disciplined. Maybe it was because she knew only one way to sing Wagner—with a pure legato line, just as the Master had taught. No barker she! Maybe it was because many of her Wagnerian performances were led by conductors like Richter and Seidl who had been trained by Wagner to keep the orchestral volume within limits. Maybe it was because she was a lifelong vegetarian and led a famously clean life. Whatever the explanation, Lilli Lehmann's art was one of the great glories of the story of opera, and one that no singer of the twentieth century came near to emulating, though there were a few brave souls who covered the same broad repertory. Of the outstanding Wagnerians, Frida Leider, Kirsten Flagstad, and Birgit Nilsson would all have the power and clarion sound of the genuine heroic soprano, but none of them had the coloratura technique and repertory, and all of them spent most of their careers battling overmighty conductors with a need to prove they possessed the biggest instrument in the house.

When Wagner produced *Tannhäuser* and *Lohengrin* in Vienna in 1875 (the price he paid for getting Amalie Materna to sing Brünnhilde in the Bayreuth *Ring*), he was closely observed by one of the Hofoper's singers, a baritone called Angelo Neumann. Neumann, who had been on the roster of the Hofoper for a dozen years, was never going to be a star singer, and it was his admiration for Wagner, both as composer and stage director, that caused him to change careers. After seeing *The Ring* at Bayreuth in 1876, he resigned from the Hofoper and became co-director of the Leipzig Opera. Within six years he had staged all of Wagner's major operas, including a full cycle of *The Ring* in 1878—a fairly faithful reproduction of the Bayreuth model, though, as Liszt tactlessly wrote to Wagner, "in some respects better even than you did in Bayreuth."[39] In 1881 Neumann took the production to Berlin, and the following year to London, performing four complete cycles in each city.

Thus, while Wagner himself was struggling valiantly to pay off the massive debt he had incurred in 1876, the center of Wagnerian opera moved, de facto, to Leipzig, the composer's birthplace. Wagner was basically supportive of Neumann's efforts and encouraged his music assistants to conduct for him, among them Seidl and Mottl, who were later reinforced by the young Artur Nikisch. There was a falling out in Berlin when Wagner stalked off the stage in the middle of Neumann's formal speech to the kaiser, but Wagner nevertheless gave Neumann the rights to perform his operas in every European city in which they had not already been seen. Neumann formed the Richard Wagner-Theater and set off on a tour of Breslau, Danzig, Magdeburg, Hamburg, Lübeck, and Bremen with a company of 134, including an orchestra of sixty. The following year he took the same company to Germany, Holland, Belgium, Italy, Hungary, and Austria, and several years later he put together another company to perform *The Ring* in St. Petersburg (1889) and Moscow (1891).

Most of the leading Wagnerian singers joined Neumann's company, and several new ones emerged from its ranks. On the female side, Therese Vogl, Amalie Materna, and Hedwig Reicher-Kindermann, all veterans of 1876, took part in the tours. Reicher-Kindermann, daughter of the man who had created Wotan in Munich in 1869–70, had sung Erda and Grimgerde (one of the Valkyrie girls) in the Bayreuth *Ring,* but in Neumann's company she graduated to larger roles. In Berlin, she was the Erda; soon afterwards, in Leipzig, she sang her first Isolde; and in London, after Vogl had sung Brünnhilde in the first cycle, she took over the role for the second and third cycles and had a brilliant success. But she was dogged by ill health. She had to leave the company after Breslau and was not able to rejoin it until it reached Italy. In Trieste, she sang the *Götterdämmerung* Brünnhilde, and twelve days later she died. She was only twenty-nine. There were contemporary reviewers who claimed she was the finest of all the first-generation Wagnerian sopranos.

One of them, Felix Weingartner, later a major conductor, then a young pupil of Liszt, wrote that the voice was "magnificent, sumptuous—the most brilliant dramatic voice I have ever heard."[40]

The "beneficiary" of this tragedy was Katherina Klafsky, a Hungarian soprano two years younger than Reicher-Kindermann, who had been gradually ascending the Wagnerian ladder, from assorted Rhinemaidens, Valkyries, and Norns to Brangäne, Venus, and Sieglinde. Now she took over Brünnhilde and made it one of the cornerstones of a substantial career based in Hamburg. She had great success in London and New York (as a member of the Damrosch company) and would have made her Metropolitan debut in 1896 at the age of forty-one, had she not died unexpectedly shortly before setting out from Hamburg.

Others also "benefited" from Reicher-Kindermann's demise, including the two outstanding Isoldes of the time. Rosa Sucher, who had married Josef Sucher, the chief conductor of the Leipzig Opera, served her Wagnerian apprenticeship in the Neumann company and was eventually selected by Cosima to be the first Bayreuth Isolde in 1886, Lilli Lehmann's claims notwithstanding. As well as having a powerful voice, she was an outstanding actress with a memorable stage personality—something that Cosima did everything in her power to stifle. The other woman with a claim on the role in 1886 was Therese Malten—not least because Wagner himself, hearing her sing Senta in Dresden in 1881, had said she would be the "ideal" Isolde. Since no performances of *Tristan* were then planned at Bayreuth, Wagner contented himself with asking her to be one of three singers (along with Amalie Materna and Marianne Brandt) to sing Kundry in the 1882 festival when *Parsifal* was first performed—and she did eventually return to Bayreuth for Isolde as well as Eva. Malten spent thirty years as a member of the Dresden company, but she was always more than just a Wagnerian: she sang regularly in French and Italian as well, with a repertory that was not as broad as Lehmann's (it took in no coloratura roles), but was unusually adventurous for a German singer at the end of the century.

Early deaths such as Reicher-Kindermann's and Klafsky's doubtless gave encouragement to those who wished to perpetuate the old myths, but the fact was that the reputation of Richard Wagner improved greatly in the years after his death in 1883. The popularity of his operas grew year by year, not only in Germany, and Neumann's touring company had a lot to do with it. As well as introducing the operas to cities that had never seen them before, it also served to prove that they did not need to be performed in specially constructed theaters: they could work quite well in normal opera houses, and nowhere more so than in New York.

The German-speaking population of New York in 1884 was estimated at 250,000. In matters musical, they were far and away the most influential group in the city. In 1842, they had been largely responsible for the founding of the New York Philharmonic. In the 1880s, though they had little enough to do with the founding of the Metropolitan Opera, they soon came to dominate it, both musically and administratively. German singers, whose salaries were partly underwritten by state-subsidized companies at home, were comparatively cheap to employ for three or four months at a time, and Leopold Damrosch, who took over the direction of the Metropolitan for its second season in 1884–85, was able to persuade his board that opera in German was the way to go (and that included performing French and Italian operas in German). When Damrosch, who had conducted every performance of eleven different operas, died of pneumonia near the end of the season, his twenty-three-year-old son Walter took over, and soon appointed Anton Seidl chief conductor. With his intimate knowledge of Bayreuth, and his experience "on the road" with Neumann, Seidl was uniquely equipped to make the Metropolitan a center of Wagnerian opera, and that is what he did. All the major works were produced, and most of the best singers eagerly made the journey from Europe. In the very first German season, Amalie Materna was Brünnhilde, Auguste Kraus was Sieglinde (she would shortly marry Seidl), and Marianne Brandt was Fidelio (she was officially designated a mezzo-soprano, although her voice ranged over almost three octaves, to D above high C). In the summer after his father's death, young Damrosch went head-hunting in Europe and returned with the nucleus of the Metropolitan's Wagner team for the next seven seasons—the bass Emil Fischer, the tenor Max Alvary, and Lilli Lehmann herself. They were joined for two seasons by Albert Niemann—still, in his fifties, the best Tristan available, and arguably the best

Siegfried as well. No other opera house, not even Bayreuth, could field casts as good as these.

Even more encouraging was the fact that North America was beginning to produce its own homegrown Wagnerian singers. Leading the way was Lillian Nordica (born Lilian Norton in Farmington, Maine). She was not a typical prima donna, even if there is such a thing. She was warm, affectionate, emotionally insecure—a thoroughly nice woman. The early part of her career, inevitably, was spent in Europe, and she did not make her debut at the Met until 1891. Although she could not be considered a serious rival to Lilli Lehmann, Lehmann nevertheless took her seriously enough to belittle her on occasion. At Bayreuth, in the summer of 1894, when Nordica became the first American to sing at the Wagner Festival, she asked a mutual friend to inquire if she might pay a call on Lehmann—a social call. "Tell her I am not taking any pupils this season," was Lehmann's reply.[41]

Nordica was one of those sopranos who went on singing florid roles while also singing Wagner—Marguerite, Violetta, and Lucia continued to be in her repertory, even as she added Isolde and the three Brünnhildes. Not only did these roles appear to keep her voice lubricated, as they did Lehmann's, but they were probably also responsible for her ability to sing Wagner with a true legato line and real richness of tone. It was when she got together with a tenor who was similarly inclined, Jean de Reszke, that she sang a series of performances of *Tristan* that may have come as close to the composer's intentions as anyone has ever come. Like Lehmann (who also claimed that her best performances of Isolde and Brünnhilde were in partnership with de Reszke), she needed a Tristan or a Siegfried who was able truly to *sing* the roles, and they have always been in short supply. Following her success with Isolde, Nordica rashly assumed she would be offered Brünnhilde opposite de Reszke's Siegfried. Her fury at discovering that her friend Nellie Melba (of all people!) had been selected to sing it, apparently at de Reszke's suggestion, led her to tear up her contract and quit the Met. The fact that it turned out to be the greatest disaster of Melba's career was no compensation. Characteristically, Nordica dusted herself off, repaired her friendships with Melba and de Reszke, and got on with the business of singing. She was still performing Isolde in 1913 at the age of fifty-six, but the following year she was killed in a freak accident on her way home from a farewell tour of Australia: her ship went aground off the coast of Java and she eventually died of exposure in an Indonesian hospital.

There would soon be many other American singers following in Nordica's footsteps, among them Olive Fremstad, a pupil of Lehmann's, but none would accomplish the feat of singing coloratura and heroic roles simultaneously. One other North American lady, however, had already done it. The Canadian Emma Albani was ten years older than Nordica and had been widely touted as a rival of Adelina Patti. She had notably failed to dethrone Patti, but she nevertheless had ambitions to take the place of the German singer Therese Tietjens in the affections of Londoners (Tietjens had died of cancer in 1877). So Albani progressively gave up the roles that had made her famous—roles that put her directly in competition with Patti, like Lucia, Linda, Gilda, and Amina—and replaced them with Senta, Elsa, Elisabeth, and, eventually, Isolde, all of them roles that Patti was unlikely to attempt. In the end, the strategy was self-defeating. The strength of her voice was its top—the chest and middle registers were not nearly so powerful—and the effort of singing so much against her natural inclinations took a severe toll. In 1896, realizing the game was up, Albani quietly retired from the opera stage and continued her career in oratorio and concert work.

These first-generation Wagnerians were distinguished, for the most part, by their determination to sing Wagner's music, if not in the Italian style, then in something that was closely related to it. The disease of Sprechgesang, though it began at Bayreuth in the last decade of the century, was not yet epidemic, and most conductors still understood the importance of containing the orchestra sufficiently to allow singers to sing rather than bark. Equally important, very few singers truly specialized in Wagner, certainly not to the point of singing little else. At Bayreuth, Cosima might have been busy preaching the official gospel, which said that her husband's works stood apart from all other operatic works and should therefore be treated differently, but the singers continued to alternate Wagner with Verdi and Massenet, Meyerbeer and Gluck. If nothing else, this ensured that a measure of lyricism was retained in Wagner's music.

Those of this first generation who recorded were well past their prime by the time they did so, so it is hard to judge how much better they might have been than their immediate successors. Of the females, it is likely that only Anna Bahr-Mildenburg, who made her debut in 1895, could be mentioned in the same breath as Lehmann and her contemporaries. Her debut, at the age of twenty-two, was as Brünnhilde in *Die Walküre,* conducted by Mahler, and it was her long collaboration with Mahler in Vienna that developed her into the extraordinary lyric-dramatic artist she became. She was another of those rare Brünnhilde/Isoldes who also sang Norma, but in her case she added too many other heavy roles (like Clytemnestra in *Salome*), and by 1916 she was unable to go on singing regularly.

So who was the greatest Wagnerian soprano of the first generation? Most people would plump for Lehmann, though there might be one or two votes for Hedwig Reicher-Kindermann, whose legend grew in the years after her early death. Yet there were many at the time who thought a Croatian soprano called Milka Ternina had a greater claim. She was fourteen years younger than Lehmann and she concentrated more intently on the German and Wagnerian repertories than did Lehmann—though she was also a famous Tosca, and the first to sing that role in both London and the United States (Puccini said she was the finest Tosca he ever saw).[42] Ternina only sang once at Bayreuth—as Kundry in 1899—and was then given a lifetime ban by Cosima for taking part in the Metropolitan Opera's 1903 production of *Parsifal,* which was staged in defiance of Bayreuth's exclusive "copyright" on the opera. Ternina never recorded—she retired in 1906 as the result of a paralysis in her facial muscles—so it is impossible to compare her technique and performance with Lehmann's, but what attracted audiences to her was her *attack*. She had a fine technique, of course, and a very dramatic voice, but it was the fire that burned within, that burst out explosively once in a while, that made people sit on the edge of their seats. She was not a particularly impressive person to look at—she was rather plump and dowdy, in fact—but there was an edge to her performance that no one else appeared to have. More than anyone, perhaps, she was able to do justice to Isolde's ecstasy and agony, to Brünnhilde's joy and fury—because these qualities (it was said) were always present in her performance, smoldering through long passages of narration and soliloquy, bursting into flames at moments of great drama.

Like Lehmann and Nordica, Ternina had the privilege of singing Isolde to Jean de Reszke's Tristan. This was a legendary performance at Covent Garden in 1898, which caused the philosopher George Moore, then only twenty-five years old, to take up his pen and write a letter to the *Daily Chronicle:* "Mlle Ternina was a woman, a sublimation of womanhood, it is true, but a woman whom Tristan could love . . . The house seemed to awaken slowly to the fact that the spectacle of the perfect incarnation of Isolde was being achieved."[43]

CHAPTER TEN

Marchesi's Pupils

"A musical experience needs three human beings at least. It requires a composer, a performer, and a listener, and unless these three take part together there is no musical experience."[1]

Benjamin Britten's observation, made in 1964 when he received the first Aspen Award, highlighted the most singular problem of twentieth-century opera. It was not that there was any lack of creativity or originality—on the contrary: there was, if anything, a superfluity—but the most creative part of the alliance, the composers, got so far ahead of the others that what Britten called "this holy triangle of composer, performer, and listener" was disrupted. The listeners did not go away (in fact, they increased their numbers by leaps and bounds as the new recording and broadcast media gave them additional means of access), but they showed comparatively little interest in their own century: instead, they turned back to the eighteenth and nineteenth centuries, and eventually to the seventeenth as well.

As for singers, they were necessarily dependent on the composers. It was true that eighteenth-century castrati and prime donne had rejoiced in their freedom to ornament and improvise, but they were doing so in the style and manner of the composer (or that's what they were *meant* to be doing: there were frequent unhappy examples of singers doing violence to both Music and the composer's intentions). Changes in the art of singing—the development of new styles, even, on occasion, of new vocal types—could almost always be put down to composers, not singers. This was certainly true of Verdi, and it was even more true of Wagner. In his lifetime, he was said to be the Great Satan, the destroyer of voices, the composer of antimusic, yet by 1900, only seventeen years after his death, he was hugely popular and there was no shortage of Wagnerian voices. That was the way it worked: singers adapted their training and their techniques to whatever new challenges the composers might provide. Thus, the spinto (or "pushed") lyric voice, increasingly called for by composers from Meyerbeer onwards, but especially by Verdi, had been unheard of in 1800, yet it was commonplace in 1900. An orchestra of Wagnerian size would have been laughable in 1800— no singer, not even Mme Catalani, could have made herself heard over it— yet no one was surprised by it a hundred years later. Verdi's requirement that Lady Macbeth should be sung in "a raw, choked, hollow voice,"[2] though it would have been anathema to any eighteenth- or early nineteenth-century singer brought up in the bel canto tradition, was perfectly acceptable in the twentieth century.

Whatever the new century held for opera in general, it was clear that the creations of the eighteenth and nineteenth centuries (at any rate from Gluck and Mozart onwards) had been so prolific and so engaging that listeners would continue to demand them. For singers, this meant that the classical Italian tradition pioneered by the great castrati and prime donne—the tradition of florid, coloratura singing which paid little attention to words and great attention to trills, ornaments, and other effects—would be kept alive. In the last part of the nineteenth century, the tradition had been notably sustained by Adelina Patti, Therese Tietjens, Christine Nilsson, and Marcella Sembrich. They very often sang Violetta and Gilda, sometimes even Elisabeth and Elsa, but the roles in which these ladies were most comfortable, and in which their listeners expected to find them most often, were the great coloratura roles of what was becoming known as "bel canto opera"—Lucia, Amina, Semiramide, Rosina, Norma, Lucrezia Borgia, and many more.

There was, therefore, a continuing need to train singers in this tradition. For ambitious young sopranos that very often meant a visit to the Ecole Marchesi in Paris's rue Jouffroy. No one who went there ever forgot it—and some never forgave it.

The school's proprietor, Mathilde Marchesi, had been born Mathilde Graumann in Frankfurt. A natural mezzo-soprano, she studied in Vienna, London, and Paris and embarked on a career as a concert singer, but apparently with the intention of moving to opera in due course. She canceled (for no very convincing reason) her scheduled stage debut in Milan, but she did make one appearance on the opera stage, in 1852, when she was thirty-one: it was an "emergency" appearance as Rosina in Bremen when the advertised singer withdrew at short notice.[3] Immediately thereafter, she married a Sicilian baritone modestly known as Salvatore Marchesi, though his hereditary titles included those of Cavaliere de Castrone and Marchese della Rajata. Mathilde and Salvatore had met two years previously, when they were both studying with Manuel García the younger in London. Initially, it was Salvatore's career that was given precedence—he had a contract to sing in Berlin—and he would continue to divide his time between singing, teaching, and writing about music, but it was not long before Mathilde became the family's principal breadwinner—as a teacher, not a singer. Within two years of her marriage she was taking pupils privately, first in Vienna, later in Cologne and Paris, then in Vienna again, until in 1881 she set up a permanent headquarters in the rue Jouffroy and continued to teach there until 1908, the year of her husband's death.

For a relative unknown's career as a teacher to take off so quickly and so permanently suggested a powerful patron, and that was certainly the case with Mathilde Marchesi. She had won the esteem of her own teacher, García, and he had quickly begun referring pupils to her, later transferring to her many of his own.

For more than two hundred years, singing teachers (many of them retired singers, including a remarkable number of castrati, who tended to be the best educated of all musicians) had been teaching Italian bel canto. The legitimacy, and therefore the authority, of these teachers was measured by their pedagogical genealogy—that is, the directness of their descent from the great teachers of previous generations. A few (not always the best) had published treatises along the way, so it is possible to follow the legitimate line all the way from Giulio Caccini in Florence at the very beginning of the seventeenth century to Mathilde Marchesi in Paris three hundred years later.

Caccini and his colleagues in the Florentine camerata had developed the initial idea of dramma per musica (later described as "opera"), but they had not set out to achieve "beautiful song." To them, words were paramount.

Their interest in adding music to plays stemmed from a belief that it was the best way to give emphasis to the drama—in fact, they thought it was exactly what the ancient Greeks had done. When he wrote the introduction to *Le nuove musiche* in 1602, Caccini was quite clear about this: he was trying, he wrote, to "introduce a kind of music in which one could almost speak in tones." But Caccini also had a wife and two daughters to think about, all of them excellent singers and members of the *concerto di donne* for which he regularly composed. No doubt egged on by them, he had begun to ornament and decorate his music in ways that were not acceptable to his more austere colleagues, and the classic Italian tradition of bel canto might therefore be said to have had its origins in Caccini's justification of such embellishments in *Le nuove musiche*. They could be used, he wrote, to "move the affections" of the audience. Nevertheless, Caccini's endorsement of ornamentation was cautious: he was much more concerned with urging composers to treat the voice entirely differently from the instruments of the orchestra, for the voice was concerned with meaning, while instruments were there only for accompaniment and emphasis.[4]

More than a century later, in 1723, Pier Francesco Tosi codified the theory and practice of Italian bel canto in his treatise *Opinioni de' cantori antichi e moderni*.[5] Tosi was a castrato. Like Mme Marchesi a century and a half later, he made only one recorded appearance on the opera stage, but he was an accomplished concert singer and became a teacher relatively early in life. First in London, then, for more than twenty years, as a musical ambassador of the Emperor Joseph I, he studied the art of singing and put together his findings in that single, highly influential publication. It contained little original thought, but a great deal of observation of accepted practice (which is what makes it so valuable as a historical document), together with a long polemic against the "modern" tendency for singers to show off their voices in flights of overembellishment that had nothing whatever to do with the opera. Like Caccini, Tosi believed that ornamentation was a valuable way of adding expression, particularly pathos, but he had a much more expansive view of it than Caccini, and that was not surprising, since Tosi was writing at a time when the da capo aria, with its requirements to embellish and improvise, was the pivot around which opera revolved—a time when singers were in control (or, according to your point of view, quite out of control). Tosi believed that all ornaments and decorations, including cadenzas, should be improvised by the singer, not written down by the composer, but he urged singers to work out these improvisations in advance—the heat of the moment was not the right time to be inventing complex musical constructions.

In its English translation, Tosi's work was known by its Italian subtitle, *Observations on the Florid Song,* but its most useful sections were concerned with the training of the voice rather than with the refinement of improvisation. There was a lot of advice—on the need for caution in extending into the upper range; on which vowels to use for vocalizations (he recommended the Italian *a, e,* and *o,* and vehemently disagreed with Caccini, as have most others, on the use of *i* and *u* for higher voices); and on the best posture, and even the shape of the mouth, for singing. But most of the treatise was devoted to straightforward instruction—basic vocal exercises, breath control, voice production ("limpid and clear," never nasal or throaty), the seamless union of chest and head registers, clear enunciation, repeated practice of messa di voce (holding a single note while taking it from pianissimo to fortissimo and back again), right up to the most complicated technical instructions about vocalization and where and when to use which ornaments (mordents, slides, trills, appoggiaturas, cadenzas). Also included were instructions about the learning of languages, acting styles, musical education, and correct manners toward one's fellow artists—but these "refined" arts were secondary to the art of singing. And since one could never entirely master the art of singing, but must study it constantly and practice it daily, the implication was that these other arts and graces paled into insignificance. To be fair, Tosi was writing about all the different styles of singing (church, chamber, and opera), and rarely addressed himself solely to the art of opera singing.

Many would follow in Tosi's footsteps, and most of them would repeat Tosi's guidelines, albeit with different emphases here and there. By the time Girolamo Crescentini published his treatise in 1810,[6] the tide had begun to turn and the singers, under the influence of Gluck and his successors, were beginning (just beginning) to acquire some discipline. Crescentini was one of the last of the great castrati (and a favorite of Napoleon's). His art was, and always had been, the art of florid singing, but he echoed Caccini rather than

Tosi when he urged that "singing must be an imitation of speech," delivered in smooth legato phrasing, elegant and flowing. What distinguished Crescentini's treatise, and set him apart from most nineteenth-century teachers, was the knowledge that he himself had been able to sing like this—witness a review in the *Allgemeine Musikalische Zeitung* when he appeared in Vienna in 1804: "His voice, employed with discreet restraint, is indescribably agreeable, round, pure and flexible; his embellishments rich in noble art and aesthetic propriety, without being overly elaborated. Especially beautiful is the pure, even, ever stronger pulsation of his heavenly voice, with which, in one passage, he makes a crescendo to the high A and then holds the tone at full voice for several measures."[7]

As opera proliferated in the nineteenth century, and the singing profession grew exponentially, so the number of teachers also grew. The Paris Conservatoire had come into existence in 1795 at the height of the French Revolution, and it was not long before Napoleonic governments were using the example of Paris to spur the founding of similar conservatories in Milan, Naples, and Bologna (all between 1804 and 1808). Later in the century, Parma, Turin, and Venice would get their own colleges of music, and the growth of similar institutions in Austria, Germany, and England ensured that there was no shortage of formal teaching. But great singers rarely emerged from conservatories. They were generally the product of individual teachers with their own independent studios (often in their own homes), and many of them were retired singers. One such teacher had been Manuel García the elder, one of Rossini's outstanding tenors in Naples and later the creator of Almaviva in *Il barbiere,* but better known to posterity as the patriarch of a great dynasty. He taught both his daughters, María Malibran and Pauline Viardot, and also his son, Manuel García the younger—but not with the results he had doubtless anticipated. The young man spent barely four years as an opera singer (a baritone) before escaping, first to the French army, then to the profession of voice teacher.

García the younger quickly became the most respected teacher in Europe, partly because of his direct succession from his famous father and even more famous sisters, but mainly because he had studied the physiological aspects of the human voice and brought a new, more scientific focus to treating and training it. That he was widely believed to have resurrected Jenny Lind's voice from the dead in 1842 did him no harm, but it was his invention of the laryngoscope in 1855 that made him world famous (it was an instrument based on a system of mirrors that enabled a doctor to examine the throat in much greater detail than ever before). He thus combined a scientific attitude with teaching skills and the firsthand experience of having had his own voice trained by his father. He was only thirty-five when he presented to the Académie des Sciences in Paris his *Mémoire sur la voix humaine* (1840), which quickly became the basis for all subsequent studies of the voice and its development. He spent the last half of his long life (he lived to be 101) in London, where he was a professor at the Royal Academy of Music from 1848 to 1895.

What García was to Paris and London, Francesco Lamperti was to Milan. As professor of singing at the Milan Conservatory from 1850, he taught a roster of singers almost as impressive as Mme Marchesi's would eventually be. His approach may have been less scientific than García's, but it was based on exactly the same principles—he taught the classic Italian style of singing that had been handed down in direct succession from Caccini, Porpora, Tosi, and the great castrati of the eighteenth century. Just as García had inherited the tradition from his father and elder sister, so Lamperti had inherited it directly from Giuditta Pasta, with whom he had worked as a young man at her academy in Como. Like Verdi, he knew most of the great prime donne of that golden era, and he was responsible for teaching many of their successors in the next generation. His famous female pupils included the Canadian Emma Albani, the Pole Marcella Sembrich, and three of Verdi's best singers—Sophie Cruvelli, the eccentric German woman who created Hélène in *Les vêpres siciliennes;* and the duo of Teresa Stolz (a Bohemian) and Maria Waldmann (an Austrian), who were the first Aida and Amneris at La Scala and later originated the female solo roles in the *Requiem*.

Lamperti's treatises and essays are very similar to García's published works—pedagogic guides to the florid style that was still required of singers in the mid-century (Lamperti's essay on the trill was dedicated to Albani, his favorite pupil)—but with this difference, that Lamperti, though he was no scientist, was less anchored in the past, and more attuned to developments in Italian opera during the last half of the century.[8] Better than most, he understood Verdi's desire to move away from the strict bel canto tradition—to get singers to sing dramatically, even at the cost of introducing ugliness into their performances. Stolz and Waldmann were products of this teaching, much to Verdi's satisfaction, and Marcella Sembrich, with a voice of great natural beauty and finely trained musical instincts (she was a virtuosa violinist and pianist as well as a singer), eventually became as dramatic a soprano as any. She had originally been a pupil of Lamperti's son Giovanni Battista, but had "reverted" to the father in 1883 and begun to acquire the much more forceful attack and the narrow, rapid vibrato that became her calling cards (they later got her into trouble when she experienced vocal difficulties in the 1890s as a result of straining her voice by singing too dramatically).[9]

If Lamperti was a pragmatist rather than a doctrinaire promoter of the old Italian method, then García the younger was probably a better theorist than he was a teacher. Aside from Lind, who consulted him in his capacity as a voice doctor rather than a singing teacher, his list of pupils was not very impressive—Erminia Frezzolini, who created Giselda in *I Lombardi* and the title role in *Giovanna d'Arco* for Verdi, was perhaps the most important of them—but his reputation for understanding the workings of the human voice was so great that his textbook, *Traité complet de l'art du chant,* published in 1840, remained in vogue for the rest of the century.[10] Like Tosi's, it was not particularly original, but it codified much of the knowledge and experience that had been handed down from generation to generation for 250 years. Part one set out the vocal exercises recommended for the proper training and production of the voice, while part two (of much greater interest to the nonsinger) was about style—it was a practical guide to the way the vocal line should be executed, ornamented, and interpreted, rather than literally reproduced. His exemplars included many of the great singers he had known— Pasta, Malibran, his father, Giovanni David (the tenor), Filippo Galli (the bass), and Giovanni Battista Velluti, the last of the opera castrati—so that the teaching he was handing down was, without question, the classical Italian method, still heavily reliant on the writings of Tosi. He dealt with breathing, enunciation, phrasing, "correct" ornamentation, use of legato, rubato, and portamento, and literally hundreds of ways in which the Italian style sought to heighten the vocal effect, even if it meant diminishing the dramatic effect, which it very often did. None of this was particularly controversial, but García is perhaps best remembered for the harm he did, quite unintentionally, by the emphasis he placed in his treatise (though not, apparently, in his regular teaching) on what he called the *coup de glotte*. Michael Scott, the modern historian of singing, has pointed out that García's stated reliance on science—on the use of the laryngoscope, for instance, to "hold the mirror up to nature"—caused several generations of singers to draw the wrong conclusions: "It encouraged the student to think of singing independently of the body, as the consequence of a mechanical operation rather than simply as a physical reflex to a mental conception. In particular, his use of the term *coup de glotte* caused no end of controversy. A correct attack is only possible with the smooth and even exhalation of the breath, and it is not contrived in the throat by some perceptible action of the glottis . . . It led to generations of students and teachers consciously trying to produce in the throat the image the term suggested and producing instead a crude—and worse, an injurious—attack . . . The fact is that to be expressive singing must be, or at any rate sound to be, spontaneous. The danger of the scientific approach, of the laryngoscope, was that it held up the mirror not only to nature but to artifice as well." [11]

Nevertheless, García's reputation as a teacher was so great in the 1850s that when one of his pupils, the little-known Mathilde Marchesi, set up for herself with his blessing and endorsement, she immediately assumed a leading position in the teaching profession.

In the course of more than half a century, Marchesi, who had no more than one or two male pupils, was responsible (or at least partly responsible) for more prime donne than any other teacher before or since. They included many of the greatest names of the era—Nellie Melba, Emma Calvé, Emma Eames, Mary Garden (but only for four weeks), Etelka Gerster, Ilma di Murska, Sybil Sanderson, Selma Kurz, Gabrielle Kraus, and the New Zealand soprano Frances Alda, who later became the all-powerful wife of Giulio Gatti-Casazza, director of the Met. Many others were important singers at the time but ultimately not famous enough to command attention in the history books, among them Anna d'Angeri, Suzanne Adams, Emma Nevada,

Mathilde Marchesi (1821–1913). One of Marchesi's pupils, Emma Eames, said of her: "She had a head for business which, with her excellent musicianship, gave her the position she occupied for so many years—that of owner, manager and teacher of the greatest school of her day." (Royal College of Music, London.)

and Antonietta Fricci. Some of these singers were genuinely formed and created by Marchesi, others, like Melba, were already well-trained singers when they came to her, but not necessarily in the Italian style.

What she taught them was in many ways anachronistic. It was what García had taught her—the eighteenth-century Italian bel canto method, shorn of all heresies such as the Garcían coup de glotte. The anachronism lay in the fact that opera, three centuries into its existence, was no longer "the Italian art form." Distinctive national styles had come into existence in several countries—France, Germany, Russia, Bohemia—and even Italian opera, in the hands of Verdi and the verismo composers, had changed course to take account of drama. On its own, beautiful singing was no longer enough. Moreover, the anachronism was magnified by the remarkable fact that, among all Marchesi's distinguished pupils, there was not one single Italian. The last female Italian who could truly be described as a member of the bel canto tradition had been Giulia Grisi, and she had retired in 1861, having hardly set foot in Italy after 1832, when she was only twenty years old. Yet the tradition was very much alive, for while the new generation of Italian singers was confronting the much more dramatic requirements of Verdi and his successors, a cosmopolitan group of non-Italians had come to dominate the bel canto world. Of them all, only Adelina Patti could claim any Italian ancestry, and she had been born in Spain and brought up on the Bowery in New York. Tietjens (German), Nilsson (Swedish), Albani (Canadian), and Sembrich (Polish) had not a drop of Italian blood between them, any more than most of Marchesi's pupils had, yet here they all were, mastering the Italian style, insisting on singing even the operas of Meyerbeer and Bizet in Italian, and perpetuating a form of opera that most people assumed was in its death throes.

But it wasn't, for the "holy triangle of composer, performer, and listener," articulated by Britten many years later, was getting out of synch. Listeners were prepared to tackle the new music of Verdi, Wagner, Massenet, Strauss, and Puccini, and they often did so with relish, but there was a proviso: however good the new works might be, they were not going to cause them to desert the old works, the bel canto operas in which singing was what mattered and dramatic values were secondary. So another generation had to be prepared, and the Ecole Marchesi was the boot camp.

The ideal Marchesi pupil had all the attributes of a Porpora pupil 150 years earlier—a wide compass, total security throughout (especially at the top), even production across the entire range, effortless attack, no forcing. The voice had to be beautiful, pure, and precise. That was all very well, but after a time it was rather boring, because it meant the singing did not reflect (let alone contribute to) the drama of the plot. Yet there were many roles in the opera repertory that could not be sung without these bel canto qualities—roles like Rosina, Amina, Lucia, and a stageful of other eighteenth-century heroines—and if the more dramatically minded operagoers of the late nineteenth century found the style bland or irrelevant, they nevertheless had to admit that, at its best, it was awesome and very exciting. It did not necessarily prepare singers to perform Verdi (after Gilda and Violetta) or Wagner (after Elsa and Elisabeth), but it was precisely the training for which other popular composers, from Gluck to Massenet, had written, and were still occasionally writing.

There was, however, one important respect in which Marchesi departed from her predecessors. A feature of her method was its concentration on *placement*—placing the voice high on the breath so that the topmost notes could be projected with maximum brilliance. For singers with technique and breath control like Melba's it was a spectacular method—but there was only one Melba. It could also be successful for young singers, whose freshness and fearlessness sometimes made up for a lack of technique. Indeed, among the collections of the Metropolitan Opera in New York is a cylinder recording made by the house librarian, Lionel Mapleson, during a live performance of Meyerbeer's *Les Huguenots* in 1902. The Queen's aria on this recording, with its demanding coloratura and sustained florid passages, has long been considered an almost perfect example of the Marchesi method in action, and an equally stellar example of Melba's extraordinary technique. Desmond Shawe-Taylor, the British authority on singing, wrote that it "flashes out with amazing brilliance and strength. There is a high C sharp, attacked in full voice, which seems to echo round the huge auditorium; there are cascades of florid singing, thrown off in a manner that might almost be called reckless." [12] But recent research has revealed that, while the recording is certainly a fine example of the Marchesi method, Melba is not the singer. It is, in fact, another Marchesi pupil, ten years younger than Melba, Suzanne Adams, and her experience illustrates an altogether different aspect of Marchesi's teaching—its dangers. [13]

Adams was an American—a direct descendant of John and John Quincy Adams, both presidents of the United States. She had gone to Paris to study with Marchesi at the age of fifteen and spent seven years absorbing the method. By 1895 she thought herself ready to make her debut at the Opéra.

Mme Marchesi disagreed: she suggested a long rest in the south of France to restore Adams's "delicate health," followed by another five years' study.[14] Adams ignored the advice and went ahead with her debut as Juliette. She must have realized very quickly that Marchesi had been right, for though she got some good notices as Juliette and Marguerite ("the virginal attitude was unmistakably not a deliberate and laborious assumption," wrote one London critic of her Marguerite),[15] her voice was still short on power and she was clearly straining it to reach into the wide open spaces of the Opéra and Covent Garden. She left the Ecole Marchesi, of course, but she continued to practice the method and eventually, in 1899, she made a very successful debut at the Met. She sang there for four seasons—as Juliette, Euridice, Micaela, Donna Elvira, and the Queen in *Les Huguenots*—not as a star who was going to unseat Nellie Melba and Emma Eames, perhaps, but certainly as a greatly admired singer. Yet within two years of that stunning recording of Queen Marguerite's aria, while she was still in her early thirties, Adams's voice was in obvious decline, and by 1905 her career was over. In 1907 she was reduced to singing in vaudeville in London. A vivid example of the dangers of the Marchesi method, said the critics. In fact (as Marchesi might have rejoined), it had little to do with the method, but it was a good example of the dangers of young and inexperienced singers thinking they knew better than their teachers, thinking they had learned it all and could do it without supervision, without constant teaching.

(A week before Mapleson's cylinder of Queen Marguerite's aria was recorded, Adams had been scheduled to sing the Queen in a gala performance of *Les Huguenots*. She had withdrawn late in the day and her place had been taken by yet another Marchesi pupil, Estelle Liebling. Liebling made no great impression on the opera stage, then or later, but she went on to become a famous voice teacher in her own right. One of her pupils, Beverly Sills, became one of the few truly brilliant coloratura sopranos of the second half of the twentieth century.[16] Thus was the authentic Italian bel canto tradition passed down to yet another generation.)

One of the obvious problems of the Marchesi method was that it required almost superhuman discipline. A few singers (and Melba was certainly one of them—"one of my most industrious, pliant and talented pupils," wrote Marchesi)[17] accepted the discipline as a duty that was properly and necessarily imposed upon them and never appeared to resent it, but most Marchesi pupils, among them the most successful, found it uncomfortable, sometime unendurable. The American Emma Eames was certainly among the most successful, but the memories of Marchesi she recorded in her auto-biography were less than charitable. She described her (probably quite accurately) as "the ideal Prussian drillmaster, a woman of much character and one to gain a great ascendancy over her pupils . . . She herself was at her piano by nine in the morning every week day, was always perfectly and rather richly dressed and with never a hair out of place . . . She had intelligence and the real German efficiency, but no intuition."[18]

Eames was four years younger than Melba, and the only thing wrong with "the world according to Eames" was Melba. The two divas were fated to bang up against each other at almost every stage of their careers, and Eames was fated to come off second best each time. It all began at the Ecole Marchesi, where Eames was enrolled in 1886, a few weeks before Melba. Eames was twenty-one years old, a New Englander (though she was actually born in China) who had had four years of quite sophisticated musical and vocal education in Boston. She had also studied the "Delsarte system of gesture," because she believed it would rid her of nervous tension and make her movements onstage graceful and natural.[19] She was, in short, a very confident and determined young lady, but one who was nevertheless deemed to need two years of the Marchesi treatment before she was ready to appear before the public. Melba, on the other hand, needed only nine months.

Helen Porter Mitchell, as Melba was then called, had been born and brought up in Melbourne, Australia, the daughter of a well-to-do suburban family. While at Girls' College, she had had the good fortune to have a more-than-competent Italian singing teacher, Pietro Cecchi, and when her early marriage broke down, leaving her with a small child, she fell back on concert singing to support herself. Cecchi was probably the only one who understood the potential of her voice at this stage, and it was with his encouragement that she hitched a lift to London with her father in 1886 and started auditioning for anyone who would listen. She got nowhere—though Sir Arthur Sullivan thought she might eventually be suitable for the D'Oyly

Nellie Melba (1861–1931) was not renowned for her tact. Dining at
Windsor Castle in 1905 after giving a concert with Mary Garden and the
tenor Giovanni Zenatello, she loudly informed the company: "What a
poor concert this would have been if I hadn't been singing!" Nevertheless,
returning to London that night by train, she shared a compartment with
Mary Garden. "Before we reached London," Garden recalled, "we had
become fast friends and this friendship lasted until she died."
(Royal College of Music, London.)

Carte chorus—so she crossed the channel to Paris (which was where she
entered an opera house for the first time in her life) and found the one person
who agreed wholeheartedly and unreservedly with Cecchi's judgement—
Mathilde Marchesi. The sixty-five-year-old teacher and the twenty-six-year-
old pupil immediately formed a mutual admiration society, and Melba, con-

veniently forgetting Cecchi, who had undoubtedly endowed her with her basic and all-important technique, never ceased to credit Marchesi as her "onlie-begetter."

Eames had a very different view of the matter: "This brilliant new soprano had little to learn and in truth was well along the road to vocal sophistication before Madame ever saw her, and lacked only taste and imagination and musical intuition," she wrote (the implication being that those were three qualities Melba never acquired, an opinion many would agree with).[20] The truth of the relationship was more likely that the teacher and pupil got along so well that the singer's qualities, which must still have been unpracticed, if not raw, when she arrived in Paris, were quickly developed into the extraordinary talent that could be compared only with that of Patti among singers in recent memory. What is certain is that within nine months of arriving at the rue Jouffroy, and armed with a new name—Melba—she made her debut at the Monnaie in Brussels as Gilda, followed by debuts in London (as Lucia) and Paris (as Ophélie). Neither of the last two was very successful, but in London she made a powerful friend, Lady de Grey, who had a great deal of influence at Covent Garden. Lady de Grey arranged for her to make a "second debut" in London in the summer of 1889, this time as Gounod's Juliette with Jean de Reszke as her Roméo. That was the real beginning.

Three months earlier, in Paris, Emma Eames had finally made her professional debut—also as Juliette, and also opposite the Roméo of Jean de Reszke. Melba, who was in the audience, helpfully went to call on Eames next day to pass on a few criticisms of her performance. But the fact was that Eames's debut had been a triumph. She was an exceptionally beautiful young woman and her grace and radiance onstage made a great impression on the audience, but it was her singing that finally brought down the house. Even Marchesi was moved by the performance and had her husband take her backstage to congratulate her pupil—and, of course, to be seen with her.[21]

Nellie Melba's name is never once mentioned in Eames's memoirs, which were published in 1927, the year after Melba's official retirement, but there are frequent and vitriolic references to "the singer who had prevented my debut in Brussels." Whether rightly or wrongly, Eames believed Melba had used her influence at the Monnaie, where she had a contract, to persuade the management not to engage Eames for the 1887–88 season. She also believed that she had poisoned her relationship with Marchesi, that she had tried to influence Gounod against her, and that she had publicly (as well as privately) been critical of that debut performance as Juliette.

Because Eames was such a rude and unforgiving woman, and because Melba was so arrogant in her superiority, there never was a truce between them. It became an unfortunate obsession for Eames—whereas Melba, who had virtual artistic control of Covent Garden for many years, and a good deal of influence at the Met as well, was careful to give the impression that she did not consider Eames any sort of competitor (while being equally careful to make sure that Eames did not sing at Covent Garden after 1901). In fact, they had an awful lot in common. They were both endowed with wonderful natural voices, to which had been added the Marchesi method and an insistence on the purity of the Italian bel canto tradition. They were both, therefore, out of step with what was happening in contemporary opera—the movement toward realism and genuine drama onstage—though they both took part in it enthusiastically, and sometimes effectively. Neither of them was much of an actor—Melba simply didn't do it, while Eames relied mainly on her great beauty and stage presence. They represented a bygone era, but one that was still much in demand in opera houses, especially traditional houses like Covent Garden and the Met where the singing was what mattered. They may have seemed a little incongruous on stage at times, but their art was beautiful singing, and they did it superbly, generally from the footlights. In his book *The Art of Singing,* the New York critic W. J. Henderson described Melba's voice in its prime: "It extended from B flat below the clef to the high F. The scale was beautifully equalized throughout and there was not the smallest change in quality from bottom to top. All the tones were forward; there was never even a hint of throatiness. The full, flowing and facile emission of the tones have never been surpassed, if matched by any other singer of our time. The intonation was pre-eminent in its correctness; the singer was rarely in the smallest measure off pitch."[22]

Encomiums for Eames's voice were not normally so uncritical, but they often used phrases like "exquisite purity" and "lovely in quality." And

Eames's reviewers often wrote openly of a criticism that applied just as much to Melba, but was easier to overlook in her case because her singing was so exquisite and often so astonishing. The problem was coldness, frigidity — the singers' detachment from, or lack of involvement in, the drama that was meant to be taking place onstage. In retrospect, this can be seen as a characteristic of the bel canto school ("in retrospect" because, at the time, in the eighteenth and nineteenth centuries, it was so often disguised by the sheer virtuosity and excitement of the singing). In *The Great Singers*, Henry Pleasants characterized it as "a kind of singing probably closer to the art of [the castrati] Guadagni, Pacchierotti and [Luigi] Marchesi than anything we are likely ever to hear. It is a sexless kind of singing, girlish rather than boyish if you like, but rarely womanly in an earthy way — suited to Elisabeth and Elsa in an obvious way, but not to Brünnhilde, Isolde, or Kundry, or to Aida or Leonora."[23]

What separated Melba, Eames, and most of the other Marchesi pupils from their predecessors was the repertory they sang. It was not the familiar bel canto repertory associated with Sontag, Lind, or even Patti. Melba sang no Mozart, only Rosina and Semiramide from the Rossini canon and Lucia from Donizetti's, no Bellini, and only the *Huguenots* Queen from all of Meyerbeer's works. Instead, she applied the method — basically the same method that Sontag, Lind, Patti, and their colleagues had used, not to mention generations of castrati before them — to a new repertory. There were French composers aplenty (Gounod, Bizet, Thomas, Delibes, Massenet), and early Wagner (Elisabeth and Elsa), and Verdi (Gilda, Violetta, Desdemona, and an Ethiopian princess who might better have been omitted), and Leoncavallo's Nedda (which was an amazing leap, but a successful one), and the God-given role of Mimi, which Melba more or less made her own at the Met, while firmly refusing to risk less lyrical, more dramatic Puccini heroines like Butterfly and Tosca. Obviously, there was a progression here, from the cascading coloratura of Lucia to the less strenuous lyricism of Mimi, but that was hardly surprising for a woman who was in her sixty-sixth year when she finally retired from the stage. Eames, in a much shorter career, omitted most of the coloratura roles; she began with the lyric ones (especially the French) and progressed to the dramatic — in her case, a good deal more dramatic than Melba: she included Sieglinde, the *Trovatore* Leonore, and Mascagni's Santuzza.

One lesson Eames and Melba had certainly learned from Marchesi was to exercise caution in what they sang—and, on the whole, they did. Neither had a huge repertory, but there were mistakes, all the same. They both sang Aida without much success (it was one of Eames's frigid performances in the role that prompted the critic James Huneker to write: "Last night there was skating on the Nile"). Once, and once only, in 1896, Melba made the terrible mistake of singing the *Siegfried* Brünnhilde, totally failing to do justice to the role and causing herself several weeks of painful vocal problems. Eames had a rather similar time with Tosca, withdrawing from her first attempt after four performances (W. J. Henderson surmised she had "Toscalitis"), but she persevered with the role and sang it right up to the somewhat premature end of her career in 1911. Puccini, who heard her as Tosca in Paris in 1904, thought she was magnificent—like a tragic Greek goddess—and you can hear something of what he must have perceived on Mapleson's cylinder recording of a Met *Tosca*. But most observers found her unemotional and undramatic in the role, as was the case with many similar roles—they found her musically precise and very beautiful, but icily detached from the drama unfolding within and around her character. Eames was very aware of the criticisms and devoted a good deal of space in her autobiography to an unconvincing defense. Melba, on the other hand, could have cared less. For her, the voice was all that mattered, and though she was four years older than Eames, she kept her instrument in such impeccable condition that she was still singing in public fifteen years after Eames had retired.

Did that have anything to do with the Marchesi method? Marchesi herself might have pointed out that Eames, having absorbed and launched herself on the basis of the method, had given up its discipline and attempted to become her own teacher, whereas Melba (with the single exception of the Brünnhilde) had remained true to the teaching and the discipline.

Because of their brilliance and their rivalry (and because they were both recorded, albeit by very primitive technology), Melba and Eames are the most notable examples of the Marchesi method, but there were many other outstanding voices for which Marchesi could take credit. One of the first was Ilma di Murska, a Croatian soprano who studied with her in the late 1850s and early 1860s. Although one of her most famous roles turned out to be Senta, di Murska was renowned as a high-flying coloratura singer with a three-octave range who generated huge excitement with her Queen of the Night, Konstanze, Lucia, Amina, and several Meyerbeer roles (Queen Marguerite, Dinorah, and Isabella in *Robert le diable*). She was, by all accounts, an eccentric lady, even by prima donna standards, and a most extravagant actress—her impersonation of the mad Lucia was so far over the top that it would have been risible had it not been for the wonderful accuracy of her singing. To add to her natural gifts, Marchesi had given her a technique in which she could have total confidence. As a contemporary writer put it: "Ilma di Murska sang the most difficult passages of ornamentation with unerring certainty; and she possessed such a memory, combined with such a dislike for the worry of rehearsals, that she would frequently learn her part by simply reading it over while she was lying in bed."[24]

For a time, di Murska was thought of as a challenger to Patti, who was much the same age—but only for a time. Another East European soprano, a dozen years younger, was not so fortunate: Etelka Gerster from Hungary eventually had to be treated for hysteria.[25] Her problems arose not from the teaching of Marchesi, which had given her a wondrous technique that enabled her to outshine most of her contemporaries in the great coloratura roles, but from her very success. Her troubles became serious when she had repeated triumphs at the New York Academy and began to be spoken of as a rival to Patti. Colonel J. H. Mapleson had both ladies under contract to the Academy for the 1883–84 season, including an ambitious coast-to-coast tour. Patti's contract required the provision of a railway coach specially outfitted for her use alone ("The bath, which was fitted for hot and cold water, was made of solid silver. The key of the outer door was of 18-carat gold," wrote Mapleson in his memoirs).[26] Inevitably, there was trouble, and it began when Gerster found out that Patti's performances had higher ticket prices than hers (which was not surprising since Mapleson had agreed to pay Patti a staggering five thousand dollars a performance). Then the two singers appeared together in *Les Huguenots*, Gerster as the Queen, Patti as Valentine. A mix-up during the curtain calls led to all the floral tributes being handed to Patti, even though many of them were intended for Gerster. The audience responded by giving Gerster a massive personal ovation, which infuriated Patti and caused her to begin an unrelenting campaign to hold Gerster (whom she referred to as "the sorceress") responsible for everything that went wrong — even a small earthquake in California was blamed on the Hungarian's "evil eye." Poor Gerster, a proud but delicate creature, was reduced to rubble, and eventually found herself expensively ensconced on the couch of Jean Martin Charcot, Freud's teacher.[27]

At just about the time Patti and Gerster were butting heads in America, the Ecole Marchesi was turning out one of its most unusual, and accomplished, pupils. If Marchesi had had her way, Emma Calvé would have stayed longer than six months, for, until Melba's arrival three years later, she probably possessed the most remarkable voice Marchesi had worked with. Calvé herself liked to say that it was actually two separate voices. It ranged from A below middle C to the E above high C, and enabled her to sing soprano or mezzo-soprano roles without difficulty. At various times she sang all the major female roles of *Le nozze di Figaro* (Cherubino, Susanna, and the Countess) and both the contralto Hérodias and the soprano Salomé in Massenet's *Hérodiade*.[28] As if this weren't enough, she also learned from Mustafà (one of the last of the castrati in the Sistine Choir and a famous teacher) a "trick voice" that she sometimes used to great effect. It was a way of producing ethereal, seemingly incorporeal high notes by keeping her mouth "tight shut" — Mustafà said she would have to practice it two hours a day for ten years before she was able to master it: in fact, it took her three years. It can be heard to good effect in the recording she made of the folk song "Ma Lisette," but it can also be heard to very bad effect on the Lionel Mapleson cylinder recording of a Met performance of *Faust*, in which she uses it, disastrously, for the final high B of the Jewel Song.[29]

Calvé had almost nothing to say about her Marchesi training, which probably indicates that she found it as hard and unrelenting as most other pupils. She was not the sort of young woman who would easily knuckle down to such an overbearing and imperious teacher, and she went through some bad times, including a dismal debut at La Scala, before she found a teacher

Emma Calvé (1858–1942), a dramatic soprano from Aveyron, in the south of France, was acknowledged to be the greatest Carmen of her day, and one of the finest Santuzzas too. The American critic Richard Aldrich described her voice as "wonderfully potent in its expression of emotion and in the variety of colour it could assume." (Royal College of Music, London.)

more to her taste—Rosina Laborde, who had been a contemporary of Pasta and Sontag. But she had learned a method from Marchesi—a method that gave her the technique on which she could always rely (a priceless gift for any singer). From Laborde she learned the art of coloring her voice, and it was this art, coupled with that hard-earned technique, that made her the finest vocal actress of her generation, a performer as much admired by the great Italian actress Eleonora Duse as she was by the composers Massenet and Mascagni. Carmen eventually overwhelmed her career—there had been no other Carmen to compare with her since Célestine Galli-Marié created the role in 1875—and it unfortunately served to hide the strength and humanity of her impersonations of bel canto heroines who had traditionally had very little flesh on them—Lucia, Amina, Marguerite. Mme Marchesi might not have boasted a great deal of Calvé as an alumna, and Calvé herself boasted not at all of her time with Marchesi, but "Calvé-the-great-Carmen" owed a good deal to those six months of her life.

Most of the young women who endured the regime at the rue Jouffroy had intrinsically powerful voices. If they were going to sing in houses like the Opéra, Covent Garden, and the Met it was a necessary precondition. But it was never a requirement for entry into the Ecole Marchesi: Madame trained voices for the concert platform as well as the opera stage, and she took as much pride in a small voice, beautifully produced, as she did in the great operatic voices that could project to the back of huge auditoriums. Sibyl Sanderson was a case in point. She had a small voice—"silvery" was a word often used to describe it—but with a range of three octaves up to the high G. A stunning beauty from California, she was an exact contemporary of Emma Eames and arrived at rue Jouffroy in the same year, 1886, at the age of twenty-one. It was said that her parents had sent her to Paris to save her from the predatory attentions of the newspaper baron William Randolph Hearst, and much later it was said that Orson Welles based the experiences of Susan in *Citizen Kane* on Sanderson's story.

This was the time of *les jeunes filles américaines* in Paris. When Sanderson arrived from California, the van Zandt scandal was still reverberating through the city. Marie van Zandt was a Brooklyn girl whose journey to Paris had included a spell in an English convent, being discovered by Patti, and being sent to Milan to study with Francesco Lamperti. In the early 1880s, she became the darling of the Opéra-Comique and succeeded in enchanting Ambroise Thomas, who declared her the perfect Mignon, and Léo Delibes, who composed the title role of *Lakmé* for her in 1883. What went wrong after those triumphs is hard to say—it's not clear whether it was a case of claques and cabals being set up to undermine her, or whether her voice was in bad shape, or a combination of both—but during 1884 and 1885 Marie van Zandt was the unwitting cause of several theatrical riots that finally caused her to quit the city, not to return until 1896.

So Sibyl Sanderson had been warned—yet she followed much the same course. Having apparently done well at the rue Jouffroy (Marchesi's daughter Blanche described her as "a kind-hearted, distinguished, most beautiful girl, without an atom of pride or jealousy, a *rara avis* in her way"),[30] she proceeded to captivate Jules Massenet. He arranged for her to make her debut (under a stage name, for some reason) as Manon in the Hague at the beginning of 1888, and he then devoted himself to writing his new opera, *Esclarmonde,* with a title role tailor-made for her. She was thus launched on Paris—along with the Eiffel Tower, which was the rival attraction—during the Universal Exhibition of 1889. Mary Garden, who was in the house on the first night, noted the audience's "gasp of adoration" as Sanderson made her first entrance[31]—and that was at the root of her problems: she was adored for her physical beauty, not for her voice, and it was her private life that very quickly became the focus of press attention. Yet the score of *Esclarmonde* suggests that her voice must have been very special and very agile, as it requires considerable weight of tone and real virtuosity—so much so that the opera has rarely been revived except for the Joan Sutherland production that originated in San Francisco in 1974 and traveled on to Covent Garden and the Metropolitan.

To begin with, this reputation did Sanderson no harm. She was in great demand throughout Europe, and Massenet was not the only composer to be enraptured—Saint-Saëns even wrote an opera that required her to undress (*Phryné*, 1893), but it all came unglued when Massenet wrote the title role of *Thaïs* for her. Given its premiere at the Opéra instead of the Opéra-Comique because Sanderson had just changed houses, it was not well received and had only fourteen performances. Once the press had got over the sensation of Sanderson's breast being revealed when her dress became unbuttoned on the first night—an accident, the management insisted, having nothing to do with Sanderson's depiction of the courtesan who becomes a saint[32]—no one had much good to say of the opera. That must have had a good deal to do with Sanderson's lackluster performance, because the production, with some additions and subtractions, eventually clocked up almost seven hundred performances at the Opéra, featuring such great stars as Mary Garden, Geraldine Farrar, and Maria Jeritza. At any rate, it was almost the end for Sanderson. After an unsuccessful debut at the Met as Manon, she got married and retired from the stage in 1897. The following year she had a stroke and suffered the deaths of her newborn child and her husband, all within a few months. After several pathetic attempts to restart her career, she died in 1903, still not forty, of a particularly brutal disease that disfigured her body and robbed her of the last semblance of her once-famous beauty. Mary Garden was one of the few people who was with her at the end.

Garden herself had escaped Marchesi's clutches. Scottish by birth but an American resident from the age of six, she had arrived in Paris as a twenty-year-old in 1895, in search of a teacher. She spent one month at the rue Jouffroy before concluding that the increasingly autocratic Marchesi, who was now in her mid-seventies, was not for her. Garden was, and would always remain, a creature of the theater: she knew instinctively that she had to be more than a good technician, more than a coloratura bird. When she wrote to try and explain this to Marchesi she received in reply a curt note that said: "Don't cry until you get out of the woods. A rolling stone gathers no moss."[33]

Garden wasted no time getting out of the woods. With a good deal of help from Sibyl Sanderson, whom she met in the spring of 1897 and with whom she lived for a time, she made her debut in Charpentier's *Louise* in 1900 and quickly made the title role her own. One day that summer she had the satisfaction of seeing Marchesi in the audience: "I prevailed upon a mutual friend to go to her, and learn, if possible, what her true impression was. Well, the famous teacher was genuinely *emotionée*—in fact, she was in tears; and she declared, without reserve, that here were effects more poignant than artificial opera had ever dreamed of."[34]

Another of the great American singers of the new century never even crossed the threshold of the Ecole Marchesi. The seventeen-year-old Geraldine Farrar, accompanied by her mother and father (who had little doubt that their daughter's voice held the key to their own prosperity), sailed for Europe in the fall of 1899 armed with a letter of introduction to Marchesi from Nellie Melba—probably the only form of introduction that could guarantee a place in Marchesi's class immediately. But Farrar never even bothered to use it, and she recalled the reasons in her memoir, *Such Sweet Compulsion,* which she claimed to have cowritten with her mother (who had actually been dead for fifteen years at the time of writing, but never mind!): "There was little to gain in submitting to a dazzling treatment whereby all voices were taught to shame the flute in impossible sky-rocket cadenzas or fall by the wayside when unable to do so. I had no true *coloratura* register and did not wish to change my own color in such mechanical attainment. I was even then aware of the monotony of beautiful even tones, when all dramatic expression was sacrificed to sound only."[35]

Farrar and Garden got it right. Whether or not their young voices would have responded to the Marchesi treatment, let alone survived it, was beside the point. The fact was that the classic Italian style of bel canto had finally been bypassed by the twentieth century. Yes, it would remain somewhat in demand, and its absence would be constantly bemoaned, because the bel canto operas would never lose their popularity—indeed, as the century progressed, more and more of them would return to the repertory. So when singers with the coloratura virtuosity of Callas, Sutherland, Sills, and Caballé infrequently appeared on the scene, there was always a welcome for them. But their performances were not as "pure," as colorless, as undramatic (as "mechanical," in Farrar's accusatory word) as those of their predecessors: they couldn't be, because by mid-century, with the advent of the stage director as an important ingredient of opera, it was no longer acceptable for singers just to sing. They were part of complex productions in which the heroines they portrayed were often "rethought" and given characterizations that the original librettists and composers would never have conceived of in their wildest imaginings. Some of them worked, some didn't, but they generally ensured that the singer had a great deal more to do than wander down to the footlights and sing.

The loudest and most uninhibited members of opera's audience have always been those who are there just for the singing—the connoisseurs of vocal style and technique. For about 250 years they constituted the vast majority of the audience: today they are a small, but very audible, minority. For good or ill (most people would say for good), the art form has moved on into much more dramatic territory, and bel canto—real bel canto, with its purity and evenness and accurate, seemingly effortless, coloratura—is something we no longer expect to hear in the opera house. But it is a shame that we almost never hear it anywhere else either.

Since we cannot properly recall it, and since recording technology could not do it justice in its final days (which were also the last days of the Ecole Marchesi, which closed its doors in 1908), it is worth trying to recreate the anticipation, the suspense, the excitement, and the *amazement* of the bel canto style in an anecdote told by Mary Garden in her autobiography, *Mary Garden's Story*. She remembered being at Covent Garden one night for a performance of *La Bohème*, with Melba as Mimì: "You know, the last note of the first act of *La Bohème* is the last note that comes out of Mimì's throat. It is a high C, and Mimì sings it when she walks out of the door with Rodolfo. She closes the door, and then she takes the note. The way Melba sang that high C was the strangest and weirdest thing I have ever experienced in my life. The note came floating out of the auditorium at Covent Garden: it left Melba's throat, it left Melba's body, it left everything, and came like a star and passed us in our box and went out into the infinite . . . My God, how beautiful it was!"[36]

How beautiful it was!

Notes

INTRODUCTION

1. Quoted in Harold C. Schonberg, *The Lives of the Great Composers* (New York: Norton, 1970; revised edition, 1981), p. 258.
2. See *Alessandro Moreschi, The Last Castrato* (Pearl Opal CD9823).
3. Patti's letter to Alfredo Barili, Dec. 8, 1905, quoted in John Frederick Cone, *Adelina Patti, Queen of Hearts* (Portland, Ore.: Amadeus, 1993), p. 244.
4. Herman Klein, *The Reign of Patti* (New York: Century, 1920).

CHAPTER ONE
Caccini's Pupils

1. 1 Corinthians, chap. 14, verse 34.
2. Anthony Newcomb, *The Madrigal at Ferrara, 1579-97* (Princeton, N.J.: Princeton University Press, 1981), pp. 7, 47.
3. Ibid., pp. 183-90.
4. G. Caccini, preface to *Euridice* (Florence, 1601 and 1615).
5. See the letter of Pietro Bardi, son of Count Giovanni Bardi, to the musical scholar Giovan Battista Doni, dated Dec. 16, 1634, reproduced in English translation in Piero Weiss, *Opera: A History in Documents* (Oxford: Oxford University Press, 2002), p. 9.
6. Caccini's *Euridice* was not the first opera to be published. Another influential member of the Florentine camerata, Emilio de'Cavalieri, wrote a work called *La rappresentatione di Anima, et di Corpo* for a performance at the Oratorio della Vallicella in Rome in February 1600. It was published in September 1600, just three months before *Euridice*. Some scholars describe *La rappresentatione* as an oratorio rather than a dramma per musica, but the first performance was undoubtedly fully staged.
7. J. Peri, preface to *Euridice* (Florence, 1601 and 1607).
8. Caccini, op. cit.
9. G. Caccini, preface to *Le nuovo musiche* (Florence, 1602).

10. Quoted in Denis Arnold, *Monteverdi* (London: J.M. Dent, 1963), p. 21.

11. See Suzanne G. Cusick in Stanley Sadie, ed., *The New Grove Dictionary of Opera* (London: Macmillan, 1992; paperback edition, 1998), vol. 1, p. 669.

12. But see S. G. Cusick, "Of Women, Music and Power: A Model from Seicento Florence," in *Musicology and Difference: Gender and Sexuality in Music Scholarship,* ed. Ruth. A. Solie (Berkeley: University of California Press, 1993).

13. Quoted in John Rosselli, *Singers of Italian Opera: The History of a Profession* (Cambridge: Cambridge University Press, 1992; paperback edition, 1995), p. 13.

14. Ibid., p. 12.

15. S. Bonini, *Discorsi e regole sovra la musica et il contrappunto* (c.1649), ed. and English trans. M. Bonino (Salt Lake City, 1979), pp. 148–49.

16. Ibid., p. 149.

17. See Clifford Bartlett, writing in the booklet accompanying the CD *Monteverdi's Orfeo, Favola in musica* (EMI Classics: CMS 7 64947 2), p. 15.

18. Alessandro Moreschi, one of the last professional castrati in the Sistine Choir, made a number of recordings between 1902 and 1904. Some are available on CD, e.g., *The Castrato Voice and the First Divas, 1902-08* (Minerva, MN-A73).

19. See Patrick Barbier, *Histoire des castrats* (Paris: Editions Bernard Grasset, 1989), in English translation as *The World of the Castrati,* trans. Margaret Crosland (London: Souvenir, 1996), p. 9.

20. See Bartlett, op. cit., p. 14.

21. Rosselli, op. cit., p. 9.

Getting Away with Murder

1. See D. Stevens, ed., *Claudio Monteverdi: Letters* (Cambridge: Cambridge University Press, 1980). Most of the relevant letters were written to his old colleague in Mantua, Alessandrio Striggio, who had been the librettist for *Orfeo* in 1607.

2. Giulio Strozzi, *Le glorie della signora Anna Renzi romana* (Venice, 1644); English translation in Ellen Rosand, *Opera in Seventeenth-Century Venice: The Creation of a Genre* (Berkeley: University of California Press, 1991), p. 232.

3. Rosand, op. cit., p. 282.

4. Ibid., p. 223.

5. Ibid., p. 224.

6. Alexandre-Toussaint de Limojon, Sier de Saint-Disdier, *La ville et la république de Venise* (Paris, 1680); English translation in Rosand, op. cit., p. 235.

7. W. Bray, ed., *The Memoirs of John Evelyn* (London, 1819), vol. 1, p. 191.

8. Quoted in Rosand, op. cit., p. 400.

9. Ibid., pp. 238–39.

10. Ibid., pp. 239–40.

11. See Luca Zoppelli in Stanley Sadie, ed., *The New Grove Dictionary of Opera* (London: Macmillan, 1992; paperback edition, 1998), vol. 4, p. 915.

294   *Notes to Pages 9–23*

12. François and Claude Parfaict, *Histoire de l'Académie royale de musique depuis son établissement jusqu'à présent* (MS, 1741: Paris, Bibliothèque Nationale).

13. J. L. Le Cerf de la Viéville, *Comparison de la musique italienne et de la musique françoise* (Brussels, 1704–06; reprint, Brussels, 1972).

14. Quoted by Lois Rosow in Sadie, op. cit., vol. 1, p. 203.

15. H. Sutherland Edwards, *The Prima Donna* (London, 1888: reprint, New York: Da Capo, 1978), vol. 1, p. 70.

16. Ibid., p. 70.

17. Parfaict, op. cit.

18. Théophile Gautier, *Mademoiselle de Maupin* (Paris, 1835).

19. Quoted in Charles Neilson Gattey, *Queens of Song* (London: Barrie & Jenkins, 1979), p. 2. The description of Maupin's adventures substantially follows Gattey's account.

20. Theodore Besterman, ed., *The Complete Works of Voltaire: Correspondence and Related Documents* (Oxford: Voltaire Foundation, 1994–2002).

21. Ibid.

22. Quoted by Winton Dean in Sadie, op. cit., vol. 3, p. 598.

23. Quoted in Edwards, op. cit., vol. 1, p. 20.

24. Ibid., p. 21.

25. Ibid., p. 25.

26. Owen Swiney, the Irish impresario, quoted by Winton Dean in Sadie, op. cit., vol. 4, p. 987. Swiney was largely responsible for bringing Faustina Bordoni to London to sing for Handel in 1726.

27. Quoted in Edwards, op. cit., vol. 1, p. 42.

28. Ibid.

29. Quoted in Gattey, op. cit., p. 5.

30. Ibid., p. 7.

31. Quoted in Patrick Barbier, *Histoire des castrats* (Paris: Editions Bernard Grasset, 1989), in English translation as *The World of the Castrati,* trans. Margaret Crosland (London: Souvenir, 1996), p. 184.

32. John Rosselli, *Singers of Italian Opera: The History of a Profession* (Cambridge: Cambridge University Press, 1992; paperback edition, 1995), p. 58.

33. Benedetto Croce, *Un prelato e una cantante del secolo XVIII* (Bari, 1946).

34. Quoted by Winton Dean and Carlo Vitali in Sadie, op. cit., vol. 1, p. 1035.

35. Quoted by Winton Dean in Sadie, op. cit., vol. 1, p. 547.

36. Ibid., vol. 4, p. 558.

37. Ibid.

CHAPTER THREE
Porpora's Pupils

1. Pietro Metastasio, *Lettere disperse e inedite a cura di Giosué Carducci* (Bologna: Zanichelli, 1883).

2. The drama was *La Nitteti* (1756).

3. Charles Burney, *Musical Tours in Europe* (1773), ed. Percy Scholes (Oxford: Oxford University Press, 1959), vol. 1, p. 78.

4. Patrick Barbier, *Histoire des castrats* (Paris: Editions Bernard Grasset, 1989), in English translation as *The World of the Castrati*, trans. Margaret Crosland (London: Souvenir, 1996), p. 93.

5. G. Sacchi, *Vita del Cav. Don Carlo Broschi* (Venice: Caleti, 1784), p. 15.

6. These and other stories about Caffarelli are chronicled in Angus Heriot, *The Castrati in Opera* (New York: Da Capo, 1974).

7. Ibid., p. 144.

8. Ibid., p. 150.

9. Quoted by Winton Dean in Stanley Sadie, ed., *The New Grove Dictionary of Opera* (London: Macmillan, 1992; paperback version, 1998), vol. 1, p. 677.

10. Quoted in H. Sutherland Edwards, *The Prima Donna* (London, 1888: reprint, New York: Da Capo, 1978), vol. 1, p. 56.

11. Ibid., p. 55.

12. Ibid., p. 57.

13. John Rosselli, *Singers of Italian Opera: The History of a Profession* (Cambridge: Cambridge University Press, 1992; paperback edition, 1995), p. 52.

14. W. A. Mozart to his father, Feb. 19, 1778, in Emily Anderson, ed., *The Letters of Mozart and His Family*, 3 vols. (Macmillan, 1938; 3rd edition, 1985).

15. Rosselli, op. cit., p. 66.

16. One of the best discussions of teaching methods in the Neapolitan conservatories may be found in Barbier, op. cit.

17. See Heriot, op. cit., chap. 3, "Life and Times of the Castrati."

18. It's at no. 15 Vico Carminiello.

19. See Rosselli, op. cit., chap. 3, "Women."

20. Quoted by Michael F. Robinson in Sadie, op. cit., vol. 3, p. 1066.

21. Hasse had already met Mozart in Vienna when Mozart was thirteen. He wrote of him then: "It is difficult not to like him. Certainly he will become a prodigy if, as he grows older, he continues to make the necessary progress."

CHAPTER FOUR

The Castrato Ascendancy

1. For a discussion of numbers, see John Rosselli, *Singers of Italian Opera: The History of a Profession* (Cambridge: Cambridge University Press, 1992; paperback edition, 1995), p. 40.

2. Alessandro Moreschi was the last castrato to sing in the Sistine Chapel choir; he retired in 1913.

3. Quoted in Charles Neilson Gattey, *Queens of Song* (London: Barrie & Jenkins, 1979), p. 34.

4. See *Alessandro Moreschi: The Last Castrato* (Pearl Opal CD9823).

5. Charles de Brosses, *Lettres familières écrites d'Italie en 1739 et 1740* (Paris, 1869), vol. 2, p. 318.

6. Quoted in Angus Heriot, *The Castrati in Opera* (London, 1956; reprint, New York: Da Capo, 1974), p. 130.

7. Ibid., p. 132.

8. Ibid., p. 88.

9. Ibid.

10. Quoted by Gerhard Croll in Stanley Sadie, ed., *The New Grove Dictionary of Opera* (London: Macmillan, 1992; paperback edition, 1998), vol. 2, p. 560.

11. John Hawkins, *A General History of the Science and Practice of Music* (London, 1776), quoted in Heriot, op. cit., p. 99.

12. Patrick Barbier, *Histoire des castrats* (Paris: Editions Bernard Grasset, 1989), in English translation as *The World of the Castrati,* trans. Margaret Crosland (London: Souvenir, 1996), p. 97.

13. The incident was reported by Burney, quoted in Heriot, op. cit., p. 99.

14. Quoted in Christopher Hogwood, *Handel* (London: Thames & Hudson, 1984; paperback edition, 1988; reprint, 1995), p. 81.

15. See Heriot, op. cit., p. 94.

16. Baron de Grimm, *Correspondance littéraire, philosophique et critique, 1753-1782* (1813), quoted in Barbier, op. cit., p. 90.

17. Barbier, op. cit., p. 111.

18. Quoted in Rosselli, op. cit., p. 38.

19. See Heriot, op. cit., p. 112.

20. Quoted by Dale E. Monson in Sadie, op. cit., vol. 1, p. 731.

21. Ibid.

22. Prologue to Gluck's *Alceste* (Vienna, 1767), reproduced in full in Alfred Einstein, *Gluck* (London: Dent, 1936; revised edition, 1964).

23. Quoted in Heriot, op. cit., p. 135.

24. Ibid., p. 137.

25. Ibid., p. 163.

26. Lord Mount Edgcumbe, *Musical Reminiscences* (London, 1834), quoted in Heriot, op. cit., p. 167.

27. See Angus Heriot, op. cit., p. 169.

28. P. Brydone, *Viaggio in Sicilia e a Malta,* Letter 36 (Milan, 1770), quoted in Barbier, op. cit., p. 100.

29. Barbier, op. cit., p. 113.

30. Ibid., p. 138.

31. Rosselli, op. cit., p. 1.

32. Barbier, op. cit., p. 112.

33. Heriot, op. cit., p. 36.

34. Ibid., p. 119.

35. See Richard Osborne, *Rossini* (London: Weidenfeld & Nicholson, 1986; paperback edition, Boston: Northeastern University Press, 1990), p. 11.

36. Barbier, op. cit., p. 234.

37. Edmond Michotte, *Souvenirs: Une soirée chez Rossini à Beau-Séjour (Passy), 1858* (Brussels, 1910), trans. Herbert Weinstock in *Rossini: A Biography* (New York, 1968; rev. ed., 1982), p. 109.

38. Barbier, op. cit., p. 235.

39. See Heriot, op. cit., pp. 197–98.

CHAPTER FIVE

Après Gluck and the Time of Mozart

1. Suggested by Michael Scott, *The Record of Singing* (London: Gerald Duckworth, 1977; reprint, Boston: Northeastern University Press, 1993), vol. 1, p. 10.

2. W. A. Mozart to his father, Feb. 19, 1778, in Emily Anderson, ed., *The Letters of Mozart and His Family*, 3 vols. (Macmillan, 1938; 3rd edition, 1985).

3. Charles Neilson Gattey, *Queens of Song* (London: Barrie & Jenkins, 1979), p. 12.

4. Quoted by Erik Smith in Amanda Holden, ed., with Nicholas Kenyon and Stephen Walsh, *The Viking Opera Guide* (London: Viking, 1993), p. 690.

5. Quoted by Kathleen Kuzmick Hansell in Stanley Sadie, ed., *The New Grove Dictionary of Opera* (London: Macmillan, 1992; paperback edition, 1998), vol. 1, p. 1094.

6. Quoted by Erik Smith in Holden, op. cit., p. 687.

7. Quoted by Kathleen Kuzmick Hansell in Sadie, op. cit., vol. 1, p. 39.

8. W. A. Mozart to his sister, Mar. 24, 1770, in Anderson, op. cit.

9. Quoted by Kathleen Kuzmick Hansell in Sadie, op. cit., vol. 1, p. 39.

10. Quoted in Gattey, op. cit., p. 18.

11. Ibid.

12. Discussed in Rupert Christiansen, *Prima Donna: A History* (New York: Viking, 1985), pp. 49–51.

13. W. A. Mozart to his father, Sept. 26, 1781, in Anderson, op. cit.

14. Julian Rushton in Sadie, op. cit., vol. 1, p. 1205.

15. W. A. Mozart to his father, Mar. 29, 1783, in Anderson, op. cit.

16. Leopold Mozart to his son, May 5, 1786, ibid.

17. In a letter to his father from Mannheim, dated Jan. 17, 1778, Mozart described some of his earliest impressions of the Weber family. In Andersen, op. cit.

18. W. A. Mozart to his father, May 16, 1781, ibid.

19. W. A. Mozart to his father, Dec. 15, 1781, ibid.

20. Elizabeth Abbott, trans., *Memoirs of Lorenzo Da Ponte,* (New York, 1929; reprint, New York: Da Capo, 1967), p. 142.

21. Clemens Höslinger in Sadie, op. cit., vol. 2, p. 498.

22. Roger Fiske, ed., *Reminiscences of Michael Kelly* (London, 1826; reprint, Oxford: Oxford University Press, 1975), p. 121.

23. Dorothea Link in Sadie, op. cit., vol. 1, p. 965.

24. Quoted by Christopher Raeburn in Sadie, op. cit., vol. 2, p. 1104.

25. W. A. Mozart to his sister, Aug. 19, 1789, in Anderson, op. cit.

26. Patricia Lewy Gidwitz and John A. Rice in Sadie, op. cit., vol. 2, p. 162.

27. W. A. Mozart to Baron Gottfried von Jacquin, Nov. 4, 1787, in Anderson, op. cit.

28. Anonymous author quoted in H. Sutherland Edwards, *The Prima Donna* (London, 1888; reprint, New York: Da Capo, 1978), vol. 1, p. 130.

29. Christiansen, op. cit., p. 56.

30. Quoted in Edwards, op. cit., vol. 1, p. 133.

31. Quoted in Scott, op. cit., vol. 1, p. 12.

32. Quoted in Edwards, op. cit., vol. 1, p. 134.

CHAPTER SIX
Prime Donne Assolute

1. Julian Budden in Stanley Sadie, ed., *The New Grove Handbooks in Music: History of Opera* (London: Macmillan, 1989), p. 171.

2. Stendahl, *Vie de Rossini* (Paris, 1824; English trans., 1956; reprint, with notes by Richard N. Coe, New York: Orion, 1970), p. 42.

3. Ibid., p. 43.

4. Quoted in William Weaver, *The Golden Age of Italian Opera from Rossini to Puccini* (London: John Calmann and King, 1980; paperback edition, New York: Thames & Hudson, 1988), p. 19.

5. Ibid.

6. J. Peri, preface to *Euridice* (Florence, 1601 and 1607).

7. Stendahl, op. cit., p. 63.

8. Quoted in H. Sutherland Edwards, *The Prima Donna* (London, 1888; reprint, New York: Da Capo, 1978), vol. 1, p. 178.

9. Stendahl, op. cit., p. 61.

10. Quoted in Rupert Christiansen, *Prima Donna: A History* (London: Viking, 1984; New York: Viking, 1985), p. 62.

11. Quoted in John Rosselli, *Singers of Italian Opera: The History of a Profession* (Cambridge: Cambridge University Press, 1992; paperback edition, 1995), p. 68.

12. Quoted in Stanley Sadie, ed., *The New Grove Dictionary of Opera* (London: Macmillan, 1992; paperback edition, 1998), vol. 4, p. 867.

13. One of the most authoritative discussions of Callas's voice may be found in "Processo alla Callas" (Callas on Trial) in the Italian weekly paper *Radiocorriere TV*, Nov. 30, 1969.

14. Stendahl, op. cit., p. 121.

15. See Henry Chorley, *Thirty Years' Musical Recollections* (London, 1862; reprint, 1926).

16. Quoted in Christiansen, op. cit., p. 72.

17. Quoted in Edwards, op. cit., vol. 1, p. 246.

18. Quoted in Charles Neilson Gattey, *Queens of Song* (London: Barrie & Jenkins, 1979), p. 42.

19. William Ashbrook, *Donizetti and His Operas* (Cambridge: Cambridge University Press, 1982), p. 203.

20. Quoted in Christiansen, op. cit., p. 84.

21. For a discussion of "birdsong," see Patrick Barbier, *Histoire des castrats* (Paris: Editions Bernard Grasset, 1989), in English translation as *The World of the Castrati*, trans. Margaret Crosland (London: Souvenir, 1996), pp. 95–96. In *Rinaldo*, Handel composed an aria for Almirena ("Augelletti che cantate," sung by a female soprano) that imitated birdsong. It had an extended introduction of two flutes and soprano recorder. During performances of the opera in London in 1711 real sparrows were let loose on the stage to heighten the effect.

22. Quoted in Christiansen, op. cit., p. 97.

23. Quoted in Gattey, op. cit., p. 41.

24. Quoted by John Warrack in Sadie, *The New Grove Dictionary of Opera*, op. cit., vol. 4, p. 456.

25. The letter was addressed to Alfred Bunn, manager of the Drury Lane Theatre, London, in 1845.

26. Quoted in Herman Klein, *The Reign of Patti* (New York: Ayer, 1920), p. 381.

27. Giuseppe Verdi, letter to Count Opprandino Arrivabene, Dec. 27, 1877, quoted in Mary Jane Phillips-Matz, *Verdi: A Biography* (Oxford: Oxford University Press, 1993), p. 642.

28. Emma Eames, *Some Memories and Reflections* (New York: Arno, 1927), p. 36.

29. See Christiansen, op. cit., p. 112.

30. *The Athenaeum*, July 1, 1876.

31. Bernard Shaw, *Music in London, 1890–94* (London, 1894; reprint, London: Penguin Putnam, 1977), vol. 3, p. 268.

32. Michael Scott, *The Record of Singing* (London: Gerald Duckworth, 1977; reprint, Boston: Northeastern University Press, 1993), vol. 1, p. 22.

CHAPTER SEVEN
The World's Showcase

1. Cited in Patrick Barbier, *La vie quotidienne à l'opéra au temps de Rossini et de Balzac* (Paris, 1987), in English translation as *Opera in Paris, 1800–1850: A Living History,* trans. Robert Luoma (Portland, Ore.: Amadeus, 1995), p. 138.

2. Paul Scudo, *Critique et littérature musicales* (Paris, 1856), p. 310.

3. Alphonse Royer, *Histoire de l'opéra* (Paris, 1887), p. 158.

4. Quoted in Barbier, op. cit., p. 147.

5. Ibid.

6. Ibid., p. 158.

7. Harold Rosenthal and John Warrack, eds., *The Concise Oxford Dictionary of Opera* (Oxford: Oxford University Press, 1964; paperback edition, 1990), p. 478.

8. Giacomo Meyerbeer, letter to Amalia Beer, Apr. 16, 1849, quoted in Heinz and Gudrun Becker, *Giacomo Meyerbeer, A Life in Letters,* trans. Mark Violette (Portland, Ore.: Amadeus, 1989), p. 123.

9. H. Berlioz, *A travers chant* (Paris, 1862), ed. Leon Guichard (Paris: Grund, 1969), p. 154.

10. Ibid., p. 170.

11. *Galignani's Messenger,* Nov. 4, 1864.

12. Camille du Locle was the director. See Hugh MacDonald in Stanley Sadie, ed., *The New Grove Dictionary of Opera* (London: Macmillan, 1992; paperback edition, 1998), vol. 1, p. 735.

13. Quoted in John Warrack, *Tchaikovsky* (London: Hamish Hamilton, 1973), p. 84.

14. Peter Gammond, *Offenbach: His Life and Times* (Tunbridge Wells: Midas, 1980; reprint, Neptune City, N.J.: Paganiniana, 1981), p. 91.

CHAPTER EIGHT
Dramatic Singing

1. G. Verdi to Felice Varesi, Jan. 7, 1847, reprinted in *Verdi's Macbeth: A Sourcebook* (original in Accademia Chigiana, Siena), p. 30.

2. G. Verdi to Giuseppina Appiani, Mar. 9, 1844, reprinted in G. Cesari and A. Luzio, eds., *I copialettere di Giuseppe Verdi* (Milan, 1913), p. 425.

3. G. Verdi to Emanuele Muzio, Mar. 7, 1853, ibid., p. 533.

4. Gaia Servadio, *The Real Traviata: The Life of Giuseppina Strepponi, Wife of Giuseppe Verdi* (London: Hodder and Stoughton, 1994: paperback edition, London: Sceptre, 1995), p. 57.

5. Ibid., p. 93.

6. G. Verdi to Giuseppina Negroni Prati Morosini, undated letter, reprinted in Cesari and Luzio, op. cit., p. 432.

7. Quoted in Francis Toye, *Verdi: His Life and Works* (London: Gollancz, 1931; reprint, 1962), p. 133.

8. Mary Jane Phillips-Matz, *Verdi, A Biography* (Oxford: Oxford University Press, 1993), p. 193.

9. Ibid., p. 194.

10. Quoted by David Kimbell in Amanda Holden, ed., with Nicholas Kenyon and Stephen Walsh, *The Viking Opera Guide* (London: Viking, 1993), p. 1133.

11. *Verdi's Macbeth: A Sourcebook,* op. cit., p. 49.

12. Quoted in Harold C. Schonberg, *The Lives of the Great Composers* (New York: Norton, 1970; revised edition, 1981), p. 258.

13. G. Verdi to Marianna Barbieri-Nini, Oct. 6, 1848, quoted in Phillips-Matz, op. cit., p. 227.

14. Toye, op. cit., p. 36.

15. Harold Rosenthal and John Warrack, eds., *The Concise Oxford Dictionary of Opera* (Oxford: Oxford University Press, 1964; paperback edition, 1990), p. 288.

16. E. Muzio to Antonio Barezzi, June 16, 1847, reprinted in L. A. Garibaldi, ed., *Giuseppe Verdi nelle lettere di Emanuele Muzio ad Antonio Barezzi* (Milan, 1931), p. 327.

17. Phillips-Matz, op. cit., p. 262.

18. Ibid., p. 317.

19. Ibid., p. 308.

20. G. Verdi to Antonio Somma, 1853, quoted in Andrew Porter, "Verdi," in *The New Grove Masters of Italian Opera* (New York: Norton, 1983), p. 218.

21. Cited by Roger Parker in Stanley Sadie, ed., *The New Grove Dictionary of Opera* (London: Macmillan, 1992: paperback edition, 1998), vol. 3, p. 1327.

22. Phillips-Matz, op. cit., p. 118.

23. F. M. Piave to C. Marzari, Feb. 3, 1853, ibid., p. 320.

24. F. Varesi to G. Brenna, Nov. 24, 1852, ibid.

25. G. Verdi to Emanuele Muzio, Mar. 7, 1853, reprinted in Cesari and Luzio, op. cit., p. 533.

26. G. Verdi to C. De Sanctis, May 26, 1854, quoted in A. Luzio, *Categgi verdiani* (Rome, 1935), vol. 1, p. 24.

27. F. M. Piave to Tito Ricordi, Apr. 1854, quoted in Phillips-Matz, op. cit., p. 328.

28. G. Verdi to V. Torelli, May 16, 1856, reprinted in Cesari and Luzio, op. cit., p, 190.

29. G. Verdi to V. Torelli, Dec. 6, 1856, ibid, p. 197.

30. Quoted in Toye, op. cit., p. 97.

31. G. Verdi to V. Torelli, June 17, 1857, reprinted in Cesari and Luzio, op. cit., p. 484.

32. Phillips-Matz, op. cit., p. 379.

33. Ibid., p. 383.

34. Ibid., p. 444.

35. G. Verdi to General Sabouroff, Mar. 19, 1862, quoted in Cesari and Luzio, op. cit., vol. 4, p. 229.

36. G. Verdi to G. Ricordi, Oct. 16, 1877, reprinted in Cesari and Luzio, op. cit., p. 624.

37. G. Verdi to Count Opprandino Arrivabene, Dec. 27, 1877, quoted in Phillips-Matz, op. cit., p. 642.

38. Teresa Stolz to Verdi and Strepponi, Mar. 18, 1878, ibid., p. 641.

39. Sadie, op. cit., vol. 4, p. 461.

40. Ibid., vol. 4, p. 549.

41. Phillips-Matz, op. cit., p. 583.

42. Ibid.

43. G. Verdi to G. Ricordi, Nov. 20, 1880, reprinted in P. Petrobelli, ed., *Carteggio Verdi-Ricordi 1880–81* (Parma: Istituto Nazionale di Studi Verdiani, 1988), p. 68.

44. William Ashbrook in Sadie, op. cit., vol. 2, p. 102.

45. G. Verdi to Teresa Stolz, Sept. 9, 1892, quoted in Giuseppe Cenzato, "Giuseppe Verdi e Teresa Stolz in un carteggio inedito," *Corriere della sera*, Oct. 30, 1932, p. 3.

46. G. Verdi to Emma Zilli, Dec. 15, 1893, in Cesari and Luzio, op. cit., p. 721.

47. Quoted in Phillips-Matz, op. cit., p. 586.

48. Robert W. Gutman, *Richard Wagner: The Man, His Mind and His Music* (London: Secker & Warburg, 1968), p. 343.

CHAPTER NINE

Heroic Singing

1. George R. Marek, *Beethoven: Biography of a Genius* (London: Constable, 1969), p. 362.

2. Ibid., p. 462.

3. Richard Wagner, *My Life* (London: Constable, 1911; reprint, 1963), p. 44.

4. Ibid.

5. William Weaver, *The Golden Century of Italian Opera: From Rossini to Puccini* (London: John Calmann and King, 1980; paperback edition, New York: Thames & Hudson, 1988), p. 83.

6. Ibid.

7. Wagner, op. cit., p. 120.

8. Ibid., pp. 275–76.

9. Ibid., p. 368.

10. Quoted by John Warrack in Stanley Sadie, ed., *The New Grove Dictionary of Opera* (London: Macmillan, 1992; paperback edition, 1998), vol. 4, p. 242.

11. H. Berlioz, *Mémoires* (Paris, 1870; English trans. by David Cairns, London: Gollancz, 1969), p. 112.

12. J. Kapp and H. Jachmann, *Richard Wagner und seine erste "Elisabeth"* (Berlin, 1926; English trans., 1944). Jachmann was Johanna Wagner's son.

13. Wagner, op. cit., p. 372.

14. Ibid., p. 272. When Cosima Wagner produced *Tannhäuser* at Bayreuth in 1891 (the first time it was staged there), she wrote in a letter to Davidson, the publisher of the *Berliner Börsen-Kurier,* that she had rejected the traditional operatic Elisabeth in favor of "a childlike virginal figure whose first terrible experience makes her a saint at the cost of her life." The singer Cosima chose was Pauline de Ahna, who later became Richard Strauss's wife—see Geoffrey Skelton, *Wagner at Bayreuth: Experiment and Tradition* (London: Barrie and Rockliff, 1965), p. 80.

15. Wagner, op. cit., p. 562.

16. Michael Scott, *The Record of Singing* (London, 1977; reprint, Boston: Northeastern University Press, 1993), vol. 1, p. 17.

17. Ibid., p. 18.

18. Wagner, op. cit., p. 745.

19. Ibid., p. 825.

20. Ibid., p. 827.

21. Ibid., p. 852.

22. See John Chancellor, *Wagner* (London: Weidenfeld and Nicholson, 1978), pp. 199–200.

23. Harold Rosenthal and John Warrack, eds., *The Concise Oxford Dictionary of Opera* (Oxford: Oxford University Press, 1964; paperback edition, 1990), p. 500.

24. Robert W. Gutman, *Richard Wagner: The Man, His Mind and His Music* (London: Secker & Warburg, 1968), p. 272.

25. Ibid., p. 273.

26. Ibid., p. 286.

27. Skelton, op. cit., p. 101.

28. Scott, op. cit., vol. 2, p. 5.

29. Geoffrey Skelton says they "ended in ridicule and failure" (op. cit., p. 20).

30. Ibid., p. 47.

31. Quoted in Ralph Sabor, *The Real Wagner* (London: Andre Deutsch, 1987), p. 271.

32. L. Lehmann, *Mein Weg* (Leipzig, 1913; English trans., 1914), p. 246.

33. Quoted in Frederic Spotts, *Bayreuth: A History of the Wagner Festival* (New Haven: Yale University Press, 1994), p. 66.

34. Gutman, op. cit., p. 51.

35. Ibid., p. 227.

36. Lehmann, op. cit., p. 235.

37. Ibid. See also L. Lehmann, *Meine Gesangskunst* (Berlin, 1902), in English translation as *How to Sing* (New York: Dover, 1902).

38. Lehmann, op. cit., p. 290.

39. Quoted in Skelton, op. cit., p. 62.

40. F. Weingartner, *Lebenserinnerungen* (Vienna, 1923), in English translation as *Buffets and Rewards* (1937).

41. Rupert Christiansen, *Prima Donna: A History* (New York: Viking, 1985), p. 178.

42. Harold Rosenthal, *Opera at Covent Garden: A Short History* (London: Gollancz, 1967), p. 68.

43. Ibid.

CHAPTER TEN

Marchesi's Pupils

1. Benjamin Britten, acceptance speech at first Aspen Awards ceremony, July 31, 1964; quoted in George Martin, *The Companion to Twentieth Century Opera* (London: Victor Gollancz, 1980; paperback edition, New York: John Murray, 1989), p. 95.

2. Quoted in Harold C. Schonberg, *The Lives of the Great Composers* (New York: Norton, 1970; revised edition, 1981), p. 258.

3. John Rosselli, *Singers of Italian Opera: The History of a Profession* (Cambridge: Cambridge University Press, 1992; paperback edition, 1995), p. 109.

4. G. Caccini, preface to *Le nuovo musiche* (Florence, 1602).

5. P. F. Tosi, *Opinioni de' cantori antichi e moderni o sieno Osservazioni sopra il canto figurato* (Bologna, 1723), in English translation as *Observations on the Florid Song*, trans. J. E. Galliard (London, 1742).

6. G. Crescentini, *Raccolta di esercizj per il canto all'uso del vocalizzo, con discorso preliminare* (c. 1810, Biblioteca dell'Accademia di S. Cecilia, Rome), quoted in Rosselli, op. cit., p. 107.

7. Quoted in Henry Pleasants, *The Great Singers: From the Dawn of Opera to Our Own Time* (London: Simon & Schuster, 1966), p. 90.

8. F. Lamperti, *Guida teorico-pratica-elementare per lo studio del canto* (Milan, c. 1864); and *L'arte del canto in ordine alle tradizioni classiche ed a paticolare esperienza* (Milan, 1883).

9. Michael Scott, *The Record of Singing* (London: Gerald Duckworth, 1977; reprint, Boston: Northeastern University Press, 1993), vol. 1, p. 27.

10. M. García, *Traité complet de l'art du chant* (Paris, 1840).

11. Scott, op. cit., vol. 1, p. 20.

12. Desmond Shawe-Taylor, EMI record sleeve; quoted in Scott, op. cit., vol. 1, p. 29.

13. Peter G. Davis, *The American Opera Singer: The Lives and Adventures of America's Great Singers in Opera and Concert from 1825 to the Present* (New York: Doubleday, 1997), p. 191.

14. Blanche Marchesi, *A Singer's Pilgrimage* (Boston, 1923; reprint, New York: Da Capo, 1978).

15. The critic was Philip Hale, quoted in Scott, op. cit., vol. 1, p. 35.

16. Ibid., p. 36.

17. Mathilde Marchesi, *Marchesi and Music: Passages from the Life of a Famous Singing Teacher* (New York, 1898), quoted in Pleasants, op. cit., p. 272.

18. Emma Eames, *Some Memories and Reflections* (New York: Arno, 1927).

19. Davis, op. cit., p. 152.

20. Quoted in Rupert Christiansen, *Prima Donna: A History* (New York: Viking, 1985), p. 126.

21. B. Marchesi, op. cit., p. 116.

22. W. J. Henderson, *The Art of Singing* (New York, 1938), quoted in Scott, op. cit., vol. 1, p. 29.

23. Pleasants, op. cit., p. 273.

24. H. Sutherland Edwards, *The Prima Donna* (London, 1888; reprint, New York: Da Capo, 1978), vol. 2, p. 217.

25. Christiansen, op. cit., p. 115.

26. Quoted in John Frederick Cone, *Adelina Patti, Queen of Hearts* (Portland, Ore.: Amadeus, 1993), p. 149.

27. Ibid., pp. 154–59.

28. Pleasants, op. cit., p. 304.

29. Scott, op. cit., vol. 1, p. 90.

30. Davis, op. cit., p. 185.

31. Ibid., p. 186.
32. According to Rodney Milnes, the American singer Carol Neblett became the first opera singer known to have appeared in the full frontal nude when she performed Thaïs in New Orleans in 1973—see Stanley Sadie, ed., *The New Grove Dictionary of Opera* (London: Macmillan, 1992; paperback edition, 1998), vol. 4, p. 708.
33. Michael T. R. B. Turnbull, *Mary Garden* (Portland, Ore.: Amadeus, 1997), p. 11.
34. Mary Garden, writing in *Theatre*, Mar. 1908, quoted in Turnbull, op. cit., p. 26.
35. Geraldine Farrar, *Such Sweet Compulsion* (New York: Greystone, 1938).
36. Mary Garden and Louis Biancolli, *Mary Garden's Story* (New York: Simon & Schuster, 1951).

Suggestions for Further Reading

ONE-VOLUME HISTORIES OF OPERA

Donald J. Grout's *A Short History of Opera* (New York: Columbia University Press, 1947), originally published in two volumes, was revised into one volume in 1965 and further revised by W. H. Williams in 1988. Leslie Orrey's *Opera: A Concise History* (London: Thames & Hudson, 1972) is available in a 1978 paperback edition, updated by Rodney Milnes. The present author's *The Story of Opera* (New York: Harry N. Abrams, 1998) has been republished in a second edition (2001).

Two scholarly and authoritative histories bring together contributions from a number of leading authorities. *The Oxford Illustrated History of Opera* (Oxford: Oxford University Press, 1994), sumptuously illustrated, is edited by Roger Parker and is now available in paperback. *History of Opera* (London: Macmillan, 1989) is a publication in the New Grove Handbooks in Music series and is edited by Stanley Sadie. Mr. Sadie has made a greater contribution to the writing and publishing of opera history than anyone else, living or dead.

REFERENCE WORKS

All other reference works—in the English language, at least—are dwarfed by *The New Grove Dictionary of Opera,* edited by Stanley Sadie and published in four volumes (London: Macmillan, 1992). Its comprehensiveness and authority make it an indispensable companion for anyone attempting to write about opera. Many other dictionaries are available: *The Oxford Dictionary of Opera,* edited by John Warrack and Ewan West (Oxford: Oxford University Press, 1998), is particularly useful. Piero Weiss's *Opera: A History in Documents* (Oxford: Oxford University Press, 2002) contains a great deal of useful material in accessible English translations, many of them by Professor Weiss.

Two other works should be present in any opera lover's library. One is *The New Kobbé's Opera Book,* edited by the Earl of Harewood and Antony Peattie (London: Putnam, 1997): this is the latest revision of Gustav Kobbé's *Complete Opera*

Book, first published in 1918. The other is *The Viking Opera Guide,* edited by Amanda Holden with Nicholas Kenyon and Stephen Walsh (London: Viking, 1993). Both of these works provide synopses of individual operas (more than five hundred in the case of *Kobbé,* fifteen hundred in the case of *Viking*) as well as some musical commentary and other useful historical information.

MEMOIRS AND LETTERS

Most European travelers of the seventeenth, eighteenth, and nineteenth centuries took in the opera wherever they went. Diarists and correspondents like John Evelyn, William Beckford, and Charles de Brosses (who was later president of Burgundy's supreme court) are therefore useful ancillary sources, but much more important are those travelers—like Charles Burney, Baron de Grimm, P. J. Grosley, and Stendahl—who stayed a while and made critical examinations, however opinionated, of the state of music and singing on the continent of Europe. Similarly, there is a host of memoirists—Richard Mount Edgcumbe, Edmond Michotte, and Henry Chorley are examples—who attended the opera regularly and wrote about it obsessively.

The most important resources of all, however, are the composers and librettists—and occasionally singers—whose letters have been preserved. They include Mozart, Monteverdi, Berlioz, Metastasio, Verdi, Wagner, Meyerbeer, Romani, Piave, and Scribe . . . to name just a few.

SINGING AND SINGERS

Henry Pleasants's *The Great Singers: From the Dawn of Opera to Our Own Time* (London: Simon & Schuster, 1966) is still the seminal work, together with W. J. Henderson's *The Art of Singing* (New York: Dial, 1938). More recently, Rupert Christiansen's *Prima Donna: A History* (London: Viking, 1985) is a useful addition. *Dieux et Divas de l'Opéra* by Roger Blanchard and Roland de Condé (Paris, 1986) is a wonderful resource, and not just for French singers. Charles Neilson Gattey's *Queens of Song* (London: Barrie & Jenkins, 1979) concentrates on nineteenth-century singers, while John Rosselli's *Singers of Italian Opera: The History of a Profession* (Cambridge: Cambridge University Press, 1992), though it deals only with Italian singers, is authoritative and minutely researched. Rodolfo Celletti's *Storia del belcanto* (Fiesole: Discanto edizioni, 1983) describes the art of opera singing up to the middle of the nineteenth century. For American singers, Peter G. Davis's *The American Opera Singer* (New York: Doubleday, 1998) is especially useful. Michael Scott's *The Record of Singing* (Boston: Northeastern University Press, 1977), though it is chiefly concerned with singers who recorded, contains a great deal of earlier history and some interesting and well-informed opinions. H. Sutherland Edwards's *The Prima Donna* (New York: Da Capo, 1978, originally published in 1888) is wildly unreliable but highly entertaining.

The castrati have a surprisingly small literature. The newest and best work on the subject is Patrick Barbier's *The World of the Castrati* (London: Souvenir, 1996), originally published in France in 1989 as *Histoire des castrats*. Angus Heriot's *The Castrati in Opera* (New York: Da Capo, 1974) contains useful profiles of the most famous castrati.

As discussed in the final chapter of this book, the history of singing (and I am concerned only with opera singing here) can be traced to some extent in the published theses of a small group of leading voice teachers between 1600 and 1900. Beginning with Giulio Caccini's *Le nuovo musiche* in 1602, they lead on to Pier Francesco Tosi's *Opinioni de' cantori antichi e moderni* (1723), Girolamo Crescentini's *Raccolta di esercizj per il canto all'uso del vocalizzo* (1810), Manuel García's *Mémoire sur la voix humane* and his *Traité complet de l'art du chant* (both 1840), Francesco Lamperti's *L'arte del canto* (1883), and Mathilde Marchesi's *Marchesi and Music: Passages from the Life of a Famous Singing Teacher* (1898)—though it has to be said that Marchesi's daughter and pupil Blanche is rather more forthcoming on the Marchesi method in her book *A Singer's Pilgrimage* (New York: Da Capo, 1978, originally published in 1923).

BIOGRAPHIES OF SINGERS

Opera singers have been written about ever since opera enjoyed its first popular success in seventeenth-century Venice. Fortunately, perhaps, singers did not begin writing about themselves very much until the twentieth century.

Some of the earliest works available—Giulio Strozzi's extravagant praise of Anna Renzi in *Le glorie della signora Anna Renzi romana* (1644) is an example—were written as publicity handouts rather than critical appraisals. They therefore have a good deal in common with some of those twentieth-century autobiographies. Inevitably, most of the best biographies are of fairly recent vintage, written by scholars able to take advantage of new discoveries, newly cataloged archives, and a mass of information that was simply not available to earlier writers. Any list of recommended biographies is bound to be subjective, but, for what it is worth, the following are all works that this writer has found useful:

Patrick Barbier, *Farinelli, le castrat des Lumières* (Paris: Editions Bernard Grasset, 1994)
Joan Bulman, *Jenny Lind* (London: J. Barrie, 1956)
John Frederick Cone, *Adelina Patti, Queen of Hearts* (Portland, Ore.: Amadeus, 1993)
Robert B. Douglas, *Sophie Arnould, Actress and Wit* (Paris: Charles Carrington, 1898)
Emma Eames, *Some Memories and Reflections* (New York: Arno, 1927)
Geraldine Farrar, *Such Sweet Compulsion* (New York: Greystone, 1938)
Roger Fiske, ed., *Reminiscences of Michael Kelly* (Oxford: Oxford University Press, 1975; originally published in 1826)

April Fitzlyon, *Maria Malibran* (London: Souvenir, 1987)

April Fitzlyon, *The Price of Genius: A Biography of Pauline Viardot* (London: John Calder, 1964)

John Hetherington, *Melba* (Melbourne: F.W. Cheshire, 1967)

Herman Klein, *The Reign of Patti* (New York: Ayer, 1920)

Lilli Lehmann, *Mein Weg* (Leipzig, 1913); in English translation as *My Path Through Life* (New York, 1914)

G. Sacchi, *Vita del Cav. Don Carlo Broschi* (Venice, 1784)

Gaia Servadio, *The Real Traviata: The Life of Giuseppina Strepponi* (London: Hodder and Stoughton, 1994)

Michael T. R. B. Turnbull, *Mary Garden* (Portland, Ore.: Amadeus, 1997)

222, 222–223, 247, 275, 282;
bel canto tradition and, 237;
Johanna Wagner and, 233–236;
orchestra, 237, 245, 246, 256,
257, 266; personality, 250; personal life, 240; reputation, 259;
singers, 226, 229, 231, 232, 237–
238, 242–244, 245, 246, 249,
252, 257, 260, 261, 265–266,
276
Waldmann, Maria, 214, 215, 216,
221, 271
Walküre, Die (Wagner), 233, 235,
247, 248, 249, 262

Weber, Aloysia, 105–107
Weber, Carl Maria von, 148, 150,
192, 226, 228
Weber, Constanze, 106

Zauberflöte, Die (Mozart), 97, 101,
102, 104, 106, 108, 227, 228,
229
Zelmira (Rossini), 128
Zeno, Apostolo, 31, 48–50
Zilli, Emma, 220, 221
Zingarelli, Niccolo Antonio, 83,
86, 91, 133, 134, 142, 168